The Dukes of Norfolk

RECUSANCY

SOLA VIRTUS INVICTA

THE
DUKES OF NORFOLK

JOHN   MARTIN   ROBINSON

PHILLIMORE

First published in 1983 by
OXFORD UNIVERSITY PRESS

This revised edition published by
PHILLIMORE & CO. LTD
Shopwyke Manor Barn, Chichester, West Sussex
1995

ISBN 0 85033 973 1

Printed and bound in Great Britain by
BUTLER AND TANNER LTD
Frome, Somerset

PREFACE

THE traveller by train along the south coast of Sussex, as he passes through the prim suburbs of Worthing and Littlehampton and the boring market gardens and greenhouses of the coastal plain is suddenly greeted by an improbable vision which combines Conway, Amiens and Claude Lorraine. The downs roll back to reveal the careful eighteenth-century planting and model farms of a great estate, a red-roofed hillside town climbing to a ridge crowned by a huge French Gothic cathedral and a still more huge castle backed by a dramatically wooded park. As an overall landscape composition it is generally considered to be among the grandest and most successful creations of the Romantic imagination. But it is much more than a piece of spectacular architectural scenery. It is the seat of the only surviving dukedom of medieval creation and the conscious expression in stone of a family history which is in many ways remarkable; it is the Valhalla of the Fitzalan-Howards.

From a distance it seems too good to be true, and, to the extent that the cathedral and much of the castle are both late nineteenth-century, it is. The impression of the secure enjoyment of continuous power and uninterrupted prosperity is also deceptive, for no other English family has had so dramatic a history as the Howards, or seen such vicissitudes of life, such heights and depths of fortune: on the one hand all the principal offices of the State, the favour of sovereigns, power, influence, riches, glory, and on the other murder, treason, attainder, imprisonment, divorce, disgrace, martyrdom and ruin. Theirs is an essentially tragic history. The first four Howard Dukes of Norfolk were all attainted. The 1st Duke was killed in battle. The 3rd Duke escaped being beheaded only because Henry VIII died on the morning his execution was due to take place. Two of his nieces who became Queens of England were beheaded. His eldest son and grandson, the Earl of Surrey and the 4th Duke, were both unjustly executed. The 4th Duke's eldest son, St. Philip Howard, died of dysentery after long imprisonment in the Tower. Philip's son died in exile, and one of his grandsons, Viscount Stafford, was also unjustly executed. The 5th Duke went mad. The 6th Duke's life was ruined by his adherence to Catholicism and the resulting exclusion from public life. The 7th Duke's wife left him in scandalous circumstances. The 8th Duke died prematurely of a terrible illness. The 9th Duke was childless, saw both his nephews die young and the extinction of his line of Howards. The 10th Duke died of melancholia and drink. The 11th Duke's first wife died in childbirth, his second wife became insane and he had no legitimate children. The 12th Duke's wife, who never loved him, left him soon after their marriage. The 13th Duke's favourite son died suddenly a few days before his twenty-first birthday. The 14th Duke died young of a painful and incurable disease. The 15th Duke's first wife died aged thirty-four after only a few years of marriage, and his only son by her was born blind and epileptic and died at the age of twenty-three. Apart from these individual tragedies the whole later history of the family is coloured by the fact that the Dukes of Norfolk were aristocratic outlaws; they were at the centre of things and yet excluded because of their adherence to Catholicism, a religious denomination which was illegal in England for three hundred years and of which they were the leading members. For centuries it has been their peculiar position to have been, on the one hand, premier English peers, great officers of State and the possessors of considerable riches, and on the other, debarred from most of the consequences and rewards of this pre-eminence by loyalty to a proscribed religion. It is this which gives the Howard Dukes of Norfolk their aura of 'fatal glory'.

CONTENTS

ACKNOWLEDGEMENTS

IN the first place I am most grateful to the Duke of Norfolk whose idea this book was, and who has helped and encouraged me at every stage of the research and writing. Other members of the Howard family who have generously provided information and hospitality, or allowed me to reproduce objects in their possession include Mr. Duncan Davidson, Lady Winefride Freeman, Mr and Mrs Stafford Howard and the late Lord Howard of Henderskelfe. My colleagues at Arundel, Miss Pamela Taylor and Mrs Ian Rodger, have helped greatly with the research. Mrs Rodger has also typed the manuscript and is responsible for many corrections and improvements to the text. Mr Howard Frith photographed a number of objects and prints for me at Arundel Castle and Mr Stephen Croad of the National Monuments Record helped with tracking down photographs of buildings and also arranged to have copied many late nineteenth-century photographs from the Arundel Castle archives. Among those who have read the whole or part of my manuscript and made helpful comments or corrections are the late Mr Rodney Dennys, Mr Peter Drummond-Murray, Mr Roger Ellis, Lord Dacre of Glanton, and the Rt. Revd. Mgr. Alfred Gilbey. My thanks are also due to Dr David Howarth, Mr Richard Sandford of the Duke of Norfolk's Estate Office in Sheffield, Dr David Postles and Miss Ruth Harman of the Sheffield City Archives, and Fr. John Sullivan at Glossop. It is not necessary to say much about the treatment of the subject except that I have modernized all dates and have also modernized the spelling of most of the earlier quotations to spare the reader tiresome chunks of olde worlde prose.

LIST OF ILLUSTRATIONS

Unless another copyright owner is stated, everything is from the collection at Arundel Castle and is reproduced by permission of His Grace The Duke of Norfolk.

East Anglia, showing estates and places where the Dukes of Norfolk had an interest.

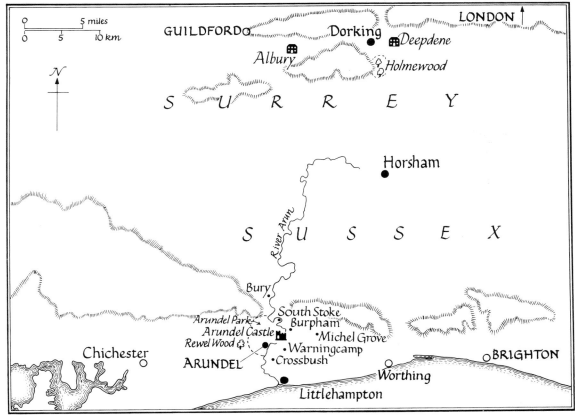

Sussex and Surrey, showing estates and places where the Dukes of Norfolk had an interest.

The northern estate.

Iohes Howard miles

Top left. Sir William Howard (d. 1308), Chief Justice of Common Pleas in the reign of Edward I and founder of the Howard Family. Drawn by Henry Lilly in 1637 from stained glass in East Winch church (destroyed).

Top right. Sir John Howard, grandfather of the 1st Duke of Norfolk. Drawn by Henry Lilly in 1637.

Sir John Howard III (d. 1436) and his second wife Alice Tendring, the grandparents of the 1st Duke of Norfolk. Drawn by Henry Lilly in 1637 from stained glass in Stoke by Nayland church in Suffolk.

The Rise of the Howards

THE story begins in a dull and windswept part of North Norfolk, at the hamlet of East Winch, a few miles from King's Lynn. A row of council cottages, the much repaired Perpendicular church of All Saints and the moat of a vanished manor-house mark the site of the original home of the Howards. Here are buried the founder of the family and several of his descendants, although the Howard mortuary chapel, despite being reroofed by the 'Collector Earl' in the seventeenth century, later fell into ruin and was finally swept away by Sir Gilbert Scott during his restoration of the church in 1875. It is now commemorated only by a brass plate, but in the church there remains a fourteenth-century font embellished with the Howard arms. 'The proudest families are content', says Gibbon, 'to lose in the darkness of the middle ages the tree of their pedigree.' This is certainly true of the Howards, whose line cannot be traced further than the reign of Edward I in the thirteenth century. The first notable Howard ancestor was Sir William Howard of East Winch, who became Chief Justice of the Common Pleas in 1297 and died in 1308. With him begins the game of political snakes and ladders which by the end of the medieval period had raised his direct male descendant to the head of the peerage of England.

In their rise, the Howards made use of all three major paths to noble status which the Middle Ages in England offered: the law, warfare and marriage. They were first raised to prominence in the person of the Chief Justice of Common Pleas in the thirteenth century; they thrived on military commands during the Hundred Years War in the fourteenth century; and they were elevated to one of the great powers in the land by Sir Robert Howard's marriage to Lady Margaret Mowbray, daughter of the Duke of Norfolk, in the fifteenth century.

William Howard, the founder of the family, is first recorded in 1277 when he bought land at East Winch, presumably out of the profits of his legal career. From 1285 onwards he was counsel to the Corporation of King's Lynn. His father John and his grandfather William lived at Wiggenhall. By the time he appears in documentary records he himself was living at East Winch, not yet in the manor-house, which he was to buy in 1298 from the Grancourts, but in a smaller house. He carefully built up his holding in the parish by purchase, acre by acre. He also added to his possessions by marriage, for both his wives were heiresses. The first wife was Alice, daughter of Sir Robert Ufford, and she brought her husband land, though they had no children. The second, another Alice, was the daughter of Sir Edmund Fitton and the heiress of Fitton Manor in Wiggenhall St. Germans, which she brought to her husband and of which only the moat still exists. In 1293 Howard was made a Justice of Assize for the Northern Counties, two years later he was summoned to Parliament as a Justice, and in 1297 he received the appointment of Justice of the Common Pleas, becoming in due course the Chief Justice of the Common Pleas, and a knight. He died in July or August 1308, leaving his family firmly established.

The Justice's eldest son Sir John Howard I further improved his position by a good marriage to Joan de Cornwall, an heiress and illegitimate descendant of Richard Earl of Cornwall and King of the Romans, younger son of King John. Her inheritance made the Howards of East Winch the most important landowners in the King's Lynn area after the owners of Castle Rising. Sir John Howard I was a Gentleman of the Bedchamber to Edward I, and fought in Scotland under Edward II, though it is not known for certain whether he was present at the English disaster at Bannockburn, which his descendants would one day avenge at Flodden. After his marriage he was appointed Sheriff of Norfolk and Suffolk, and Governor of Norwich for a time. He died in 1333 and was buried at East Winch.

His son Sir John Howard II had the good fortune to be brought up in the King's Household as a result of his mother's Plantagenet connections. He was one of the knightly companions who helped the young Edward III to break the power of Mortimer and shut away the Queen-Mother, the 'she-wolf of France', in Framlingham Castle. Howard was made a knight-banneret and Admiral of the North Seas in 1335. In the latter post he was paid the large sum of £153 7s. 6d. for himself and his men in 1336. He helped to ferry Edward's armies to France and also carried out various raids on the French coast. The first of the family to be involved in such naval warfare, he began a Howard tradition which lasted for three hundred years and culminated in Lord Howard of Effingham's defeat of the Spanish Armada. He was Sheriff of Norfolk in 1345 and lived to a good old age; the exact date of his death is not known but he was still alive in 1388. The font in East Winch church was presented by him, or his son, and bears his arms together with those of his wife Alice de Boys, another heiress, who brought to the Howards the manor of Fersfield near Diss, of all the old Howard estates the only one which despite every vicissitude remained Howard property down to modern times. Some of the land there and the manor remain in the possession of the present Duke of Norfolk, the only material link with the pre-ducal Howard past.

Top left. The font in East Winch church, showing the Howard arms and the original font cover now lost. Drawn by Henry Lilly in 1637.

Top right. Katherine, first wife of the 1st Duke of Norfolk. Memorial brass in Stoke by Nayland church. Drawn by Henry Lilly in 1637.

Margaret, second wife of the 1st Duke of Norfolk. Drawn by Henry Lilly in 1637 from stained glass in Long Melford church.

Sir John's eldest son Sir Robert Howard predeceased his father, having how-ever succeeded in making the most splendid match so far, with Margaret, daughter of the 3rd Lord Scales of Newcells. As a result of this marriage their descendants became the heirs to the Scales barony, though as it turned out this title, which should have been the culmination of the Howards' rise in the world, was to elude them, and the estates so carefully built up over a century and more were to be lost. The heir to Sir John Howard II was his grandson Sir John Howard III of East Winch and Fersfield. He married twice, firstly Margaret Plaiz, daughter and heiress of John Plaiz of Tofte, an alliance which made his descendants heirs to the barony of Plaiz of Tofte in addition to the Scales barony and also brought them substantial estates in Essex, Hertfordshire and Cambridgeshire. On the strength of these estates John Howard became Sheriff of Essex and Hertfordshire under Henry IV and Henry V and sat in Parliament as Knight of the Shire for Cambridgeshire. Margaret died in 1381 and two years later he married Alice, daughter and heiress of Sir William Tendring of Tendring Hall, Stoke by Nayland, in Suffolk, the house which was to replace East Winch as the chief Howard seat in the fifteenth century. Like his grandfather, he held the office of Admiral of the Northern Seas on the resumption of war with France. When he was nearly eighty, he went on a Pilgrimage to the Holy Land and died at Jerusalem on 17 November 1437.

His eldest son Sir John Howard IV, who had married Joan Walton, heiress of Wyvenhoe in Essex, had died in his father's lifetime and unfortunately had had only a daughter, Elizabeth (born in 1410), who married John de Vere, 12th Earl of Oxford; she took most of the now substantial Howard estates, including East Winch, and the Baronies of Scales and Plaiz to the de Veres, while the male Howard heir John V, son of Sir John III's second son Sir Robert Howard (who had also predeceased his father), inherited only a tiny fraction of his grandfather's estates.

Sir Robert Howard had a distinguished fighting career on land and sea. He was a near contemporary of King Henry V, having been born in about 1385. He may have been present at Agincourt, and certainly commanded the English fleet which ravaged the French coast south of Calais. His military prowess and his now established family background enabled him to make the most brilliant marriage of all and one which was 'the foundation of all the subsequent glories of the Howard line'. This was in about 1420, to Lady Margaret Mowbray, elder daughter of Thomas Mowbray, Duke of Norfolk and Earl Marshal of England, the great-great-grandson of Edward I and Margaret of France, who had been banished by Richard II for quarrelling with Bolingbroke and had died in exile in Venice. The death within sixty years of four Mowbray Dukes of Norfolk without a direct male heir was to leave the Howards as the senior co-heirs to the Mowbray estates and the successors to the Bigods, Warennes and Mowbrays. John Howard V, who was born in 1421 or 1422, therefore made up in birth for what he lacked in land when on his grandfather's death he was left only with Fersfield and Tendring.[1]

He took up residence at Tendring Hall and in about 1443 married Katherine Molines. He continued the family tradition by fighting in France; in 1451 he was among the English troops under the command of Lord Lisle and took part in retrieving Bordeaux. In the mid-1450s he was back in England, and following the lead of his powerful Mowbray cousins he threw in his lot with the Yorkists. He acted as the administrator of the Duke of Norfolk's estates, being appointed the Duke's chamberlain or agent-in-chief, and holding the stewardships of various estates in East Anglia. As a result of Mowbray support he was elected to Parliament in 1455 as the Yorkist Knight of the Shire for Norfolk, much to the annoyance of the Pastons and their friends, who grumbled that he had 'no livlihood in the shire nor conversement' and that it was an 'evil precedent for the shire that a strange man should be chosen and no worship to my Lord of York nor to my lord of Norfolk to write for him'.[2]

Howard took part in the second battle of St. Albans and the decisive victory at Towton on 29 March 1461 which established the Duke of York on the throne as Edward IV in place of Henry VI. He was knighted by Edward after the battle and from that moment was constantly in the service and good favour of the King, who appreciated his combination of administrative ability and military prowess. He was made a King's Carver by Edward's first civil patent and is said to have had 'great fellowship' with the King. He was appointed Sheriff of Norfolk and Suffolk and Constable of the castles of Norwich, Harwich and Colchester, and from 1466 to 1474 held the important post of Treasurer of the Household as well as acting as deputy Earl Marshal at the tournament between Lord Scales and the Bastard of Burgundy in May 1467.[3] He was also appointed to administer the de Vere estates after the execution of the Earl of Oxford, and this, together with the administration of the Mowbray estates and his public offices, substantially increased his stature in his native East Anglia as well as at Court. The culmination of this phase of his career was his ennoblement by Edward IV as Lord Howard in the late 1460s, though the exact date, rather curiously, is not known. Several writers have been misled by the writ of summons to the Lancastrian Parliament on 15 October 1470 into assuming that he was created Lord Howard by writ during Henry VI's brief restoration. But he is already referred to as Dominus de Howard in a commission dated November 1467 appointing him an envoy to France, and he is referred to as Lord Howard when summoned to Pontefract by Edward IV in September 1469. He must therefore have been created Lord Howard by Edward IV some time before Henry VI's return to the throne in 1470. The writ of summons to the Lancastrian Parliament is merely that which was sent to every existing peer regardless of Yorkist or Lancastrian loyalty and was not a new creation in that year. His first wife having died in 1465, he remarried in 1467, at about the same time as his ennoblement. His second wife was Margaret Chedworth, widow of John Norreys.

In 1470, when Edward IV was captured by Warwick the King-Maker, and Henry VI briefly restored to the throne, Howard was one of the party of Yorkist nobles who rescued Edward from Middleham Castle and carried him to the Continent. On Edward's return in 1471 Howard hastened to Suffolk with his son (who had been in sanctuary at Colchester) and proclaimed Edward King again.[4] They then gathered a force of soldiers and joined Edward at Barnet Heath, where Warwick was defeated and killed on Easter Sunday 1471. Howard also took part in the battle of Tewkesbury, the last battle of the so-called 'Wars of the Roses'. He was rewarded by being made a Knight of the Garter and was sent with Lord Hastings to claim Calais for the Yorkists; this mission he accomplished without loss of blood, and he was appointed Governor of the town. During the next few years he was much occupied with Anglo-French affairs, and in 1475 was one of those who accompanied Edward on his sham military expedition to France, which concluded without any fighting at the Treaty of Amiens and meeting with Louis XI at the château of Picquigny. Howard stayed behind as a hostage for the withdrawal of the English troops from France after Edward had agreed not to go to war against Louis XI.

In 1481 there occurred the event which was to have so great an effect on the Howard fortunes. Lady Anne Mowbray, only daughter and heiress of the 4th Mowbray Duke of Norfolk, died without issue at Framlingham Castle, leaving Lord Howard as senior co-heir to the Mowbray estates. Edward IV, however, had already married Lady Anne to his younger son the Duke of York, creating him Duke of Norfolk in right of his wife. Following the marriage, an Act of Parliament had been passed giving the prince the enjoyment of the Mowbray estates for life even if his wife predeceased him,[5] so that Howard found his inheritance blocked for the immediate future by the King's younger son. This in itself was reason enough for Howard to support Edward's brother, Richard Duke of Gloucester. They both had much to gain from the bastardization of Edward's sons: Richard the throne, and Howard the Mowbray inheritance, which was rightfully his, and possibly also the Dukedom of Norfolk.

In 1482, during the last year of Edward's reign, Howard was involved in the Anglo–Scottish war where he served as King's Lieutenant and Captain-at-Sea under Gloucester. He commanded the English fleet in a successful naval action in the Firth of Forth in the course of which he captured and burnt the Scottish fleet. This is one of the earliest great English naval victories. Howard's flagship was called the *Mary Howard*, and his personal expenses on the expedition are recorded in his 'Household Books', which also list the twelve volumes he took with him to read on the expedition. They were all in French and included manuals on chess and dice as well as chivalric romances such as *La Belle Dame sans Merci*, *Ponthus et la Belle Sidogne* and *Sir Baudin Conte de Flandres*. There were two works recently printed by Caxton as well as several which had been produced in the last ten years in Lyons or Paris, so he was obviously up to date in his literary interests.[6]

On the death of Edward IV, Howard bore the banner royal in the funeral procession, and immediately joined with Northumberland, Buckingham, Hastings and Lincoln in supporting Gloucester's title of Lord Protector of the Kingdom and guardian of the young princes in opposition to the Queen and the Woodville connection. Edward Hall in his *Chronicle* (1548) states that Howard was 'one of the priviest of the Protector's Council and doing' and that he was one of the Lords who induced the Queen to allow the Duke of York and Norfolk to leave sanctuary so that he could be put in the Tower with his brother Edward V. Neither were to be seen again. On 15 May the 'Household Books' record that Howard presented the Lord Protector with a gold cup and cover. On 28 June 1483, barely a week after Richard's accession to the throne, Howard was created Duke of Norfolk, Marshal and Earl Marshal of England, and granted his share of the Mowbray estates. At the coronation of Richard III on 6 July, Norfolk officiated as Lord High Steward as well as Earl Marshal. On 25 July he was created Lord Admiral of England, Ireland and Aquitaine, Surveyor of Array in Norfolk, Suffolk and eleven other counties, Steward of the Duchy of Lancaster and a member of the Privy Council. So his support for Richard III was handsomely recognized. Or was it perhaps rather more than mere support for which he was being rewarded?

His creation as Duke of Norfolk and succession to the Mowbray estates implied that the Duke of York and Norfolk was already dead, though Richard III's declaration that Edward IV's sons were illegitimate would perhaps have been enough to remove the obstacle to Howard's inheritance. Ever since Payne Collier in 1844 put forward his fanciful supposition that the perfectly straightforward references in the 'Household Books' to such commonplace items as feather mattresses and lime were connected with the murder of the princes in the Tower (the mattresses to suffocate them and the lime to calcine their bodies), the accusation has floated in the air that the Duke, as Constable of the Tower, was responsible for murdering the princes on Richard's behalf. The trouble with this theory is that he never was the Constable of the Tower. Though on 10 February 1479 John, Lord Howard, was granted the secondary reversion of the office for life after John Sutton, Lord Dudley, and Richard Fiennes, Lord Dacre, he never in fact succeeded to the office; Richard III appointed Robert Brackenbury Constable of the Tower on 17 July 1483, and Brackenbury seems to have retained the post throughout the reign.[7] So though Norfolk certainly had nearly as strong a motive as Richard III for wishing the princes dead, he did not have the opportunity to kill them himself. No writer at the time suggested that anybody other than Richard was responsible for their murder, though it is true that none of the commentators on the event was entirely disinterested.

Much light is thrown on the Duke's life in the crucial years surrounding his elevation to ducal status by his 'Household Books', which give a day-to-day record of his expenses. 'My Lord's letters patent of the Dukedom' cost him £3 with an extra 18s. and 3d. for the 'sealship' of them. The Mowbray Dowager Duchess was still living at Framlingham, so he continued in his old house at Tendring. The charges of his household were, however, much augmented after he became a Duke. He now travelled around with an entourage of a hundred and thirty horsemen; and in addition to the Auditor, Steward, Treasurer, Clerk of the Kitchen, Groom of the Hall and two chaplains who had formed the principal officers of his household as Lord Howard, he now had a private secretary as well. His staff also included the unusual extravagance of *two* fools, and a princely chapel establishment with a regular choir, including Nicholas Stapylton, William Lindsey, 'Little Richard' and half a dozen 'children', who were provided with food and clothing as well as wages. Music played a large part in his life both before and after he became a Duke. There was a house organ as well as a chapel organ at Tendring and considerable sums were paid for 'a prick song book', 'a missal of pricked song', 'an anthem for a chapel' and a 'song book of four anthems'. There were also frequent payments to harpers and to minstrels and for repairing musical instruments. The Duke was also a patron of the theatre. At Christmas in 1481, for example, 'the Earl of Essex's Men, players' were paid for performing at Tendring. As was expected of any great medieval nobleman, he distributed alms with princely munificence in London, in East Anglia and on his journeys. He was bountiful to the poor; he contributed to the education of youths at Cambridge; and he gave money to the clergy and holy men, including, most interestingly, 'gentlemen hermits'.[8]

Following the death of Richard III's only son Edward, Prince of Wales, in 1484, and that of Queen Anne less than a year later, Richard III applied for a papal dispensation to marry his niece Elizabeth, daughter of Edward IV. Sir George Buck in his *Life of Richard III* quoted a letter (then preserved in the Howard archives but now lost), supposedly from Princess Elizabeth to the Duke of Norfolk, in which she assured him that he was the man upon whom she most relied in consequence of the love her father had borne him, and entreating him to contrive a marriage between her and her uncle, the King.[9] Norfolk may well have had a hand in helping to forward this proposed match, but to no avail, for both he and the King were shortly to lose their lives on the battlefield, and although Elizabeth of York was indeed to become Queen of England it was to be as a result of marrying Henry Tudor.

On 1 August 1485 Henry landed at Milford Haven in Wales, the southern English coast being too carefully guarded by Norfolk's ships; he then marched eastwards into the Midlands gathering strength as he went. Norfolk at once rallied to Richard III and on 13 August wrote to Sir John Paston arranging to meet him at Bury St. Edmunds and asking him to bring with him a company of well-armed men dressed in the Howard livery.[10] He remained loyal and ignored the famous verse supposedly nailed to his gate the night before he joined the King:

> Jack of Norfolk be not too bold
> For Dickon thy master is bought and sold

He owed everything to the Yorkists, to Richard III most of all, and, unlike the Stanleys and Northumberland, he was not prepared to switch his allegiance, a decision which was to cost him his life. The Duke joined Richard III at Leicester on 16 August and then encamped at Sutton Heath, near Bosworth. In the battle which took place on 22 August he led the van and was cut off from Richard when the turncoat Stanley led his troops into the gap between the van and the King. The Duke's visor was struck off in a hand-to-hand fight with the Earl of Oxford and, his face being unprotected, he was shot through the head by a stray arrow and fell dead. Edward Hall's words in his *Chronicle* are the Duke's most appropriate epitaph: 'He regardeth more his oath, his honour, and his promise made to King Richard, like a Gentleman and a faithful subject to his Prince, absented not himself from his master, but as he faithfully lived under him, so he manfully died with him, to his great fame and laud.'[11]

The Duke seems to have been treated with greater respect in death than the King. Instead of being slung over a horse and taken to Leicester he was carried through Northamptonshire, Huntingdonshire and Cambridgeshire to Thetford in Norfolk, where he was solemnly interrred in the Cluniac monastery founded by Roger Bigod, alongside the Mowbray Dukes of Norfolk, rather than with his parents at Stoke by Nayland, in Suffolk. Two months later he was posthumously attainted, but he had died and been buried as Duke of Norfolk.

Thomas, 2nd Duke of Norfolk (1444–1524), the victor of Flodden.

The Flodden Duke

THE chief source for the details of the life of Thomas, 2nd Duke of Norfolk, is his epitaph, an unusually long autobiographical inscription which once adorned his monument in Thetford Priory, and though now destroyed, was recorded in the seventeenth century by the antiquary John Weever.[1] It gives the chief points of the Duke's rise in the world, a rise which was broken only by the dramatic watershed of Bosworth in which his father was killed, he was wounded and the Dukedom attainted.[2] His career is a classic demonstration of how it was possible to acquire power and riches in the late Middle Ages as a result of political sagacity, good marriages, fortunate accidents, and proximity to the King's person. The 2nd Duke of Norfolk was a steadfast man, loyal to the King and his own guiding principles of enlightened self-interest, a good soldier, competent administrator and an able diplomat. He was described by his contemporary, Polydore Virgil (no lover of Yorkists), in the *Historia Anglicana* as a 'Vir prudentia, gravitate et constantia praeditus'.

Born at Tendring Hall, Stoke by Nayland, in 1443 or 1444, he was the eldest son of John Howard V and a cousin of John Mowbray, Duke of Norfolk, and also of the Earl of Oxford, the two greatest magnates in East Anglia. His father had not yet been knighted or ennobled when his son was born but had already started out on the path that was to take him to great heights, and his son with him. Thomas was educated at Ipswich Grammar School and lodged with the mayor of that town while pursuing his studies; but his interest in literature, revealed later in his and his wife's patronage of the poets Alexander Barclay and John Skelton and in his commissioning an English translation of Sallust's *Bellum Jugurthinum*, probably came from his sojourn at the Burgundian Court and from his own family, especially from his well-read father,[3] rather than school. Thomas completed his education, in conformity with the practice of the time, by personal and military service in the household of a great man. In his case, because of his father's strong support for the Yorkists and his Mowbray connections, he was able to obtain a place in the household of the King and entered the service of Edward IV as a 'henchman' *circa* 1466, thus establishing that close proximity to the monarch which was to last through four reigns and was one reason for his success.

After a period at the English Court, he spent further time, together 'with divers other Gentlemen of England', at Dijon in the service of Charles the Bold, Duke of Burgundy, Edward IV's brother-in-law whose Court was among the most civilized, extravagant and magnificent in Europe. It must have made a considerable impact on the young Englishman. The ceremony which attended the Duke's meals and every other aspect of his life verged on the megalomaniac, and its complex protocol served as a model for the other Courts of Europe. Charles was also a generous patron of the arts. He would not retire at night without listening to chivalrous romances or classical myths for at least two hours. He was also an accomplished player on several musical instruments and had been taught keyboard composition by Dufay. In these literary and musical tastes young Howard would have seen a larger-scale reflection of his own.

On his return to England, he was made an Esquire of the Body to Edward IV 'and he was about him at his making ready both evening and morning'. On 14 April 1471 he fought at the Battle of Barnet where he was 'sore hurt' but recovered. He likewise took part, with his father, in Edward IV's expedition to France in 1475 and was with the King when he met Louis XI, 'the universal spider', at Picquigny on the Somme. There Edward was bribed to give up his plans for invading France, thus abandoning the Burgundians. It was as a direct result of this arrangement that Charles the Bold was defeated and killed in battle by the French on 5 January 1477, his corpse being found in a frozen puddle stripped of its gilded armour and half eaten by wolves, identifiable only by its affectedly long finger-nails.

On 30 April 1472 Howard made a rich match, Elizabeth Tilney (widow of Humphrey Bourchier), whom the Pastons had been hoping to catch and were disappointed at losing to the Howards. She brought to her husband a life interest in a dozen manors including Ashwell Thorpe, which they made their home. This helped to enhance Howard's position in East Anglia and he spent most of the following years in residence there, playing an active role in local affairs. He became Sheriff of Norfolk and Suffolk in 1476 and MP for Norfolk in 1478. On 18 January of the latter year he was also created a Knight of the Bath.

His great leap forward, however, occurred in 1483 as a result of the Howards' support for Richard III. When his father was created Duke of Norfolk on 28 June 1483, he was created Earl of Surrey, a Knight of the Garter, and a member of the Privy Council. On 7 July he carried the Sword of State at Richard's coronation and was Steward of the Household for the first two years of the reign. The Howards' support for Richard III which brought them such spectacular rewards also nearly ruined them. Thomas was wounded and taken prisoner at the Battle of Bosworth and spent the first three and a half years of Henry VII's reign in the Tower, from which he wisely refused to escape when offered the opportunity while the King was out of London.

Though he succeeded to the Dukedom of Norfolk on the death in battle of his father, he lost it almost immediately when both he and his father were attainted by the first Parliament of Henry's reign. He was also degraded from the Order of the Garter. This dramatic reversal of fortune however proved not to be a final catastrophe but merely a temporary set-back. Thomas Howard was one of those who benefited from Henry VII's politic clemency, aimed at winning over former opponents to his own service by the carefully regulated distribution of judicious rewards. Early in 1489 Howard was freed from the Tower, the attainder against him and his father reversed and the Earldom of Surrey restored to him, as were his wife's properties. At this stage, though, the Dukedom of Norfolk and the Howard–Mowbray estates were withheld from him. He was expected to prove himself first and to earn the return of his patrimony as part of a general reprieve for those Yorkists who showed themselves to be trustworthy. Surrey was of special importance to the Tudors as the best military leader in the country. Over the next thirty-four years he slowly won back the lost possessions of his family, and, as it turned out, with interest. Acts of Parliament in 1490 and 1492, for instance, restored his right to all his father's property, only excluding personal grants from Richard III; in 1507 he was given entry to the residual Mowbray estates on the death of the Mowbray Dowager Duchess of Norfolk, and two years later the whole of his landed inheritance was restored to him.

The point of Henry VII's methodical mercy was to ensure that Surrey worked faithfully in the royal service; and this he did, becoming as loyal a servant of the Tudors as he had been of Edward IV and Richard III. The Howards' position was based on service to strong monarchs, not on adherence to faction. They served the principle of strong monarchical government rather than personalities, as is illustrated in the famous and no doubt apocryphal words, attributed to Surrey by William Camden, of the Earl's supposed defence of his allegiance to Richard III after Bosworth, an incident which later came to be enshrined in Whig mythology and was, for example, painted for the 11th Duke of Norfolk by Mather Brown:

Sir, he was my crowned King. Let the authority of Parliament place the Crown on that stake and I will fight for it. So would I have fought for you had the same authority placed the Crown on your head.[4]

Once Richard III was dead, Surrey had everything to gain from serving Henry VII, and serve him he did as soldier, administrator and diplomat; his career of public service extended uninterruptedly from 1489 till two years before his death at an advanced age in 1524.

Surrey was appointed Chief Justice in Eyre North of the Trent in 1489, a post he held till 1509. On 20 May the following year he became Vice-Warden of the

Memorial to Thomas Howard, 2nd Duke of Norfolk, formerly at Thetford Priory and then at Lambeth, but now destroyed. Drawn by Henry Lilly in 1637.

East and Middle Marches, ostensibly as the deputy of the youthful Prince Arthur, who was the titular Warden, but effectively as the Lieutenant of Northern England.[5] The immediate cause of these appointments was an outbreak of serious rioting in the North against Henry's new taxes, riots which had claimed the life of the Earl of Northumberland. Surrey was successful in putting down the revolt in 1489, and a further outbreak of trouble in 1492. He was Lieutenant of the North for ten years, residing for much of that time at Sheriff Hutton, near York, of which royal castle he was Steward and Constable. His duties were civil and military, including the publication of royal proclamations and administration of justice as well as suppressing riots and disturbances. He had a council at Sheriff Hutton staffed with its own officials, from which developed the Council of the North, based after the dissolution of St. Mary's Abbey, in the King's Manor at York. In 1497 Surrey led a successful military expedition into Scotland which destroyed Ayton Castle and resulted in a temporary Anglo–Scottish truce on 3 September aimed at putting a stop to Border raids. Surrey's first wife died while he was in the North, in April 1497. On 8 November of the same year he remarried, in the chapel at Sheriff Hutton, Agnes Tilney.

He surrendered most of his posts in the North in the winter of 1499/1500 and returned to Court, attending the King and Queen on their State visit to Calais in May and June of 1500. The following year he was reappointed to the Privy Council and on 16 June was made Lord Treasurer of England, an office which he was to hold for twenty-one years. It made him head of the Exchequer and one of the three chief executant officers of the Crown, alongside the Lord Chancellor and the Privy Seal.

His faithful and conscientious service in the North had been rewarded, and he remained one of Henry VII's leading ministers for the remainder of the reign. He combined his role at Court and the Council table with a series of diplomatic missions of varying degrees of success. He was chosen to accompany Henry VII's daughter Margaret Tudor to Edinburgh and to give her away in marriage, on the King's behalf, to James IV of Scotland. This marriage was to lead to the succession of the Stuarts to the English throne in the person of Margaret and James's great-grandson James I and VI. The Scottish King, overlooking the Ayton raid of 1497 and unable to see into the future, made a great fuss of Surrey, treating him with marked attention and giving him generous presents. Other diplomatic employments took the Earl to France, Spain and the Pope. No doubt his youth at the Burgundian Court stood him in good stead when it came to dealing with Continental princes.

On his death-bed in 1509, Henry VII finally restored all the family estates to Surrey, and as a mark of special trust appointed him one of the executors of his will. At this time Surrey moved at last into the ancestral castle of the Bigods and Mowbrays, and the 'silver lion floated once more over the Towers of Framlingham'. The accession of a new King altered the character of the Court. Henry VII's exaggerated care over money gave way to princely extravagance. As Lord Treasurer Surrey adapted from being miserly to being open-handed with the Crown's revenues and he, together with his two sons, Thomas and Edward, and his son-in-law Knyvett (who were the King's age), found themselves in great favour. Surrey was appointed Earl Marshal at the coronation, an office which he held for life and which in the long run was to become synonymous with the Dukedom of Norfolk. Thus at the opening of the new reign the future looked promising for the Howards, though events turned out not to be quite as smooth as expected, largely because of the rise to power of Thomas Wolsey.

Henry VIII as a young man was not interested in the dull details of day-to-day government. Wolsey, an energetic and ambitious priest who was prepared to work non-stop from six in the morning till late at night, proved to be the King's deliverer from the tedium of routine government and gradually came to fill the vacuum caused by the King's lack of interest. He soon became indispensable and was rapidly promoted to Grand Almoner, to Bishop of Lincoln, to Archbishop of York, Lord Chancellor, Papal Legate and a Cardinal, a unique concentration of power. The rise of this clerical upstart naturally caused consternation amid the established governing class and led to strong differences of opinion and mutual jealousies. Wolsey seems to have resented the military Howards' favour with the war-like young King and hated the arrogance of the great nobles like the Duke of

Buckingham. Surrey on his side was worried by the financial extravagance of the Cardinal's grandiose foreign policy.

The immediate result was that Surrey, disapproving of the way things were going, obtained leave of absence from Court in September 1511 and retired temporarily to his estates in East Anglia, leaving Henry and Wolsey to push forward with their plans for a Continental war. They signed a treaty with Ferdinand of Aragon in November whereby, while the Spanish were waging war against the French in Italy, the English would open a second front in northern France. Surrey's sons and son-in-law all took a prominent part in the initial stages of the French campaign, Thomas as a commander on land, while Edward and Knyvett fought at sea, the former being appointed Lord Admiral of England. Knyvett's death in battle in 1512 led to Edward Howard's rash engagement with the French at Brest in 1513, in the course of which he too was killed. 'Sir Edward hath made his vow to God that he would never see the King in the face till he had revenged the death of the noble and valiant Knight Sir Thomas Knyvett.' The death of these two young men, both great favourites and contemporaries of the King, had a damaging effect on the Howard interest at Court as it removed the two members of the family who were the closest to Henry VIII. In his will Sir Edward Howard left the well-being of his two bastard sons to the King and Charles Brandon (later Duke of Suffolk) respectively; he also left his greatest treasure, 'St. Thomas's Cup', to Queen Katherine of Aragon. Though Thomas Howard, Surrey's eldest son, was appointed Lord Admiral in succession to his brother, he earned the King's displeasure by preparing at Plymouth when Henry thought he ought to have been crossing the Channel. The Howards, at Wolsey's instigation, were not allowed to conduct Henry VIII to France but were left behind to guard the kingdom, so that Wolsey alone could have the King's ear once the army had sailed across the Channel. This was the unpromising background to the greatest triumph in the history of the Howard family and it was later to be seen as the working of divine providence, when Surrey's smashing defeat of the Scots at Flodden overshadowed Henry's paltry success in France.

Almost as soon as Henry and the army had left, James IV invaded England. The Lord Lyon King of Arms travelled to France and officially declared war on Henry VIII on 13 August 1513. Surrey, who had been in London engaged in routine duties as Lord Treasurer, had already learnt that the Scottish King had gathered together an army of fifty thousand men, crossed the Tweed, captured Norham Castle and was ravaging Northumberland. As soon as this news had reached him on 22 July, he had left for the North. He reached Pontefract Castle on 1 August and spent the rest of the month making preparations and assembling an army of twenty thousand men with, by Tudor standards, commendable speed and efficiency. He was joined some days later by his son Thomas Howard, who landed at Berwick with five thousand seasoned troops from the French campaign. The two forces joined together and marched on to meet the Scottish army, reaching Wooler Haugh on 7 September. There Surrey found that the Scottish King and his troops had taken up a strong position on Flodden Hill, the most easterly spur of the Cheviots, 'a ground more like a camp or fortress than any meet ground to give battle on'. As the Scottish forces outnumbered his own by nearly two to one Surrey decided not to risk a frontal attack on this well-defended position but sent a challenge to James IV inviting him to join in battle on the flat ground between Flodden and Wooler. James replied to this with an illogical snub: 'it became not an Earl thus to challenge a King'. At this stage Surrey's son Thomas Howard suggested the *ruse de guerre* which was the cause of the English success. He advised his father to pretend to march round Flodden Hill as if about to invade Scotland and to cut off James IV's supplies. This was adopted. The English army broke camp and marched north crossing the Twill, but then suddenly swerved westward directly behind the Scottish army. The manœuvre was successful, and James, frightened by the English tactic, abandoned his camp, setting fire to the huts in which his soldiers had been quartered, and moved across to Branxton Moor. The smoke from the burning huts blowing eastward proved very useful to Surrey, as he was able to advance under its cover and to divide his army into two parallel lines, the centre of the front line led by Thomas Howard, its right flank by Sir Edmund Howard (Surrey's youngest son) and the left by Sir Marmaduke Constable. The centre of the rear line was commanded by Surrey himself, while his right and left were commanded by Lord Dacre and Sir Edward Stanley respectively. The two English lines drawing closer together then advanced and the attack began. The first engagement on 9 September went more in the Scots' favour than the English. Lord Home and his Borderers were able to overwhelm the English 'front right' under Edmund Howard but then dissipated their advantage by looting his camp and sitting out the rest of the battle. The wild Highlanders then swept down in wave after wave led by Lennox and Argyle and were destroyed by the English artillery. Those who were not blown to pieces refused to ask for quarter and were cut to pieces instead. The superior quality of the English artillery was a decisive factor in the battle and helped to make up for the much smaller size of the English army. Surrey was able to defeat the main Scottish charge in the centre led by James IV himself, who had been rashly encouraged by the seeming success of Home's forces. Thereafter the English victory was a foregone conclusion. The fighting went on into the twilight and by the morning of 10 September 1513 the King of Scotland, two of his Bishops and the chief of his nobility (nine earls out of a total of twenty-one, and eleven barons out of twenty-nine) were dead and the remnants of the Scottish army were in full flight; over ten thousand Scots are reputed to have been killed as opposed to four hundred English losses. The sword, dagger and ring were removed from the body of the Scottish King as trophies (to be long preserved as relics in the Howard family[7]), while the King's corpse itself was taken to England to be presented in due course to Henry VIII, at Richmond, before being buried in the charterhouse there. The English troops dispersed to their various counties of origin. The Lancashire archers are commemorated in one of the most moving of English war memorials, the stained glass east window of Middleton Church, erected by Sir Richard Assheton and incorporating little, named portrait figures, not of those who died but of those who safely returned home.

Surrey had won a decisive victory which not only saved England from Scottish invasion in 1513 but ended the Scottish military threat forever and left the Scottish nation leaderless. 'This noble act was done by the help of Almighty God to the high honour of the King's highness', and was a personal victory for the Howards. They were suitably rewarded when, in a magnificent ceremony at Lambeth Palace on Candlemas Day 1514, Surrey was 'honourably restored unto his right name of Duke of Norfolk'[8] He wore splendid crimson robes for the occasion and was ceremonially presented with the patent of the dukedom by Garter King of Arms. He was also granted an honourable augmentation to his arms, namely: 'in an escutcheon or, a demi-lion rampant, pierced through the mouth with an arrow, within a double tressure flory and counter flory gules', in other words the lion of the Royal Scottish arms chopped in half with an arrow stuck down its throat, a graphic memento of the victory. Lastly Norfolk was presented with a group of thirty manors and an annuity of forty pounds by Henry VIII. For the remainder of his life the old Duke was to be treated with the deference usually reserved for princes of the blood.

Despite this extraordinary show of favour, Norfolk found his influence at the Council table gradually eroded by Wolsey, who from 1515 was the King's chief adviser. This did not in fact reduce the amount of public business with which the Duke was involved, although whether he enjoyed much of what he was called upon to perform must remain a matter for conjecture. In 1514 he escorted Princess Mary, the King's young sister, to France for her marriage to the elderly King Louis XII. Norfolk himself had opposed the marriage, but Wolsey had pushed forward regardless, and Norfolk unintentionally offended the Princess by dismissing all her English attendants (chosen by Wolsey) as soon as they were on French soil. In the event the marriage only lasted eighty-three days before Louis died, and Mary was able to marry Charles Brandon, Duke of Suffolk, with whom she was already in love, and return to England with him. On 15 November Norfolk performed another official ceremony which could not have been entirely to his satisfaction. This was to escort Wolsey from the High Altar to the West door of Westminster Abbey after the ceremony in which Wolsey had received his Cardinal's hat. The following year he was appointed a commissioner for the formation of a 'Holy League' between England, Spain and the Emperor 'for the defence of the Catholic Church against heresy', which he must have found more congenial.

Norfolk's last major enterprise in public life was the suppression of the 'May Day' or 'Prentice Riots' in 1517 in the capacity of Earl Marshal. These riots in the City of London were caused by English jealousy at the growing prosperity of immigrant artificers, and have a familiar ring. A priest, Fr. Beale, and a broker called Lincoln had stirred up agitation against foreigners and had been imprisoned for threatening French and Flemish merchants with violence. This culminated in the rioting of a group of English apprentices who liberated their imprisoned colleagues and then ransacked the establishment of a merchant from Picardy called Meutas, killing several of his servants. Norfolk and his son, together with the Earl of Shrewsbury and a troop of one thousand three hundred East Anglians marched on London and put down the riot on 1 May. The ringleaders were arrested and a proclamation published ordering that 'women should not meet together to babble and talk' and that 'all men should keep their wives in their houses', which throws interesting light on whom the Duke considered to be responsible for stirring up all the trouble. Henry VIII wanted wholesale executions, but Norfolk succeeded in persuading him to take a more lenient course. Though Lincoln and thirteen other leaders were hanged, the remainder, to the number of over four hundred, were pardoned after presenting themselves to the King, clad only in their shirts and carrying rope halters round their necks, begging forgiveness. An attractive postscript to this is that on Norfolk's death he was remembered by the London apprentices who sent some of their members as representatives to his funeral at Thetford.[9]

Finally while Henry and Wolsey were in France for the junkettings of the Field of the Cloth of Gold, Norfolk acted as the 'guardian of the realm'. But Wolsey was already planning an event which would lead indirectly to Norfolk's retirement in disgust from public life. This was the destruction of the magnificent Duke of Buckingham, whose royal descent from Thomas of Woodstock made him too dangerous to be allowed to live, and who had made no effort to disguise his contempt for Wolsey, thus gaining the Cardinal's enmity. A few months after Wolsey, Henry VIII and Buckingham had returned from the Field of the Cloth of Gold Buckingham was arrested, to the astonishment of all Europe. He was accused of High Treason on the flimsiest of charges and subjected to a travesty of a trial in May 1521 over which Norfolk was forced to preside as Lord High Steward. Buckingham had been his friend for thirty years, his eldest son had married Buckingham's daughter, and they agreed on almost every political issue. The poor old man was therefore completely broken by this unwanted duty. When the subservient jury of twenty peers had condemned Buckingham, and Norfolk came to pronounce the sentence of attainder and death, he burst into tears and it was some time before he could falter out 'the words of doom'. Soon afterwards he

Framlingham Castle. The Howard arms in the gatehouse, which was rebuilt by the 2nd Duke of Norfolk.

Framlingham Castle, Suffolk, inherited by the Howards from the Mowbrays in 1483.

resigned the Lord Treasurership and all his other official duties except for that of Earl Marshal and made his way to Framlingham, never to take part in public affairs again. He spent the last two years of his life in quiet retirement in his castle, which he had already much embellished and improved, having rebuilt the gatehouse with a proud display of the Howard arms in a cartouche over the entrance archway, and having added a splendid array of ornamental brick chimneystacks to the battlemented walls of the Bigods and Mowbrays.

The Duke died on 21 May 1524 aged eighty and was given a funeral which was the last of its kind. 'No nobleman was ever to be buried in such style again.' His will too, signed on 31 May 1520, was also the last in which a subject spoke of himself as 'we'. The chamber of state, the great hall and chapel at Framlingham were hung with black cloth and escutcheons of arms while the Duke's body lay in state for a month before the altar in the chapel 'which his grace [had] kept prince like for he had great pleasure in the service of God'. Three solemn masses were sung daily with nineteen mourners kneeling round the hearse, while every night it was watched by twelve gentlemen, twelve yeomen, two yeoman ushers and two gentleman ushers. On 22 June the Duke's coffin set out from Framlingham on the twenty-four mile journey to Thetford, the ancient burial place of the Earls and Dukes of Norfolk, Bigods, Mowbrays and now Howards; the coffin was placed in a chariot drawn by three horses bedecked with black trappings and gold escutcheons and was accompanied by nine hundred mourners, including four hundred torchmen in black gowns with hoods, friars, chaplains, standard- and banner-bearers, lords, knights, esquires, gentlemen of the household, and the Duke's treasurer and comptroller. His helmet with crest (which now hangs in the Howard chapel at Framlingham) was borne by the Windsor herald, and hatchments of his arms were carried by the Carlisle herald, Clarenceaux King of Arms and Garter King of Arms. The journey took two days and the procession rested overnight at Diss where a solemn dirge was sung in the church and alms distributed, as had also occurred in all the churches along the way. A substantial portion of the population of East Anglia must have witnessed this gigantic cavalcade and thousands benefited from the distribution of alms.

On arrival at Thetford Priory, the Duke's coffin was received at the church door by the Bishop of Ely 'in pontificalibus' and by the Abbots of Wymondham and Thetford and the Prior of Butley, all wearing their mitres. The body was carried by six gentlemen and six knights to a fabulous catafalque in the middle of the black-draped choir of the abbey church. This unimaginable structure was an enormous heraldic fantasy of black and gold adorned with seven hundred lights, a hundred wax effigies of black-gowned bedesmen holding rosaries, eight 'bannerols' showing the Duke's illustrious descent and marriages and no fewer than a hundred hatchments of his arms. There the Duke's body rested in state overnight. The services of the funeral itself began at five o'clock in the morning with three consecutive requiem masses of increasing grandeur, the first sung by the Prior of Butley, the second by the Abbot of Wymondham, the third and final one, a pontifical High Mass of requiem, celebrated by the Bishop of Ely. They were followed by the heraldic ceremonies which marked the obsequies of a dead duke, including a procession of hatchments of his arms carried by the heralds and presented to the Bishop. The high point however was the dramatic entry into the church of a knight dressed in the dead Duke's armour with visor closed, carrying his battleaxe head down, and mounted on a horse with cloth of gold trappings. This awesome apparition rode slowly up the nave of the church to the choir screen where it presented the dead Duke's axe, still head down, to the Bishop.

There followed a sermon of the same heroic character preached by Dr Mackerell. It lasted an hour and the theme was 'Behold the lion of the Tribe of Judah triumphs.' So effective was this piece of oratory that the congregation fled from the church in terror. The Bishop then consecrated the new burial vault under the choir which the Duke had just had built for his family and which may still be seen today in the midst of the ruins of the abbey church. Finally the body was interred, the Bishop throwing a symbolic handful of earth on to the 'noble corpse' and sprinkling it with holy water while the chief officers of the Duke's household broke their staves of office and threw the pieces into their master's tomb.[10]

It is as well that the Duke died when he did. He would not have welcomed the bloody deterioration of public life under Henry VIII, or the religious revolution that would shortly destroy much of what he prized including the monastery of Thetford, for he was to be the last as well as the first of his family to be buried in his new vault there. Within twenty years the whole ethos of which his funeral was a last, but by no means undistinguished, witness would have been undermined. The 2nd Duke of Norfolk, whose obsequies marked the end of the Middle Ages in England, was the patriarch of the entire Howard family, and from him are descended all the titled Howards now in existence: the Norfolks, Suffolks, Carlisles, Effinghams and Howards of Penrith.

The 3rd Duke of Norfolk

THE Flodden Duke was succeeded by his eldest son Thomas, an unscrupulous and brilliant man who for long periods was the most powerful nobleman in the kingdom, the scheming Machiavellian uncle of two Queens of England and the leader of the conservative reaction at the Court of Henry VIII; he was chiefly responsible for the overthrow of both Wolsey and Thomas Cromwell, and almost single-handedly stopped the latter's political and religious revolution in the 1530s. He has the distinction of being immortalized in literature and art, by Shakespeare and Holbein. Holbein's famous portrait shows the Duke holding the Earl Marshal's gold baton and the Lord Treasurer's white staff, and confirms contemporary descriptions that he was small, sallow, clean-shaven and aquiline, his face thrown into relief by the dark hair which, with characteristic conservatism, he wore falling over his ears in a long-abandoned fashion giving him a subtle distinction and emphasizing his connection with a remote and feudal past.

The impression he made was of an intelligent, kindly man, approachable and unpretentious; he was famous for the informality of his manner and his easy way with all classes. This outward appearance was deceptive for he was in fact cunning, ruthlessly ambitious and without mercy. His military methods seemed, even to contemporaries, to be exceptionally and calculatingly cruel. It was best not to trust this seemingly amiable, honourable soldier-statesman, as the participants in the Pilgrimage of Grace found when he instituted a reign of terror after they had put down their arms. Henry VIII, himself not the most merciful of men, once felt obliged to apologize to the French for the Duke's 'foul warfare', and after one particular Scottish raid it was announced that the Duke had left 'neither house, fortress, village, tree, cattle, corn nor other succour of man'. He was among the most oppressive and conservative landowners in early sixteenth-century England, and one of the very few to retain villeinage on his estates. In Norfolk, of four privately-owned manors which still retained bondmen or serfs in the 1540s, three belonged to the Duke of Norfolk, and in Suffolk five of the six manors retaining villeins belonged to him. His former serfs complained to the Lord

Hans Holbein. Thomas, 3rd Duke of Norfolk, Earl Marshal and Lord Treasurer of England in the reign of Henry VIII.

Protector, Somerset, in the 1550s that the Duke had used towards them 'muche more extremitie than his Auncestoures did'. Kett's rebellion in East Anglia in 1549 was largely a cheerful reaction to the Duke's overthrow.[1] Marillac, the French ambassador, was disgusted by the Duke's heartlessness at the time of the execution of Queen Katherine Howard, while the Duchess of Norfolk said of her husband in a letter to Cromwell, 'he can speak fair as well to his enemy as to his friend . . . he neither regardeth God nor his honour'. Such were the qualities essential for survival at the Court of Henry VIII.

The Duke's dissimulation extended into every aspect of his life. There was for instance a notable discrepancy between his public show of open-handedness, and his private meanness. He was ready to receive and feed two hundred poor persons or travellers every day in a manner becoming a great ducal household, yet he balked at paying small allowances to his wife and son. The Earl of Surrey was always short of money and judging from his earliest surviving letter seems to have been dependent on loans from friendly local abbots, while the Duchess of Norfolk spent much of her time writing to the King and Council complaining of her shortage of money and the Duke's miserliness towards her. The Duke owned fifty jewelled rosaries, but was strangely mean in small ways and, for instance, wore his fur-lined dressing-gowns till they were rubbed bare. The key to his behaviour was a deep instinctive conservatism which made him hostile to any hint of change or manifestation of popular unrest, and he was prepared to go to any lengths to preserve the status quo and his own place in it. Perhaps his most revealing remark was when he snapped back at a clerk in the Exchequer in 1540: 'I have never read the Scripture nor ever will read it. It was merry in England afore the new learning came up; yea, I would all thinges were as hath been in times past.'[2]

He was born at Ashwell Thorpe, the Tilney house, in 1473 and was brought up there with his brothers and half-brother Lord Berners, the translator of Froissart's *Chronicles, Huon of Bordeaux*, and other French romances. Nothing is known of his early education, but he learnt to speak fluently in French, Italian and Spanish. In 1495, when he was twenty-two, he married a royal princess in Westminster Abbey, Lady Anne Plantagenet, daughter of Edward IV and sister-in-law of Henry VII. It is possible that he had been betrothed to her eleven years earlier, before Bosworth, but if this was so it is not documented. This marriage, although magnificent, was unprofitable and unproductive, for his wife had no dowry and during fourteen years of marriage her four sons all died in infancy. After her death Norfolk, at the age of forty, in about 1512 married Elizabeth Stafford, daughter of the Duke of Buckingham (who was beheaded nine years later by Henry VIII). This marriage began well and produced two sons and a daughter, but eventually turned sour when the Duke became infatuated with Bess Holland, the daughter of his steward at Kenninghall. After several years of bitterness and quarrelling, the

Duke and Duchess finally separated in Lent 1534. The Duchess left Bess Holland
in command at Kenninghall and retired to Redbourne in Hertfordshire where she
lived in modest circumstances and bombarded the Duke, the King and Thomas
Cromwell with a succession of letters retailing her wrongs at her husband's
hands: amongst other indignities he had cut her head and 'He keeps that harlot
Bess Holland and the residue of the harlots that bound me and pynnacled me and
sat on my breast till I spat blood, and I reckon if I come home I shall be poisoned.'[3]

The Duke protested to Cromwell in reply:

My good lord, if I prove not by witness, and that with many honest persons, that she had
the scar In her head XV months before she was delivered of my said daughter, and that
the same was cut by a surgeon of London for a swelling she had In her head of drawing
of 2 teeth, never trust my word after ... surely I think there is no man alive that would
handle a woman in child bed of that sort; nor for my part would not so have done for all
that I am worth.[4]

He later told Cromwell that if she 'continues her false and abominable lies and
obstinacy against me I shall ... lock her up'.[5] The Duchess referred to Bess with
more bitterness than truth as 'a churl's daughter and of no gentle blood' and 'that
drab'. This unpleasant domestic squabble spread its taint throughout the Duke's
life, and the household dissensions, jealousies and hatreds that grew out of it were
to have serious repercussions.

Up to the age of thirty-six the 3rd Duke, then known as Lord Thomas Howard,
does not seem to have achieved much, as his early life was hampered by the
straitened circumstances of his father following Bosworth. It was only in 1509
with the accession of Henry VIII that he came into his own, and it was primarily
his ability in the military field that led to his advancement. The young King
wanted a belligerent foreign policy and a 'glorious' war against France, England's
traditional enemy. In the early sixteenth century English society in its higher
ranks was still largely geared to war. The nobility held fighting to be a major
raison d'être, and prowess in fighting to be the distinguishing hallmark of their
class. The Howards formed part of an hereditary military caste, nourished on the
cult of war and chivalry, which had always provided the natural leaders of the
army and navy. The accession of a war-like King provided them with an outlet for
their energies and talents on land and sea.

Henry VIII was keen to revive the military glories of Henry V's wars and was
anxious not to associate the Tudors with the surrender of the traditional English
holdings in France. Hence throughout his reign he mounted a series of expensive,
and in retrospect futile, campaigns against France, designed to impress upon the
French King the gravity of the English threat. Thus the intermittent besieging of
Boulogne by the Duke of Norfolk 'came to be considered the sine qua non of
Tudor generalship'.

Henry VIII went to war with France for the first time in 1512. On the ill-fated Guienne expedition Thomas Howard emerged as almost the only commander of the English forces who could be relied on when the English were betrayed by their ally Ferdinand of Aragon and the army almost mutinied. As Howard wrote to his father 'Would to Christ the King and his counsel had put no more trust in the King of Aragon's fair promise.'[6] While Thomas was active in France, his younger brother Edward was at sea as Lord Admiral in charge of the English fleet in the Channel, which provided the essential back-up to any Continental expedition. He was killed in a foolhardy attack on the French fleet at Brest in April 1513, dramatically tearing his admiral's badge (a golden whistle) from round his neck and diving to his death as the French soldiers closed in round him. Thomas was appointed Lord Admiral in his brother's place on 4 May and became responsible for making the Channel safe for the crossing of the English army under Henry VIII's own leadership; however, contrary winds confined him to Plymouth at a critical moment and earned him the King's displeasure for appearing to vacillate. Henry crossed to France in August 1513 where he took part in the Battle of the Spurs and the capture of Tournai. The Howards however, as has been mentioned already, were left behind at Wolsey's instigation, to look after the Scottish Border. The Scottish campaign and the victory at Flodden, which was such a personal triumph for the Howards, overshadowed the King's Continental escapades. Thomas played a leading role, under his father, in the strategy of the battle, and as a reward was created Earl of Surrey at the same time that his father was restored as Duke of Norfolk at the ceremony in Lambeth Palace on Candlemas, 1514.

From then on Thomas played an increasingly active role in public affairs, both as a military commander and as an administrator. In the ten years between 1514 and 1524, when he succeeded to the Dukedom, he held four important posts: he was Lord Admiral throughout, Lord Deputy of Ireland in 1520 and 1521, Lieutenant General of the Anglo-Imperial army in France in 1522 and King's Lieutenant on the Northern Border in 1523 and 1524. This record of conscientious service to the Crown firmly established his position in national affairs, but his responsibilities lay heavily on him and damaged his health. At one stage he told Wolsey: 'I am marvellously afeared that I shall consume and waste away . . . the flush that I had is clean gone . . . I never slept one whole hour without waking, my mind is so troubled for fear that anything should frame amiss.'[7]

As Lord Admiral he was responsible for building up English naval power in the Channel, which was a necessary part of Henry's ambitious Continental foreign policy. Much of Howard's time was taken up with detailed day-to-day administration, the fortification and garrisoning of naval bases and the victualling of fleets. One of his improvements was to divide the North Sea and Channel into three different administrative zones. He did not fight any battles at sea but concentrated on shipping troops across to France, and on raiding the French coast.

He enjoyed this ravaging warfare and wrote eloquently to the Privy Council in 1514 of his achievement in Normandy where 'no house [was] left unbrent'. In order to facilitate his naval activity, he was later created 'Lord Admiral of the Holy Roman Empire and its dependant states' by Charles V, a position which gave him the use of the ports in the Low Countries, a considerable advantage in the Channel.

Surrey's appointment as Lord Deputy of Ireland in 1520 and 1521 was not so much a promotion as an ingenious attempt on Wolsey's part to remove him, for he was developing into a serious threat to the Cardinal, and his absence was necessary while Wolsey encompassed the destruction of his father-in-law, the Duke of Buckingham. Then, as at many times before and since, Ireland meant political death for any Englishman unfortunate enough to be entrusted with ruling it. When Surrey arrived, the country was in its usual state of anarchy, with Norman barons and Gaelic chieftains warring with each other. The O'Mores, O'Neills, Desmonds and O'Byrnes all rose at different times, and he was engaged in a series of military expeditions to try to restore order. This thankless task was made even worse by Wolsey's deliberate policy of keeping him short of money. He arranged truces between the Desmonds and Ormonds, with the O'Mores, and persuaded the McCarthy and O'Donnell to agree to hold their lands from the English Crown. However, he remained sceptical about such efforts, thinking the Irish people to be of 'small trust'. His treasurer agreed with this view, and called them 'naturally covetous and deceitfully subtle people'. Surrey declared to Wolsey that 'this land will never be brought to due obeysaunce but only with compulsion and conquest'.[8] Henry VIII was then merely Lord of Ireland; Surrey was among the first to propose the establishment of a kingdom of Ireland, which came into effect in 1542 when Henry assumed the Kingship. Surrey's policy was to offer the chieftains and nobles security of tenure of their lands, and assistance against marauding neighbours, in return for allegiance to the English Crown. In his reports to Henry VIII he outlined two alternative policies for controlling Ireland: the relatively peaceful conquest of the country by winning over the great chieftains, or the complete extermination of the Irish race. The latter was considered too expensive and so Surrey attempted to persevere with the former. The imprisonment of Kildare, however, caused ill-feeling and sparked off a series of rebellions at Easter 1521. After an ineffective expedition against the insurgents, during which he went down with dysentery, Surrey finally lost interest in Irish affairs and begged to be recalled. His petition was granted and in April 1522 he left Ireland for good with little or nothing achieved. Ormond was appointed in his place.

After a spell of recuperation with his family at Tendring, which his father had made over to him on moving to Framlingham, Surrey returned to sea; he escorted Charles V on his trip to England in 1522, and also attacked and burnt several more châteaux and towns in Normandy and Picardy. The next year he was appointed Lieutenant-General of the English army against Scotland, following the return of the Scottish Regent, Albany. In 1523 and 1524 he led a series of destructive raids over the Border, which were intended to deliver a salutary reminder of Flodden to the Northern Kingdom. During this period he was based at the royal castle of Sheriff Hutton near York.

In all this Surrey proved himself loyal, hardworking and conscientious. His frequent letters to Wolsey and the Council were scrupulously obsequious, but after his succession to the dukedom in 1524 they concealed a stubborn determination to acquire power at the Council table as well as in the field; such an ambition required the destruction of Wolsey. The Cardinal stood in the way of the Howards' attempt to secure control of the government, and they saw him also as arrogant and 'jumped-up' (a butcher's boy) and responsible for the unjust execution of Norfolk's father-in-law the Duke of Buckingham. The Duke's Irish exile had been the last straw and to some extent explains his savage outbursts of hatred. The chance for revenge came with the failure of Wolsey's extravagant foreign policy at the Treaty of Cambrai in 1526 when both France and the Emperor ignored England; and Wolsey's ruin was completed by his inability to secure a papal annulment of Henry's marriage to Catherine of Aragon. Norfolk conspired with his niece Anne Boleyn, and on 18 October 1529 had the satisfaction of receiving from Wolsey the Great Seal, the badge of supreme power. He subsequently contrived the Cardinal's removal from Whitehall to his diocese of York; 'if he go not away shortly I will rather than he should tarry still, tear him with my teeth', a savage remark which contrasts tellingly with his accustomed air of mild affability. For the next three years Norfolk was in command, as President of the Council. In 1530 through an unpleasant piece of intrigue, he was able to secure Wolsey's arrest for High Treason, but the Cardinal died at Leicester Abbey on his way back to London before any action could be taken against him.

Norfolk had triumphed but, though a good soldier and a competent administrator, he had not the originality of mind to make a great statesman and was unable to further the matter of the King's divorce, which in turn led to the promotion of Thomas Cromwell to the inner ring of the Council. Cromwell gradually took over control of affairs, carrying through the revolution that destroyed the medieval Church and made England a sovereign national State. His Treason Act of 1534, which enabled a 'traitor' to be condemned to death without trial, by Act of Attainder, provided a terrible weapon for the reigning power to use against its enemies, and was to claim its share of Howards.

During these years Norfolk attempted to strengthen his position by arranging marriage alliances between the Howards and the royal family. He betrothed his daughter Mary to Henry VIII's illegitimate son the Duke of Richmond and toyed with the idea of marrying his eldest son the Earl of Surrey to Princess Mary. At first he was aided in his endeavours by his niece Anne Boleyn (his sister's daughter) who, as the King's mistress and later wife, was happy to forward her uncle's and the Howard fortunes; though she soon tired of this, however, and turned against Norfolk and this was partly the reason for his callousness towards her when she was condemned for adultery. He took an active part in preparing the charges and presided over her trial as Lord High Steward. He even encouraged Henry to declare their daughter Elizabeth illegitimate, presumably in order to improve Richmond's chance of being legitimized and succeeding to the throne; but if this was so the scheme was thwarted when Richmond died at the age of seventeen in 1536, with his marriage to Mary Howard still unconsummated. He was buried in the Norfolk vault at Thetford Priory. The fall of Anne Boleyn opened the way for Henry to marry Jane Seymour, a representative of the opposition to the reactionary Howards. When she produced a legitimate son and heir to the throne, the Seymours were established as the Howards' most dangerous long-term enemies.

The years 1536–40, during which he struggled with Cromwell, are the most exciting of Norfolk's life. The story of the 3rd Duke in this period is essentially that of the English Court, and almost the history of England itself. The execution of Anne Boleyn for adultery and the rise of the Seymours, reduced the Howard stock at Court. But the Duke waited patiently for an opportunity to make a come-back. It soon arrived in the Pilgrimage of Grace. The Duke eagerly welcomed this crisis, and his behaviour in 1536 has always been interpreted as a notable landmark in the gradual degradation of his character which was brought about by the struggle for power. Chapuys, the Spanish ambassador, reported that the prospect of dealing with the rebels made Norfolk 'exceedingly happy', for he knew that the rebellion would probably destroy Cromwell. Norfolk was Henry's ablest, almost his only, military commander, and therefore indispensable to the King in putting down the northern revolt, though the Duke agreed with the demands of the Pilgrims for the restoration of 'true religion' and certainly shared their hatred of Cromwell:

> Crom, Cram and Riche,
> With L.L.L. and their liche,
> As some men teach,
> God them amend.

The Duke's cruel and bloody subjection of the North after the risings was pursued with a thoroughness intended to demonstrate his dutiful devotion to the King's wishes. It has been suggested that there was a direct conflict between Norfolk's personal beliefs and his acts, and that he sacrificed men whose ideals he shared in order to re-establish his position at Court. The extent to which the Pilgrimage of Grace was a genuine religious movement as opposed to a popular rebellion is still a matter for controversy. Norfolk probably saw it more as the latter, and as a strong supporter of the status quo he would have had little hesitation in supporting the King against the rebels, even if he did personally sympathize with some of their claims.

At first the King and Cromwell were reluctant to give Norfolk a free hand because they did indeed suspect his loyalty. He was therefore especially keen to prove himself and to serve the King's wishes. He offered to send his son to the King 'to be pledge for my truth, which though by this dealing may give occasion to be suspected, shall never be deserved'. Despite Cromwell's reluctance to rely on the Duke, events played into his hands. The rebellion seemed daily more serious and Norfolk was rapidly promoted to sole command, appointed Lieutenant of the North and given authority to march to Doncaster with an army. Once there he informed the King that the best way to deal with the situation was to grant an amnesty to the rebels and to pacify them without fighting, if possible. The King approved this and Norfolk sent the rebels an ultimatum which led to a meeting with their leaders at Doncaster Bridge on 27 October. Norfolk then went back to Court to discuss the situation further with the King, before returning in December with the false promise that the King would consider their demands if the Pilgrims laid down their arms and returned peacefully to their homes. Once they had dispersed, the time came for retribution. Norfolk wrote in February 1537 'Now shall appear whether for favor of these countrymen I forbore to fight with them at Doncaster as you know the King's Highness showed me it was thought by some I did. Those that so said shall now be proved false liars.'⁹ (Cromwell in reading this must have realised that the Duke was referring to him.)

Courts Martial were set up to deal with the Pilgrims, as it was feared that local juries would not condemn them. The Duke was satisfied with the results: 'though the number be nothing so great as their deserts did require to have suffered, yet I think the like number hath not been heard of put to execution at one time'. All the leaders were hanged including the abbots of Kirkstall, Whalley, Jervaulx and Fountains; altogether 222 to 250 persons were executed. The Duke reported with relish on 18 April: 'These countries thanked be God be in such order that I trust never in our life no new commotions shall be attempted. And surely I see nothing here but too much fear.'¹⁰

After the defeat of the rebels, Cromwell pushed on with his programme, though his own end too was now in sight; beginning in 1537 the great monasteries were dissolved, as their lesser brethren had been already, and in 1538 shrines and pilgrimages were also abolished. Cromwell destroyed much of value: a form of religion, noble buildings, works of art and great libraries, as well as causing a major redistribution of land in England. But the relative ease with which he initially broke with Rome and carried through his revolution was deceptive. In 1538 began the series of religious struggles and problems which have continued in some corners of the British Isles down to the present day, though the Elizabethan Church Settlement, with its careful balance of traditional organization and Protestant theology, achieved an admirable working ecclesiastical compromise in most of the south of England. In 1538 there occurred the first contest of the English Reformation, with Norfolk and Bishop Gardiner of Winchester as leaders of the conservatives, and Cromwell and Archbishop Cranmer at the head of the radicals. Norfolk won this first round, although at the end of the reign he lost the battle to the Protestant Seymours.

The conservatives' success was demonstrated in the Parliament of April 1539 with the passing of the Act of the Six Articles which solemnly enforced belief in all the important doctrines and practices of the old religion: transubstantiation, communion in one kind, clerical celibacy, the perpetual obligation of vows of celibacy, the utility of masses and prayers for the dead, and the necessity of auricular confession. This schema was drawn up largely by Gardiner and Norfolk, and it effectively set at naught all the labours of the Protestant party. The failure of Cromwell's attempt to secure a Lutheran bride for Henry VIII following the death of Jane Seymour in 1537 gave the reactionaries the opening they wanted. Cromwell's choice of Anne of Cleves was a misjudgement because Henry found her physically repulsive, and though he went through with the marriage for diplomatic reasons, he parted from her on amicable terms immediately afterwards. Cromwell's dragooning of the King into the Cleves' marriage, together with general royal unease over the extent of the religious revolution, helped to wreck his political position. The conservatives grew in strength throughout 1540 and Norfolk's embassy to Francis I in order to secure a new Anglo–French alliance raised the Duke once more in the King's favour. He and his supporters realized that if they were to gain lasting influence over the King they must provide him with a new wife who would be sympathetic to their point of view – as their opponents had done with Jane Seymour and, less successfully, with Anne of Cleves. Norfolk's choice fell on one of his pretty nieces, Katherine Howard, daughter of the Duke's dead brother Lord Edmund Howard. Katherine had been brought up by her devout step-grandmother Agnes (Tilney), Duchess of Norfolk, in the supposedly convent-like atmosphere of the old manor-house at Horsham St. Faith. In fact she had been seduced at the age of fourteen and had already had two lovers before she was brought to Court by her uncle and introduced to the King, on whom her youthful prettiness and purportedly virginal charms soon had the desired effect. Katherine married Henry quietly at Oatlands on the day that Cromwell was executed.

Cromwell had been arrested on 10 June 1540 by the Duke of Norfolk at the Council table: 'My Lord of Essex, I arrest you of High Treason . . . You are a traitor,' he shouted as he tore the George from the Minister's neck and trampled it under his heel. 'You shall be judged by the bloody laws you yourself have made.'

John Howard, 1st Duke of Norfolk. A sixteenth-century portrait pair for Lord Lumley and displaying the characteristic Lumley *cartellino*.

Mather Brown. The Earl of Surrey defending his allegiance to Richard III before Henry VII. Painted for the 11th Duke of Norfolk.

Cromwell was condemned by Act of Attainder, the instrument of judicial murder which he had invented to dispose of the Countess of Suffolk, and was beheaded. His removal left Norfolk once more in control and in an apparently impregnable position. He and Gardiner began to look ahead and plan to retain power by securing the regency, once the King, whose decline was obvious, was dead. Norfolk's triumph, however, proved to be short-lived; within a year the unexpected fall of Katherine Howard threatened to bring about his complete eclipse and ended the chance of carrying through a successful reaction in the long term, though in the event the Duke himself narrowly escaped the worst.

Poor Katherine! To Henry she had seemed a 'rose without a thorn'. Though perfunctorily educated she was pretty, sympathetic and kindly. Marillac, the French ambassador, tells us that her countenance was delightful, her figure slender and that she dressed in the French fashion. She behaved well to her predecessor Anne of Cleves and, less wisely, to her old friends and supporters. She made Francis Dereham, with whom she had had midnight frolics in the 'Maids' Chamber' at Horsham St. Faith, her secretary. It is unlikely that there were any further relations between them, but such an appointment was nevertheless an act of folly. Henry was deeply infatuated with his lovely young wife, and following their return from a northern tour (intended to soothe the bitter feelings left by the aftermath of the Pilgrimage of Grace), in the autumn of 1541 he ordered a public Form of Thanksgiving to Almighty God to be read on All Saints Day, for having blessed him with so loving and virtuous a wife; this in fact never took place, for in the interval Cranmer handed the King a note to be read in private which contained a detailed account of Katherine's previous liaisons and indiscretions.

This came as a great shock to the King. Quite apart from his feelings, his self-esteem was sorely wounded. 'Henry who had pretended to a wonderful sagacity on the subject in the case of Anne of Cleves, had not discovered any lack of virginity in Katherine Howard.' He ordered a secret inquiry, which confirmed the worst: Henry Mannock the music master's lewd behaviour at the virginals, Katherine's 'betrothal' to Francis Dereham before her marriage and her continued intimacy with him, as well as her friendship with Thomas Culpepper after her marriage. Katherine was interviewed by four Privy Councillors including Norfolk and Cranmer. At first she denied everything, but Cranmer was able to gain her confidence and to 'comfort her by your Grace's benignity and mercy. There followed much weeping and sobbing and pangs of contrition' and she made her confession. Dereham, Culpepper, Lady Rochford (Katherine's lady-in-waiting) and Katherine herself were all executed. Norfolk however extricated himself. He denounced his niece's behaviour with tears in his eyes for the King's grief. Chapuys reported that the Duke had said that he wished, 'God Knows Why', that Katherine were burned. He laughed when sentence was passed against her.

Marillac wrote ironically of this disgraceful behaviour 'it is the custom and must be done to show they do not share the niece's crime'.

In the short-term the Duke was saved by another military crisis when in 1542 there was a renewal of trouble on the Scottish Border. Norfolk was appointed Lieutenant and Captain General of the army and hurried to the North with his son. He laid waste the richest part of the eastern Border counties with his usual thoroughness, while the main Scottish army was annihilated by the Warden of the Western Marches, Sir Thomas Wharton, at Solway Moss. Almost contemporaneous with the Scottish campaign was a renewal of war with France. Henry VIII in person led a huge army to the Continent, in which both Norfolk and his son the Earl of Surrey served. This campaign saw the final flare-up of the King's military ambition. Boulogne was captured and Landrecy and Montreuil unsuccessfully besieged at a cost to England of two million pounds; nothing was achieved beyond the ruin of the financial indepence of the Crown, the debasement of the currency and the undermining of the prosperity of the country. Norfolk had the political sense to realize the futility of the war, and once back in England did his best at the Privy Council table to persuade the King to give up Boulogne. This policy was not helped by the Earl of Surrey's enthusiastic letters which, with their detailed reports of the defence of the city against the French, unwittingly fed the King's delusions of military glory. In the end the King bowed to the Privy Council's persuasion, peace was made and Boulogne handed back to the French under a treaty negotiated by Hertford in 1546.

As Henry VIII's reign drew to a close, the politics of the Court degenerated into a life-and-death struggle between the Howards and Seymours for the Protectorship of the young heir, Prince Edward. The Seymours held the trump card, in that Edward was Hertford's nephew. The fate of the Howards in 1546 was, however, not so much determined by the machinations of their political and religious opponents as by the divisions and dissensions within the family itself. The Duke had sacrificed his family to Court intrigue and dynastic ambition. He had separated from his wife in order to live with Bess Holland and had turned his children against their mother: 'never a woman bare so ungracious an eldest son, and so ungracious a daughter and so unnatural'. Anne Boleyn's lack of co-operation had wrecked the Duke's marriage proposals for his son the Earl of Surrey in 1529 and led to bitter hatreds. Once the Duke of Richmond died, Norfolk lost interest in his only daughter Mary. A proposal to marry her to one of the Seymours and thus to heal the breach with the Howards' arch-enemies had foundered over the opposition of her brother, the Earl of Surrey. The Duke had refused to assist in her attempts to obtain her dowry from the King in the years 1537–8 because he did not want to incur the King's further displeasure during a difficult period. As a result the Duchess of Richmond held her father and brother responsible for her state of impoverished widowhood, and added personal hatred to the differences of religion arising from her support for the new theology which the Duke and Surrey loathed. Thus when it came to the final political struggle of Henry VIII's reign, the House of Howard was divided against itself and was also hampered by a dangerous heir, in the proud, tactless Earl of Surrey whose rash words and lack of guile undermined much of the wily Duke's careful scheming.

The arrest and trial of Surrey was the preliminary to trapping Norfolk himself. On his return to London from Kenninghall, following his son's sudden arrest, he too was put in the Tower and an Act of Attainder against him was rushed through Parliament. Norfolk wrote a grovelling last letter to the dying King, abandoning his son and admitting himself guilty of acts which were not in fact treasonous. This proved ineffective and he was condemned to death in January 1547. The legal chicanery of the Duke's attainder arouses a certain sympathy for his ruthlessly single-minded struggle for survival, his ambition and greed. But his luck held and the death of Henry VIII on the very morning of the day on which he was due to be beheaded saved the Duke's life, because it was not wished to open the new reign with an execution and bloodshed.

The Duke's arrest and imprisonment sparked off a celebratory rebellion in his native East Anglia, where the populace rose under Kett's leadership in response to what seemed the end of the Howard sway and the collapse of the focus of local government. They destroyed the fences round Kenninghall park and sacked the Earl of Surrey's house in Norwich. The Duke's former villeins petitioned the Duke of Somerset (the title to which Hertford had now risen) for their freedom: 'We pray that all bonde men may be made free for God made all free with his precious blood shedding.'[11]

The Duke spent the whole of Edward VI's reign imprisoned in the Tower. Somerset's triumph however proved short-lived. He was a hopeless administrator and he was in turn destroyed by the opportunist John Dudley, Duke of Northumberland, who after Somerset's execution, superseded him as Lord Protector. On the death of Edward VI, and accession of Mary in 1553, Norfolk was released, the attainder against him reversed and his titles and estates restored to him on 3 August. He was re-installed a Knight of the Garter and member of the Privy Council on 10 August. As Lord High Steward he had the satisfaction of presiding over the trial and condemnation of Northumberland in the same month. As Earl Marshal he presided at Mary's coronation in October, the enthronement of a Catholic monarch to the sound of trumpets and according to ancient rituals. This event highlighted the Howards' return to power. The following year, despite his advanced age, he was once more put at the head of military affairs when he was appointed Lieutenant-General of the army to suppress Wyatt's rebellion. He died at Kenninghall on 25 August 1554 aged eighty and the greatest nobleman in the country. Not only had he survived, he had triumphed.

He left to his grandson, who succeeded him as 4th Duke of Norfolk, East

Kenninghall Place, Norfolk. The remaining portion of the great house built by the 3rd Duke of Norfolk 1523–7 as the chief family seat, but largely demolished in 1650.

Castle Rising, Norfolk. Given to the 3rd Duke by Henry VIII as a reward for his service. Staircase to the keep.

Anglian estates which he had greatly extended and consolidated in his lifetime, a new mortuary chapel at Framlingham and a rebuilt seat at Kenninghall, which was not only one of the finest Tudor houses in England, but to all intents and purposes the capital of an independent principality. Surprisingly little is known of the appearance of this house, which had come to the Howards from the Mowbrays. It was rebuilt by the 3rd Duke as his principal seat, in preference to Tendring, Framlingham Castle or Castle Rising, in 1526–7, with further additions (at a cost of £348 1s. 8d.) in 1532. He chose Kenninghall because of its central position on his East Anglian estates, close to the Norfolk–Suffolk border. It was set in a park of seven hundred acres enclosed by the Duke with fences all around, and 'well stocked with deer'. The house itself formed an H shape with open courtyards facing north and south, and was built of red brick ornamented with diaper patterns and with tall chimneys and Gothic traceried windows. Kenninghall was largely demolished unrecorded *circa* 1650 and only part of one wing now survives, long used as a farmhouse but still owned by the Duke of Norfolk.

The best picture of the interior comes from the 'Inventorye of the Goods late the Duke of Norff' made by the Crown at the time of Norfolk's arrest and attainder in 1547. The house was divided into different apartments for different members of the family: the Duke, Bess Holland, the Duchess of Richmond, the Earl of Surrey; and the household officers: the Steward, Treasurer, Comptroller, Seneschal, Auditor, Tutor, Secretary and so forth. Each apartment comprised an appropriate number of rooms richly furnished with tapestries, over fifty of which are listed in the inventory, and which varied in subject from the historical and mythological to the religious: the Siege of Paris, the Story of Hercules, Christ's Passion, and six 'verdures' with the Norfolk arms in the centre. The chapel was furnished with two organs, an altar picture on 'wainscot' of Christ's birth, passion and resurrection, illuminated Mass books and a large quantity of embroidered vestments, including forty-two copes. It was served by six domestic chaplains and a full complement of lay clerks and choristers. Other public rooms included a great hall, presence chamber and a tennis-court.[12]

As well as Kenninghall, the 3rd Duke's building activity included the provision of a new mortuary chapel, for his ancestors and descendants, in the parish church at Framlingham. In the fifteenth century the Howards had been buried at Stoke by Nayland, in Suffolk, but after the Mowbray inheritance, had taken over the ducal vault at Thetford Priory in Norfolk: the first and second Howard Dukes of Norfolk, as well as the Duke of Richmond, had been buried there. When the priory was dissolved in 1539 the Duke, who was interested in his family memorials, had written to Henry VIII asking that Thetford should be made into a college served by secular priests, or that alternatively it should be given to him so that he could maintain it as the family burial place. In the event he was allowed to purchase the priory and its lands on very favourable terms – for £1,000 in fact.

The Commissioners who visited Thetford at the time of the Duke's overthrow, noticed that the church was still properly maintained and richly decorated. For some reason, however, the Duke nevertheless decided to make a new Howard vault at Framlingham and to transfer his ancestors' coffins there. He demolished the old chancel at Framlingham in 1545 and started to rebuild it on a larger scale with wide aisles for tombs. This work was incomplete at the time of the Duke's attainder and the structural work was finished after his fall by Edward VI. The tombs which adorn it were commissioned after the Duke's death by his executors in the late 1550s, and perfectly represent the courtly Renaissance taste of the leaders of the Catholic reaction in the mid sixteenth century. This magnificent series of Franco-Italianate designs includes the tomb of the 3rd Duke himself, the Duke of Richmond, and (completed last) the first two wives of the fourth Duke. They remain today as the finest expression of the Howards' position in the mid sixteenth-century as the richest and most powerful family in England. They are all by the same group of unknown sculptors. The Duke of Richmond's has panels of Old Testament scenes and is dated 1555, while the 3rd Duke's is dated 1559 and is a large tomb chest with baluster shafts, effigies of the Duke and his wife, and statues of the Apostles in shell-headed niches which are the last major display of religious imagery in sixteenth-century English art and outstanding pieces of sculpture which can bear comparison with anything of their date in northern Europe.[13]

The 3rd Duke had inherited large estates in East Anglia based chiefly in South Norfolk round Kenninghall, and comprising a large part of East Suffolk stretching from Bungay in the north to Stoke by Nayland in the south. He augmented his landed income by various official salaries and pensions such as the Lord Treasurership, the Stewardship of Augmentation and the Stewardship of Winchester. His combined income in the 1530s amounted to about £3,000, of which after niggardly allowances to his wife and son 'remayneth to me clear' £2,638. He greatly increased the family patrimony in the late 1530s and 1540s by the acquisition of the lands of various dissolved religious houses including Sibton, Coxford, Castle Acre, and the Grey Friars at Norwich as well as Thetford Priory. Their revenues added a further £850 per annum to his income. He was also appointed Chief Steward of the Suppressed Lands South of the Trent.[14] His part in the dissolution of the monasteries, like much of the rest of his career, has been criticized for its cynical opportunism, and much has been made of the fact that he, a leading Catholic reactionary, should have profited so handsomely from the dissolution of religious houses. But surely as the heir-in-chief of so many of the founders of the religious houses in question, it was perfectly fair, once the monasteries had been dissolved, that he should have reclaimed his share of the land which his ancestors had piously given away? He had a stronger claim to ex-monastic land than, for instance, Cromwell's minions like the Russells and

Framlingham, Suffolk. The tomb of the Duke of Richmond, bastard son of Henry VIII, who married Mary, daughter of the 3rd Duke of Norfolk.

Framlingham, Suffolk. The tomb of the 3rd Duke of Norfolk and his second wife, Elizabeth Stafford, daughter of the Duke of Buckingham.

Wriothesleys. Whatever the morality of it all, the perquisites of the dissolution vastly increased the Duke's already impressive territorial influence in East Anglia and he was able to leave to his heirs an estate unequalled in private hands, but so large that it was deemed a threat to the Crown and was broken up within one generation, never to be reconstituted.

The Poet Earl

HENRY Howard, Earl of Surrey, was the ideal of the *uomo universale* in the Renaissance sense, distinguished as a poet, a scholar and soldier, perhaps the closest that sixteenth-century England came to producing Castiglione's model courtier, not that this prevented him from being unjustly executed on a charge of treason at the age of thirty. His great gifts were counterbalanced by a corresponding number of flaws in his character, above all arrogance and lack of tact. He represented the quintessence of the old nobility of high descent: the heir of the Mowbrays and Howards, and through his mother Elizabeth Stafford (daughter of the attainted Duke of Buckingham) the descendant of a ducal family even more illustrious than the Norfolks, the representative of the de Bohuns and Woodstocks. His awareness of this genealogy and his Plantagenet connections, combined with an innate pride, was to be the cause of his destruction. But his poetry is still read; with Sir Thomas Wyatt he was responsible for those experiments which transformed English poetry in the early sixteenth century: the elegant assimilation of Italian models, the perfecting of the sonnet and the evolution of blank verse. 'The influence of Surrey's genius upon our language and our literature did not perish with him. That has been permanent.'

He was born in East Anglia in 1517 (the exact date is not known) and lived in the country until he was thirteen, moving from family estate to family estate according to his grandfather's and father's established routine, from Tendring Hall and Framlingham in Suffolk, to Hunsdon in Hertfordshire and Kenninghall in Norfolk, with the ducal household of ninety servants including six chaplains, fools, choirboys, ushers, scullions, grooms of the chamber and all the rest. From the 3rd Duke of Norfolk's household books it is possible to re-create the young earl's daily routine beginning with Mass at six a.m. followed by breakfast, which he ate in the nursery till he was five or six and thereafter with his parents. A typical breakfast included a chine of beef, joint of mutton, buttermilk, six eggs, a chicken and a bottle of beer. His mornings were spent with his tutor studying the classics and sciences. Dinner was at twelve o'clock and comprised three courses:

Framlingham, Suffolk. The tomb of Henry, the Poet Earl of Surrey and his wife. At the foot kneel his two sons, Thomas 4th Duke of Norfolk and Henry Earl of Northampton, who erected this tomb to his father in 1610.

roast capon, boiled beef or venison, custard; a sweet course; rabbit, chicken pasties, roast pork, fish, almond tarts and baked apples. After dinner he spent some time in lighter studies than the morning: music and foreign languages. Evening prayers were at three p.m. and were followed by supper, a long and elaborate meal with appetizers of plums and grapes, gingerbread and jellies, oysters from Colchester and on Fridays eight or nine different kinds of fish. After supper there were games and music, and bedtime was at nine o'clock. This ordinary routine was broken on holydays and anniversaries when his studies gave way to hunting and other outdoor pursuits.[1]

Surrey's tutor was John Clerk, an Oxford scholar and Fellow of Magdalen, who had travelled in France and Italy and spoke the languages of those countries as well as Latin. He was one of a group of scholars and men of letters who existed within the Norfolk orbit and included John Skelton, a protégé of the Duchess, who became the Poet Laureate. Clerk had entered the Norfolks' employment as the Duke's secretary before becoming Surrey's tutor, and his career was to be closely associated with the Howard family. He too was to come to a tragic end, for, like his employers, he was committed to the Tower accused of *lèse-majesté* and to avoid public shame hanged himself in his cell on 10 May 1552. He had considerable influence over Surrey, introducing him to Latin, French, Italian and Spanish before the age of twelve. In the dedication of his *Treatise of Nobility* to the Duke of Norfolk, Clerk commended Surrey's youthful translations from those languages, and his *De Mortuorum Resurrectione* was dedicated to Surrey himself.

The Duke took great pride in his son's accomplishments. In 1529 Eustache Chapuys, Charles V's ambassador in London, reported a supper party at Whitehall and that the Duke had 'during the repast showed me a letter from his son in very good Latin, which he desired me to read and give my opinion upon, adding that he was much pleased with the youth's proficiency and advancement in letters'. The Duke, though it was out of his way, accompanied Chapuys home 'as friends' and told him *en route* that Henry VIII had entrusted him with the education of his bastard son the Duke of Richmond and that Surrey was to be Richmond's 'preceptor and tutor, that he may obtain both knowledge and virtue, so that a friendship thus cemented promises fair to be very strong and fair; and will be further consolidated by alliance; for the King wishes the Duke to marry one of my daughters'. This was all part of Norfolk's clever scheme for strengthening the Howard position at Court. The connection with the Duke of Richmond was specially significant as there was at one time a possibility that, for want of any other son, he might be legitimized as heir to the throne. In the event, however, nothing came of Richmond's youthful companionship with Surrey for he died of consumption at the age of seventeen before he could fulfil the role for which he had been prepared.

In the spring of 1530 Surrey gave up his quiet life in the country for the Court and he and Richmond, who was two years his junior, resided at Windsor till 1532 when they both accompanied Henry VIII to France to meet Francis I at Calais and remained to pass a year at the French Court. As Norfolk had hoped, Richmond and Surrey became friends and Surrey was idyllically happy at Windsor, later recalling his time there in a rare autobiographical poem:

> . . . proude Windsor, where I in lust and joye,
> With a Kinge's sonne, my childishe yeres did passe,
> In greater feast than Priam's sonnes of Troye.

He went on to recall the details of that 'place of bliss': the large green courts, the wild forest, the silver mead where 'with reins awailed and swiftly y-breathed horse, with cry of hounds and merry blasts between' they had chased the fearful hart, or the tournaments 'with sleeves tied on the helm, On foaming horse, with swords and friendly hearts', the tennis, dancing, and

> The secret thoughts imparted with such trust,
> The wanton talke, the divers change of play,
> The friendship sworn, each promise kept so just,
> Wherewith we passed the winter night away.

The sojourn at the French Court was an important element in the completion of Surrey's education, as well as cementing the Anglo–French alliance against the Emperor, Richmond and Surrey being guarantees 'for the greater security of the treaty'. At Fontainbleau and the Louvre he was able to see the effects of Francis I's importation of the Italian Renaissance to France and probably met there Alemmani, a Florentine poet resident at the French Court. In France he also read the work of Molza, one of the earliest translators of the Aeneid.[2]

Richmond and Surrey spent twelve months in France, and on their return Richmond, now aged fourteen, was married to Surrey's sister. In his ambitions for his son and the general advance of the family, Norfolk had been angling for another royal alliance, namely the betrothal of Surrey to Princess Mary, but by that stage Anne Boleyn's compliance with her scheming uncle's dynastic plans was beginning to wear thin. The Duke had overreached himself and nothing came of the proposal. Instead Surrey was hurriedly married in 1532 to Lady Frances de Vere, daughter of the Earl of Oxford. Norfolk told Chapuys, with characteristic duplicity, that he had arranged the Oxford marriage for his son because he did not wish to appear to be intriguing for the princess. Surrey went to live with his wife in 1535 and, like many arranged marriages, theirs turned out to be perfectly happy. A son was born in March 1536 and christened Thomas; he was to succeed his grandfather as 4th Duke of Norfolk.

In the following years Surrey was closely associated with his father in the power struggle to secure the Howard interest amidst the potentially fatal shifts of Court politics: the trial and execution of Anne Boleyn, the fall of Cromwell, the death of the Duke of Richmond, the advance of the Seymours, the Pilgrimage of Grace, and the struggle at the end of Henry's reign for the Protectorship. But Surrey lacked his father's cunning and discretion. In 1537 he risked the traditional punishment of having his hand chopped off at the wrist for striking Hertford at Court and was imprisoned for a time at Windsor where he wrote the poem recalling his youth in the castle. Even more serious was his obdurate opposition to the proposed marriage of his sister to Sir Thomas Seymour (Hertford's brother), an abortive arrangement of Norfolk's for healing the dangerous breach between the Howards and the Seymours. The Duchess of Richmond and Surrey had a public argument over the proposed marriage in the long Gallery at Whitehall in the course of which Surrey taunted his sister with the suggestion that if she wanted to use her body for the good of the family why did she not become the King's mistress like Madame d'Estampes in France? The Duchess never forgot nor forgave her brother for those bitter words and was to repeat them against him at his trial. Surrey however was successful in thwarting the marriage and the Duchess was doomed to a life of Calvinist widowhood.

Despite his rash tongue Surrey remained in favour at Court; indeed Henry VIII seems to have regarded him with indulgence almost, but not quite, till the end. The comic failure of the Cleves marriage and the fall of Cromwell brought the Howards back into control. The years 1540–1, as has been discussed already, saw the culmination of their prestige and power in the reign of Henry VIII with the marriage of the King to Norfolk's niece Katherine Howard. Surrey was created a Knight of the Garter in spring 1541 (being installed on 22 May), appointed a Commissioner for the Coastal Defence of Norfolk, and joint steward with his father of the University of Cambridge. This triumphant phase did not last long and the hard-won Howard supremacy was soon undermined by Henry VIII's discovery of Katherine Howard's sexual infidelities and her subsequent trial and execution, which Surrey attended.

As in the past, Norfolk and his son attempted to maintain the royal favour during this difficult period through a display of indispensable military service. In 1542 war broke out with Scotland and Surrey accompanied his father on a raiding expedition to the North which was distinguished by the ferocity of Norfolk's burning and pillaging; Kelso was razed to the ground. After the humiliating defeat of the Scots at Solway Moss by a small English force under Sir Thomas Wharton (which took place before the Howards could cross from the Eastern Marches to the West), Surrey left his father on the Border and returned to London. There he celebrated his return by leading a convivial riot through the City, firing stones from crossbows at the windows of Sir Richard Gresham's house and those of other leading citizens as well as at the brothels in Southwark, a matter which came to the notice of the Privy Council and led to Surrey and his companions being put in the Tower for a time before receiving the King's pardon. There he wrote a satire beginning: 'London, hast thou accused me of breche of lawes?'

This was not the first time that Surrey had spent a spell in prison for boisterous conduct. In July 1542 he had been imprisoned in the Fleet for challenging John à Leigh, a fellow courtier, to a duel but had been released on writing a humble letter of apology to the Privy Council. The investigations of 1543 uncovered a number of incidents which later became the fuel for serious accusations by his enemies. The gossip of some of the maids in Mrs Arundell's house, where Surrey lodged in the City, for instance, was carefully noted, to be exploited when the moment seemed right.

In October 1543 Surrey had the chance to fulfil his ambition to take part in full-scale Continental warfare. He joined the English and Spanish army en-

camped before Landrecy in the Low Countries and was present at the unsuccessful attempt to take that city. Charles V wrote to Henry VIII, praising Surrey in
glowing terms: 'And as to what we have written in commendation of the son of
our cousin the Duke of Norfolk, for his eagerness in learning the Arts of War, he is
shown such an excellent example of your men that he cannot fail to profit
thereby; while all of our side respect in his person, and deservedly so, the courage
of the father, and the noble nature of the son.'[13] The following summer he returned
to the war in France with his father. Boulogne was successfully taken by the
English, largely due to the treason of the French Governor Vervin who was later
beheaded by the French for surrendering the city, but Norfolk and Surrey with
inadequate forces and supplies were unable to take Montreuil. In the assault on
that town Surrey was injured and nearly killed, but his life was saved by his squire
Thomas Clere who rescued him under heavy bombardment and in the process
received a wound from which he himself died. Surrey wrote a commemorative
sonnet which his grandson Lord William Howard of Naworth later caused to be
inscribed above Clere's tomb in the Howard chapel at St Mary's Lambeth. It is
Surrey's finest epitaph and 'perhaps the most perfect of its kind in our language':

> Norfolk sprung thee, Lambeth holds thee dead;
> Clere of the County of De Cleremont, hight
> Within the womb of Ormond's race thou'rt bred,
> And saw'st thy cousin crowned in thy sight.
> Shelton for love, Surrey for lord thou chase;
> (Aye me! while life did last that league was tender)
> Tracing whose steps thou sawest Kelsal blaze,
> Landrecy burnt, and batter'd Boulogne render.
> At Montreuil gates, hopeless of all recure,
> Thine Earl, half dead, gave in thy hand his will,
> Which cause did thee this pining death procure,
> Ere summers, four times seven thou coudst fulfill,
> Ah Clere! if love had booted, care or cost,
> Heaven had not wonne, nor earth so timely lost.

After a brief period of convalescence at home in East Anglia, Surrey returned
to France in July 1545, and throughout the campaign that summer he was
gradually promoted; on 26 August he became Governor and Commander of
Guisnes; and on 3rd September he, rather than Lord Grey de Wilton, was
appointed Lieutenant General of the English army and Captain of Boulogne. He
was only twenty-eight and his promotion was unprecedented for one so young.
On taking command his first step was 'to rid all harlots and common women out
of Boulogne' and to instil a greater degree of military seriousness into the defence
of the town. He obviously enjoyed his post at Boulogne and the war against the
French and wrote frequently to Henry VIII with long detailed accounts of the

defence. These letters helped to fuel the King's illusions of military glory, much to the annoyance of Norfolk and others on the Privy Council who were trying to prevail upon the King to abandon Boulogne, since its defence was proving an impossible drain on England's finances. The Privy Council sent a letter to Surrey asking for his detailed views on the situation at Boulogne, hinting that he should provide them with a good excuse for abandoning the town. To make this clear Norfolk sent a private covering letter to his son: 'Have yourself in await, that ye animate not the King too much for the keeping of Boulogne; for who so doth, at length shall get small thanks . . . look well to what answer ye make to the letter from us of the Council. Confirm not the enterprises contained in them.'4

On 7 January the following year Surrey led a skirmish to intercept a French victualling convoy at St. Etienne. This expedition was a partial failure. Much of the convoy was destroyed but the English were forced to retire and several men of high rank were killed. Surrey's enemies were able to use the incident to arouse the distrust of the King towards one so young. As a result Surrey was relieved of his command and Hertford was appointed Captain of Boulogne in his place. Sir William Paget advised Surrey to swallow his pride and to serve under Hertford but this was more than he could stomach and he returned to England in June 1546. Hertford announced that Surrey had misused his office and set about reversing many of his actions, dismissing those appointed by him and finally signing a treaty with Francis I whereby Boulogne was handed back to the French, much to Surrey's chagrin. Paget in his letter to Surrey had written 'in my opinion, you should do well . . . to make sure by times to his Majesty to appoint you to some place in the Army; . . . Whereby you should the better be able hereafter to serve . . . which should be to your reputation in the world.'5 Surrey however ignored this sound advice and allowed himself to be both outmanœuvred by Hertford and represented in an unfavourable light, possibly thereby sowing the mistrust in the dying King's mind which was to grow into a savage resentment against Surrey and to cost him his life.

During his periods of leave from the French wars Surrey had devoted himself to building and poetry. He had begun a new house on St. Leonard's Hill in Norwich in 1544. This he named Mount Surrey. No accurate record of the external appearance of this architecturally important house is known to survive, though it seems to have been an Italian Renaissance design, since in the eighteenth century it was called 'purely Grecian'. In the garden were cheerful little gazebos redolent of Surrey's military enthusiasms for they were made to look like toy forts with ornamental cannon mounted on top. The interior of the house was richly fitted with Turkey carpets and tapestries, as can be seen from the inventories of Surrey's possessions made by the Crown after his attainder. The house was sacked but not destroyed during Kett's rebellion and later fell into ruin; not a stone now remains.

Surrey continued the tradition of patronage established in the Howard family. The younger Thomas Churchyard, for instance, began his career as a gentleman retainer in Surrey's household, later becoming a prolific but uneven Court poet under Elizabeth. He paid tribute to Surrey in a poem published in 1580:

> More heavenly were those gifts he hid, than yearthly was his forme,
> An Erle of title; a God of spirite; a Tullie for his tong;

As tutor to his children Surrey appointed Hadrianus Junius, hitherto physician to the Duke of Norfolk. Surrey also had in his house a number of Italian protégés including a jester called Pasquil, and his own manners and dress were said to be Italianate.

His personal literary achievement was, of course, more important than his patronage of others. He and his friend Sir Thomas Wyatt were the two principal English poets of the early sixteenth century. Surrey's experiments with verse, especially the evolution of English blank verse, greatly enriched English literature. His translations of the second and fourth Books of the Aeneid are the earliest English poetry to be published in blank verse. His succinct and simple adaptations of classical and Italian models transformed English poetic forms; the sonnets have always been considered perfect models of carefully polished poetry and his epitaphs and love odes, which are temporarily less fashionable, were more highly regarded than Wyatt's rather earthier work well into this century. The distinctive features of his poetry are dignity and compression. He was able to convey in a single line or even a word the sense that other poets took a quatrain to express. The epitaph to Clere, for instance, is a complete biography indicating in a short space the deceased's county of origin, ancestry, military career, character, the name of his mistress, the manner of his death and place of burial, as well as the fact that he was Surrey's loyal squire. Surrey's poems earned immediate popularity, as is attested by the large number of early editions. They were first printed in June 1557, and in the course of that and the following month they went through four impressions; they were reprinted in 1565, 1567, 1569, twice in 1574, and again in 1585 and 1587. Much of his literary output, apart from his translation of Virgil and paraphrases of the Psalms, consists of fashionable platonic love poetry such as the famous sonnets to 'Fair Geraldine', but beneath the polish and conventional sentiments there can be detected a more sombre strain, a strong satirical sense and an almost prophetic awareness of the dangers of too elevated a station:

> The lofty pine the great wind often rives;
> With violenter sway fall turrets steep;
> Lightnings assault the high mountains and clives.

Badge of the Pilgrimage of Grace showing the Five Wounds of Christ. It was carried by Thomas Constable of Everingham, who was among those executed by the 3rd Duke of Norfolk.

The Poet Earl of Surrey. A posthumous portrait painted in the early seventeenth century for the Collector Earl of Arundel, probably by an Italian artist. The architectural framework may have been designed by Inigo Jones as part of the decoration of Arundel House in the Strand.

His own life and death is the classic demonstration of the fickleness of fate and the fragility of greatness. The Duke of Norfolk survived, but Surrey fell victim in the power struggle between the Howards and Seymours for the Protectorship during the minority of the young Edward VI. Surrey was too haughty to stoop to his father's cringeing duplicity. He made no attempt to conceal his resentment of the climbing 'new men', or to lower his voice when insulting the powerful: Cromwell was that 'foul churl'; Hertford was the 'upstart'; Paget was a 'catchpole' and 'mean creature'. In a well-known passage by Constantine Barlow, Dean of Westbury, Surrey was described, not without reason, as 'the most proud, foolish Boy that is in England'.[8]

Hertford and his henchmen stored away their resentment, and then when their moment came, set about the destruction of their rival. Following Surrey's City 'riot', the gossip of the maids in Mistress Arundell's house had been heeded by the Privy Council: 'That once when my lo. of Surrey was displeased about buying of cloth she told her maids in the kitchen how he fumed; and added "I marvel they will thus mock a Prince". "Why," quoth Alys her maid, "is he a Prince?" "Yea, Mary, is he" quoth this deponent, "and if aught should come at the King but good, his father should stand for King."' One of the maids, Joan Whetnall, suggested the idea which was to be developed into the principal indictment against the Earl at his trial in 1547, 'talking with her fellow touching my lo. of Surrey's bed, she said the arms were very like the King's'.

Henry VIII, on his deathbed, was roused to sudden resentment against Surrey; 'it was notorious how the King had not only withdrawn much of his wonted favour, but promised impunity to such as would discover anything concerning him'.[9] No convincing explanation has ever been put forward for the King's passion to see Surrey dead. He may, of course, have read the poem on Sardanapalus and taken it as a personal insult:

> Th' Assyrian King, in peace, with foul desire,
> And filthy lust that stain'd his regal heart, . . .
> Who scarce the name of manhood did retain,
> Drenched in sloth and womanish delight.

Whatever the reason, witnesses were soon rushing to ingratiate themselves by furnishing the Privy Council with an array of evidence of almost ludicrous triviality. Sir Richard Southwell seems to have opened the campaign with the information that Surrey had a shield of arms at Kenninghall which constituted treason.

Surrey was quietly arrested at Whitehall in December 1546 and conveyed to the Lord Chancellor's House at Holborn. A Spanish merchant who was in the palace at the time described how he saw a captain of the guard come into the great hall in the early afternoon with twelve halberdiers whom he told to wait in an adjoining place. When Surrey came out from dinner the captain approached him with 'My Lord, I would your lordship should intercede for me with the Duke your father in a matter in which I need his favour, if you will deign to listen to me . . .' and so led him outside where the halberdiers took charge and conveyed him to Whitehall stairs and a waiting boat. Nobody missed him till that night.[10] The following day he was interviewed by the Privy Council and on 12 December was placed in the Tower with his father.

A commission was dispatched to Kenninghall to institute a thorough search. The Duchess of Richmond and Bess Holland both agreed to give evidence against Surrey and were dispatched to London. The Countess of Surrey who was expecting another baby and who might have been an inconveniently 'prejudiced' witness, was left behind in the country. Surrey's trial presented the sad spectacle of a family divided against itself. The divisions and jealousies which had long been simmering in the 3rd Duke's household now broke out, with tragic results. The spiteful Duchess of Richmond declared that her brother had found in an old tale of chivalry certain heraldic arms attributed to Lancelot of the Lake. As the designs had pleased him, he had placed them in one of the quarters of his escutcheon! Worse, she claimed that he had placed over this escutcheon the cap of maintenance, royal crown and the King's cipher H.R. Bess Holland, who hated Surrey because he had never concealed his disapproval of her liaison with his father, also testified against him. She reported that the Duke himself had told her that Surrey had 'placed the Norfolk arms wrong'.

The main strand in the case against Surrey was that he had used the arms of Edward the Confessor, which privilege 'appertain only to the King of this Realm', and this *lèse-majesté* was construed as a claim to the throne and treason. Surrey must however have known of the ruling of the chapter of the Kings and Heralds of Arms in 1473–4 that his great-grandfather Henry Duke of Buckingham might bear the arms of Thomas of Woodstock 'alone without any other Armes to be quartered therewith', and he would also have known of Richard II's ruling in favour of his ancestor Thomas de Mowbray that he could bear the arms of Brotherton alone, and that Richard II had also granted the Mowbrays the right to bear the arms of Edward the Confessor.[11] These armorial precedents must have encouraged Surrey to flaunt the evidence of his royal descent, despite the fact that he had the fate of Edward Duke of Buckingham before him as a warning of the likely result of such pretention.

In August 1546 Surrey had shown Sir Christopher Barker, Garter King of Arms, a 'scutcheon of the arms [of] Brotherton and St. Edward and Anjou and Mowbray quartered, and said he would bear it'. Garter declared that he had protested against this 'improper' heraldry. Surrey also proposed to remove the label from the arms of Brotherton, thus in effect turning it into the old Royal Arms of England.[12] He was tried at the Guildhall in the City of London on these unfounded and frivolous charges. 'It was even urged against him that he had waved his Lion's tail, but even this enormous crime might be defended, as in the patent 17th Richard, the Mowbrays and their heirs were authorised to wear the crest of England, with a difference of a crown as its collar.'[13] A servile jury had been specially selected from those known to be hostile to him. The Earl 'as he was of a deep understanding, sharp wit and deep courage, defended himself many ways; sometimes denying their accusations as false, and together weakening the credit of his adversaries'.[14] The cross-examination went on for eight hours, and at the end the desired verdict was forthcoming and he was condemned to death.

He was beheaded in private on Tower Hill on 19 January 1547, and was buried at All Hallows By The Tower, though his body was removed to the Howard chapel at Framlingham in 1614 and a monument erected to him with effigies of himself and his wife. His coronet lies not on his head but beside him on the cushion as a mark of his attainder. No historian has suggested that he was other than innocent. His execution was 'generally condemned, as an act of high injustice and severity, which loaded the Seymours with a popular odium that they could not overcome. He was much pitied, being a man of great parts and high courage with many other noble qualities.'[15] Did the old Duke of Norfolk as he lingered in the Tower recall the lines in Surrey's translation of the Aeneid where Priam reproaches Pyrrhus for killing his son Polites?

> If in the Heaven any justice be
> That of such things take any care, or keep,
> According thanks the Gods may yield to thee,
> And send thee eke thy just deserved hire,
> That made me see the slaughter of my child . . .

The 4th Duke of Norfolk

THE 4th Duke of Norfolk, who was executed and attainted for attempting to marry Mary Queen of Scots, is the tragic hero of the Howard family. He was the last of the 'overmighty subjects' to survive from the Middle Ages and his death in 1572 marks the end of an epoch in the aesthetic and religious as well as the political history of England. He was as much a victim of the greatness of his position as his own personal failings, and the story of his fall and the events leading up to his death at the age of thirty-four are as complex and improbable as a Verdi opera. The Duke, a sincere Protestant throughout his life, is supposed to have been a leading conspirator in an international Catholic plot involving the Pope and Philip II of Spain to overthrow Elizabeth, replace her with Mary Queen of Scots and to restore the Catholic religion in England. Norfolk's purported behaviour is so unlikely that some historians have thought that he must either have taken leave of his wits or been blinded by overweening ambition.

The Duke had weaknesses, lacked foresight and made mistakes, and these were cleverly exploited by the superior political skill of his enemies. But despite his failings, he was a man 'of more than ordinary integrity and depth of character', popular, handsome and able. Though it cannot definitely be proved one way or the other, it is highly likely that the Duke was deliberately and cold-bloodedly misrepresented as a principal conspirator in a plot of which he was essentially ignorant and innocent. False evidence of treason was manufactured to bring him to the block; the task of his opponents was made easier, in that, although not guilty of treason and almost certainly ignorant of Ridolfi's 'plot' for the invasion of England, he was not entirely free from guilt, for he had re-opened correspondence with Mary Queen of Scots despite his promise to Elizabeth not to do so. That was his fault, but it was not a heinous fault, and there was no reason in the first place why he should not have aspired legitimately to the hand of Mary Queen of Scots. Even to contemporaries, the Duke was a figure of controversy.

Incredible it is how deeply the people loved him, which he had purchased through his bounty and singular courtesy, not unbecoming so great a prince. The wiser sort of men

After Hans Eworth. Thomas, 4th Duke of Norfolk (1536–72).

After Hans Eworth. Mary Fitzalan, daughter of the 12th Earl of Arundel, first wife of the 4th Duke of Norfolk and heiress of Arundel Castle.

were diversely affected about him. Some were terrified with the greatness of that degree which, while he lived, seemed to threaten the state by means of him and his faction. Others were moved with pity towards him, as being a man of so noble descent, singular goodness of nature, goodly personage and manly countenance, who might have been both a great strength and ornament to his country, had not the cunning practices of malicious adversaries, and his own false hopes, attended with a show of public good, diverted him from the first course of life.[1]

Thomas Howard, 4th Duke of Norfolk, was in fact one of the half dozen principal actors on the early Elizabethan stage. His attempt to marry Mary Queen of Scots and his execution for treason are part of national history. Almost every aspect of his life is documented with unusual precision and this makes him the first Englishman, other than royalty, for whom a full biography is possible. He was born at Kenninghall, the principal seat of the Howards, at thirty-six minutes and seven seconds past two o'clock in the morning of 10 March 1538. As a child he lived at Kenninghall, his tutor being the internationally known scholar Hadrianus Junius. He was only eight when his father was executed, his grandfather imprisoned and Kenninghall confiscated by the Crown. He and his brother and sisters were handed over to their aunt, the Duchess of Richmond, to bring up in her house at Reigate, and she appointed John Foxe, the martyrologist, to be their tutor. It was no doubt the Duchess's Calvinist household and the influence of Foxe which moulded the Duke's sincere and life-long inclination to Protestantism. On the accession of Mary and the restoration of the Howards to power, he was restored as Earl of Surrey, created a Knight of the Bath and joined the household of Bishop Gardiner. Subsequently he was appointed one of the seven Gentlemen of the Bedchamber to King Philip II and attended the ill-fated marriage of Philip and Mary at Winchester Cathedral.

He succeeded his grandfather on 25 August 1554 as 4th Duke of Norfolk, Earl Marshal of England and the greatest landowner in the kingdom, the heir to fifty-six manors, thirty-seven advowsons and 'many other considerable estates' which, during his minority, were administered by the Crown. Six months later, in Spring 1556, he married Lady Mary Fitzalan, daughter and heiress of Henry, 12th Earl of Arundel and Lord Steward of the Royal Household. A son was born to the seventeen-year-old Duchess on 28 June 1557 but she never recovered and died eight weeks later to the great grief of the Duke. Short though this marriage was, it had the important result of bringing to the Howards Arundel Castle and the Fitzalan estates in Sussex. The Duke, in common with the practice of the time, soon remarried, this time Margaret Lady Dudley, daughter and heiress of Lord Audley of Walden. The Duke's eldest son by this marriage, Thomas (later Earl of Suffolk) inherited Audley End in Essex.

The accession of Elizabeth I established on the throne a cousin of the Duke's, for Elizabeth's mother Anne Boleyn was the granddaughter of the 2nd Duke of

Norfolk. As Earl Marshal he organized the coronation ceremony in Westminster Abbey and as Chief Butler he organized the feast in Westminster Hall. He was made a Knight of the Garter on St. George's Day, and as premier peer and cousin of the Queen he must have looked forward to a brilliant future. He was the kingdom's sole duke and greatest magnate, the richest man in the land. In his native East Anglia his influence was absolute. His lands there formed a private franchise, 'the Liberty of the Duke of Norfolk', over which the Duke exercised the rights of justice as well as all the usual privileges of landownership, and which had been founded by King Edward IV for John 3rd Mowbray Duke of Norfolk in 1468. It was the largest private franchise to survive and comprised the entire hundreds of Launditch, South Greenhoe, Earsham and Guilt-Cross (where Kenninghall lay) with fourteen other manors in Norfolk, nine parishes in Suffolk, the rapes of Bramber and Lewes in Sussex, the manor of Reigate and Dorking in Surrey and the lordship of Harwich and Dovercourt in Essex. There were also outlying estates in Devon, Shropshire, Ireland, and a coalfield in South Wales. Altogether he controlled six hundred square miles. His extraordinary territorial rights and privileges were equalled in mid-sixteenth century England only by the royal duchies of Cornwall and Lancaster and the episcopal palatinate of Durham. His total income was £4,500 per annum, but he always found it difficult to live within his means because of the expenses of public service and the extravagances of Court life. He had to borrow money and to seek the advice of Sir Thomas Gresham, the greatest financial expert of the day. It may have been his need for money which led him to the Florentine banker Roberto Ridolfi in 1569. He also invested in various mercantile enterprises, of which the most successful was the establishment of Flemish weavers (refugees from the Duke of Alva's persecutions in the Low Countries) in Norwich.[2]

The Duke's estates were not only the source of his income, they were his power base, the foundation of his political role, local and national. His position in East Anglia was strengthened by being appointed Lord Lieutenant of Norfolk and Suffolk in 1559. His political patronage was decisive in local parliamentary elections and in all East Anglian affairs. His desire for a commensurate role in national affairs, however, was to create enemies who were to be responsible for his undoing.

His life was spent in regular perambulations between his three houses and the Court, perambulations of considerable pomp and pageantry, for he was licensed to travel with a hundred retainers, heralds and servants. His principal seat, Kenninghall, remained in essence the house built by his grandfather, but he further embellished it with pictures and tapestries. This collection of tapestries was the finest in England. The pictures included the Holbeins of the 3rd Duke (protected by a curtain) and the Poet Earl, and many European and English royal portraits in the Long Gallery, including Louis XI, Francis I, Charles IX, Ferdinand of Spain, the Queen of Hungary, the Count of Nassau and Richard III. There were also a number of Continental subject pictures, some with gold backgrounds: Christ and the Apostles, the Battle of Pavia, 'Lucretia', a 'woman with a child in her arms' and a naked woman as 'a mirror of death'. The house was also full of musical instruments, as in his grandfather's time, and he maintained a professional choir, while his staff of domestic chaplains was the largest body of ecclesiastics in the county, with the exception of the chapter of Norwich Cathedral. The Duke's own apartments included a bathroom furnished with '12 pieces of copper great and small to bathe in'.[3]

The ducal palace in Norwich, then the second city in England, was greatly enlarged by the 4th Duke. It formed a quadrangle with a conduit in the middle, and its general appearance must have resembled the Great Court at Trinity College, Cambridge. A grand gateway in the middle of the south side gave access from the High Street. The north and south ranges were three storeys high while the other two were four. The first floor of the south side comprised a long gallery with the Duke's closet at one end and the Duchess's at the other. He kept many of his books in his rooms at Norwich, the Latin works in presses in the Council Chamber and the Italian books in the closet off the Long Gallery. The Great Hall and presence chamber as well as fifteen other important rooms, occupied the west range while the east wing contained the apartments of the steward and other principal officers of the household. The Duke also built a bowling-alley one hundred and eighty feet long and a large covered tennis-court. He later boasted that when in his tennis-court at Norwich he considered himself the equal of the Queen of Scotland: 'his estate in England was worth little less than the whole realm of Scotland, in the ill state to which the wars reduced it; and that when he was in his own tennis court at Norwich, he thought himself as great as a King'.[4]

In London the Duke bought the Charterhouse from Lord North for £2,000 in 1564 and renamed it Howard House. He greatly altered the buildings, continuing these architectural improvements right up to his final imprisonment. He enlarged the Great Hall, built a Long Gallery and the great staircase – all in an unusually refined Renaissance style, the Hall screen, for instance, being much purer in its detail than is usual in this kind of English woodwork. The alterations to the Charterhouse, together with the magnificent Franco-Italianate Renaissance tomb erected to his first two wives at Framlingham, are all that survives of the Duke's architectural ventures and give some idea of the unrecorded splendours of the Norwich palace and Kenninghall. The Duke's artistic patronage, like much of the rest of his life, marked the end of an era; it was the last and not the least distinguished flicker of the early sixteenth-century English Renaissance inspired by French and Italian example.

The 4th Duke, like many of his ancestors and descendants, was a patron of scholarship and learning. His secretary William Barker, who was to be at least

Framlingham, Suffolk. The tomb of Mary Fitzalan and Margaret Audley, the first and second wives of the 4th Duke of Norfolk.

The Charterhouse, the 4th Duke of Norfolk's London house, where he carried out many architectural improvements in the years leading up to his trial and execution.

partly responsible for his ruin, was an accomplished translator of the classics from Italian, Latin and Greek and was probably responsible for the English version of Xenophon's *Cyropaedia*.[5] The Duke took an active interest in Cambridge, of which he was Lord Steward, and was created MA in 1564; he was a great benefactor of Magdalene College, contributing £40 per annum until the Court was completed. He arranged for his sons to attend St. John's after his death. John Foxe, who returned to England in 1559, dedicated the English section of his *Church History* (published in Basle) to the Duke, 'all powerful and pious . . . my Maecenas'. Norfolk replied in Latin as a compliment to his old tutor and helped find him a place. He was also a patron of the theatre, and his band of players was one of the four leading dramatic companies in the country in the early years of Elizabeth's reign. Such private companies were important in providing a framework for the flourishing Elizabethan theatre. The Duke combined literary concerns with a passion for sport, and he himself compiled with William Parr, Marquess of Northampton, *Orders Laws and Rules for Coursing the Hare* published *circa* 1562 and still in print in the early nineteenth century.

The Duke's concern for regulating and codifying activities had its most lasting effect in his reform of the College of Arms, which body he controlled as Earl Marshal. He established the organization of the College in the form which still exists. Set up by Richard III in 1484, the early history of the College had been disturbed by internecine disputes among the heralds. The 4th Duke secured a new Royal Charter of incorporation for the College in 1555 and initiated the custom of regular visitations of the country to investigate claims to bear arms. He installed the College in premises in Derby Place in the City – the site which it still occupies, although the College was rebuilt after the Great Fire – and established the supremacy of Garter over the other heralds. He also showed concern for the College records and set out regulations for the care and conduct of the College library.[6]

The Duke's first significant official appointment was the Command of the English army sent to the Border in 1560 to counter French influence in Scotland, a military expedition sometimes known as the War of the Insignia. It was his first visit to the North, the domain of the Percys, Cliffords, Nevilles and Dacres; still feudal and Catholic, with its own loyalties and traditions very different from the South or East Anglia. The English expedition, in the conduct of which the Duke distinguished himself, and the Treaty of Edinburgh which concluded it, ensured the withdrawal of French troops from Scotland and finally broke the 'auld alliance' between Scotland and France; it was the first in the chain of events that led to the Act of Union in 1707.

On his return to London the Duke made a bid for political influence. He was admitted to the Privy Council in 1562 and soon found himself one of the three principal contestants for power at Court alongside 'Mr Secretary' Cecil (later Lord

Burghley) and Robert Dudley (soon to be created Earl of Leicester). Norfolk's antipathy to Leicester and his struggle to gain the Queen's confidence rapidly became the basis of a major division of the Court and drew its bitterness from the opposite views held over a suitable marriage for Elizabeth. Leicester was for a French alliance and Norfolk for a Spanish. At Court Norfolk's supporters wore yellow and Leicester's purple and blue. In 1566 both peers were invested with the Order of St. Michael by Charles IX of France, in return for his Garter, at a splendid ceremony in the chapel at Whitehall. The Queen used the occasion to reconcile the two men and to allay the jealousy between them.

Two years before this event, Norfolk's second wife had died after giving birth to another son, William. This third great tragedy in his life affected him more deeply than his father's execution or his first wife's death. They had been married for five years and had been exceptionally happy together. His third marriage was in January 1567, to Elizabeth, daughter of Sir Thomas Leyburne and widow of Thomas Lord Dacre of Gilsland, one of the most powerful magnates of the North. Under the terms of the marriage contract Norfolk was entrusted with the wardship of her son, the five-year-old George Lord Dacre, and married his three step-daughters to his own sons, Anne Dacre to the eldest, Philip Earl of Surrey, Mary Dacre to the second, Thomas (later Earl of Suffolk) and Elizabeth Dacre to the youngest, William. This was among the most remarkable marriage contracts of the sixteenth century, comparable to Bess of Hardwick's marrying her children to her Shrewsbury step-children. Little George Dacre died in 1569, crushed while practising vaulting over a wooden horse which fell on top of him. Mary also died young. As a result Elizabeth and Anne became coheiresses to the Dacre estates in Cumberland and Yorkshire. The Duke made elaborate arrangements to secure these Dacre lands for his sons Philip and William and their descendants, with such success that the arrangements survived his attainder and the northern Dacre estates are still held by the Howards four hundred years later. *

Only nine months after his marriage the Duke was again bereaved when Duchess Elizabeth died in childbed on 4 September 1567. The baby was also lost. His grief made the Duke ill and he did not recover till Spring 1568. At Easter, however, he was well enough to accompany his brother Henry to Oxford where they were both created MAs. While there he met Gregory Martin, a fellow of St. John's, and engaged him as a tutor for his children. In May 1568, after an absence of sixteen months, he returned to Court where the struggles over the pros and cons of a French or a Spanish marriage for Elizabeth were still in progress.

It was at this moment that Mary Queen of Scots fled from her kingdom to England. Elizabeth appointed Norfolk a commissioner, with Sir Ralph Sadleir and the Earl of Sussex, to go north to York to investigate the charges brought against

---

* Chiefly the Earl of Carlisle and the Howards of Castle Howard, Corby Castle and Greystoke.

Mary of complicity in her husband Darnley's murder, and from that moment his destiny was set. In York Norfolk met John Leslie, Bishop of Ross, Mary's special ambassador to England, and there followed complicated negotiations and inquiries with the Regent Moray's commissioners and the Scottish lords. Norfolk was shown some of the 'Casket letters', reputedly Mary's love-letters to Bothwell. On 16 October Norfolk and the Scottish Secretary, Maitland of Lethington, went hawking to Cawood, in the course of which expedition Maitland suggested that the way to cut the Gordian knot was for Norfolk to marry Mary Queen of Scots and restore her to her kingdom. That would save her from dishonour and cement the Anglo–Scottish alliance. The idea suggested by Maitland developed rapidly in Norfolk's mind, and the more he thought about it, the more he liked it.

As the inquiry, faced with a mass of contradictory evidence, was unable to come to any conclusion, Elizabeth adjourned the session at York and called a full Privy Council in London to look further into the matter. Before returning south Norfolk lingered behind to inspect the defences of the Border. Elizabeth, by this stage, was beginning to suspect the Duke's partiality for Mary. She asked him to his face whether he intended to marry her. He replied that 'no reason could move him to like of her that hath been a competitor of the Crown; and if Her Majesty would move him thereto he will rather be comitted to the Tower, for he meant never to marry with such a person, where he could not be sure of his pillow'. But these hints from the Queen and others helped Norfolk to make up his mind and what had been only a vague idea developed into a serious project.[7]

The Duke was England's richest peer and a widower. In theory there was no insurmountable obstacle in the path of his fourth, last and most splendid matrimonial venture. It was not far-fetched or disloyal for a Howard to entertain the project of marrying the Queen of Scots. Such a plan however would depend for its success on the goodwill of a great many people, not just Queen Elizabeth but also those who had her confidence and the conduct of affairs, of whom Burghley was the most important. The Duke, however, without realizing fully what he had done, had alienated his former friend Burghley, and Burghley's faction, by opposing his anti-Spanish policy in the Privy Council. Norfolk's pro-Spanish attitude over the Spanish pay ships issue in 1569 brought Burghley literally to his knees in the Privy Council and only Elizabeth's direct intervention had protected the Secretary from extreme censure. The Duke however, did not seem to have grasped the seriousness of his act and never realized that he had forfeited Burghley's friendship. Even on the brink of his execution he could still write: 'I wold hope that my good Lord Burley for the olde love, good wyll and frendshype that he hathe borne to me ther wofull father wold be intreatyd to extend hys charytable and fryndlye favor nowe in fatheryng them whoe are otherwyse destytute, and I wold hope that they schall be as obedyent to hyme as ever they were to me.'[8]

One of the Duke's chief failings was a disregard for humbler people's pride and feelings. He took everything and everybody for granted and could not grasp the fact that a seemingly friendly or servile exterior could conceal disloyalty or even personal hatred. The Duke's opinions and his bid for political influence threatened to bring about the ruin of Burghley's own carefully built edifice of political power. The Chief Secretary was determined to prevent that happening. The Duke almost by accident drifted into a life-and-death struggle with somebody for whose political ability and sharp intellect his own easy-going, patrician character was not a match.

Burghley watched and waited, and when Norfolk made his one fatal error, he pounced. That error was not to take the Queen into his confidence over his marriage plans. By mid-May 1569 Mary had been acquainted with Norfolk's proposals, and the two had exchanged tokens, almost the equivalent of a betrothal. But the Duke had not yet mustered the courage to inform Elizabeth of his intentions. On the Royal Progress that summer Elizabeth gave Norfolk three opportunities to tell her about the marriage but he let them slip and thereby lost her confidence, leaving the field open for his enemies to misrepresent his intentions.

This failure to take the Queen into his confidence was perhaps not so much pusillanimity on Norfolk's part as a response to Leicester's advice. The two noblemen had, on the surface at least, made up their quarrel. They now shared a pro-Spanish, anti-Burghley policy on the Council. Leicester advised Norfolk that Elizabeth would almost certainly accept his proposals if he, the Queen's special favourite, were to break the news to her. Norfolk agreed to let him proceed as he suggested. The Queen however first heard of the proposal from another source, the Scottish Regent, Moray, who had originally supported the idea, but in 1569 turned against Norfolk.

The discontent of the northern Earls in 1569 and their known intention to place Mary on Elizabeth's throne and to restore Catholicism, gave Burghley his opportunity to represent Norfolk as plotting behind Elizabeth's back and aiming at nothing less than her throne by marrying Mary. Burghley was thus able to use the Norfolk marriage as a way of re-establishing his own supremacy in the Council and to toughen Elizabeth's attitude towards Mary Queen of Scots. On 6 September Norfolk went to the Queen at Titchfield and belatedly explained his intention to her, but it was too late. She would not accept it, for it was too much of a threat to her own position. The Duke found that he was shunned by the other courtiers and, too late, realized that all was not well. He grew uneasy and quitted the Court. On 26 September he went to Kenninghall, missing a request from Elizabeth that he should join her at Windsor where she had retreated for safety's sake. This was his second major mistake.

Nobody knew where he had gone and it was therefore possible to suggest to

Elizabeth that he was on his way north to join the disaffected Earls, for he alone with his power and popularity could have been the leader of a successful revolt against the throne. In fact he spent a week quietly on his Norfolk estates, indecisive and unwell. On receiving the forwarded summons from Elizabeth, he set off for Windsor on 1 October and on arrival was immediately placed under arrest and sent to the Tower under suspicion of treason. He remained there for ten months, in the same room in the Constable's Lodgings as had been occupied by his grandfather. Meanwhile, evidence of a conspiracy was pieced together. Leicester confessed in melodramatic circumstances to his attempts to aid Norfolk's marriage project, and was forgiven by the Queen. Moray sent to her Norfolk's correspondence with him. The Duke's supporters and friends were questioned, but not enough evidence to condemn him of treason was forthcoming. The northern Earls rebelled in November and were ruthlessly suppressed seven hundred and fifty rebels were executed under martial law, their estates redistributed, the old feudal loyalties destroyed. The North did not recover economically for two centuries. In 1570 followed Pius V's long delayed and disastrous bull 'Regnans in Excelsis' excommunicating Elizabeth as a heretic, which provoked a spate of penal legislation against Catholics. These two events created an atmosphere in which Norfolk appeared too dangerous to be allowed to live and Mary Queen of Scots' case could not be dealt with rationally. At this stage, however, there was not yet enough evidence to enmesh the Duke and he was allowed out of the Tower, under surveillance, to Howard House where he employed his time in further building improvements.

Over the following two years the complexities of the Ridolfi Plot were revealed to the world and, like a fly in a spider's web, Norfolk was firmly trapped in the centre as 'principal counsellor and director of Ridolfi to persuade to the Duke of Alva – the Pope and the King of Spain to have foreign force to invade this realm and Ireland and to have maintained the Scots Queen in this realm by force'.[9] The curtain on the first act in this drama rose in the early Spring of 1571 when Charles Bailly, a young Fleming employed as a secretary by the Bishop of Ross was arrested on entering the country, purportedly carrying letters from Roberto Ridolfi, a Florentine banker and Pope Pius V's *nuncio segreto* in England, who had just left in the opposite direction. Bailly had been expected by the authorities and was taken to Lord Cobham, the Warden of the Cinque Ports, who for reasons which have never been convincingly explained allowed the letters to go forward to the Bishop of Ross. It is clear that Burghley knew about these letters from the start and they were meant as bait for Ross, although the pretence was that they were only discovered by a process of brilliant deduction on the part of Walsingham's secret service.[10]

Bailly was committed to the Marshalsea prison where he was spied on by William Herle, a pirate in Burghley's employ, disguised as an Irish priest. In prison he was allowed to build up an incriminating correspondence in cipher with Ross. (This ruse proved so successful that it was repeated ten years later to bring Mary Queen of Scots to the block.) Poor Bailly, who was only a youth and not used to English ways, went to pieces in prison and on being moved to the Tower, where he was racked, 'confessed' that Ridolfi had left England carrying instructions from Mary Queen of Scots to the Duke of Alva, the dreaded Spanish governor of the Netherlands, Philip II of Spain and the Pope, urging them to invade England and cast out Elizabeth, substituting Mary and Catholicism in her place.

Ridolfi himself was almost certainly a double agent. He had spent the winter of 1569 in the house of Walsingham, the head of Elizabeth's secret service, and had very probably been 'turned round' there. Alva was not impressed by his proposals and informed Philip II that he was like a man who had 'learned his lesson parrot-fashion'. He did not even know where Harwich was, the port where Alva's army was supposed to land. Ridolfi went on to Rome, claiming that Alva's intransigence and lack of co-operation alone had caused the plot to fail. He spent the remaining forty years of his life in his native Florence, enjoying a well-earned and prosperous retirement. He was the only one of the 'conspirators' to escape. In Florence he told the Grand Duke of Tuscany of 'his plans' and the Grand Duke obligingly passed on the information to Elizabeth.

In London Burghley's and Walsingham's spies were busily at work. Ross was arrested and taken to the Tower where he too 'confessed' and 'related the inner history of the Ridolfi Plot with as much detail as if he were dictating his memoirs'.[11] He was told that the other 'conspirators' had already confessed and that his deposition would not be used to incriminate them, merely to clarify his own standing in the matter. Naturally the Bishop was keen to show that he was innocent and that, if there was a plot, it must be the work of others. The signed report of his examination on 26 October was written by Sir Thomas Smith in a flowing narrative which left out many key phrases such as 'Barker said' or 'Ridolfi stated'. Very little of what Ross 'confessed' was first-hand knowledge; it consisted chiefly of what Ridolfi and the Duke of Norfolk's servants had reported to him. Nevertheless it was used to incriminate the Duke.

The involvement of the Duke of Norfolk was the most obscure part of the whole Ridolfi conspiracy and meant inventing a little sub-plot to the main action in the form of a further rising of Mary's northern supporters. The Duke was betrayed by his servants who intercepted and meddled with his correspondence in order to give a treasonable slant to otherwise relatively innocent transactions. The immediate cause for involving him was the discovery of a bag of gold which was to be conveyed from Howard House to Mary's supporters in Scotland. This money came from De la Mothe Fénelon, the French ambassador in London, and was to be sent from him to Scotland on behalf of Mary. The Duke was aware of this transaction and had given his permission, after initial doubts, for his servants to carry the money, an exceedingly rash act in the circumstances and a sign of his blindness to danger. The messenger employed to take it to Scotland, and informed that it was £50 of silver going to the steward of the Dacre estate in Cumberland, took the bag straight to the Privy Council. A letter in cipher was then found, or more likely planted, in the bag which 'proved' the Duke to be the mysterious 'Quarante' of Ridolfi's cipher correspondence. Round this was woven the fable that the Duke was sending money to Mary's supporters in northern England so that they would rise in support of Alva's invasion. The Duke's servants were interrogated and confessions extorted by threats of the rack, his steward Bannister and his secretary Barker providing false evidence against their master. Barker was now an old man and his mind may have been failing for he kept changing his story. Nevertheless it was his shaky accusations which were used to damn the Duke.[12]

Norfolk was arrested and placed once more in the Tower. While there he supposedly wrote a letter to his London house revealing the hiding-place, under a tile in the roof, of his own code to the cipher and handed it to a messenger who promptly took it to Burghley. Howard House was searched and a further treasonable letter in cipher was 'found' casually concealed under a mat. The trial took place in Westminster Hall on 16 January 1572, and the peers in judgement against Norfolk were carefully chosen from his rivals and enemies. The evidence against him consisted of the written confessions and declamations of absent persons (most of them imprisoned in the Tower) and in some cases extorted by torture, or the threat of torture, despite the fact that 'Mr. Treasurer and Mr. Chancellor, sworn, did testify that Barker made all these confessions freely without compulsions'. None of the witnesses were allowed to appear in person at the trial, although the Duke specifically asked that Ross should be questioned to his face.

The Duke's defence was the same as in the letter which he had already written to Queen Elizabeth and which is now preserved in the archives at Hatfield: that he had attempted to marry Mary Queen of Scots without Elizabeth's permission, that he had renewed his endeavours after his promise to the contrary. That he was aware of certain letters but gave no consent thereto, though he had undutifully concealed them. That he had sent letters and money to Scotland 'in doing whereof I did too much forget myself'. But he denied any part in the rebellions and intrigues, inciting foreign princes to invade England or any harm to the Queen.[13] There is nothing in the evidence against him to prove that he was not speaking the truth. He was nevertheless found guilty of treason and condemned to death.

The Duke was not deliberately guilty of any treasonable act, though he had certainly concealed information and continued with his plans to marry Mary Queen of Scots against Elizabeth's wishes. This enabled him to be irretrievably compromised and destroyed by his political opponents, just as his father had been before him, and his son would be afterwards. Ironically, the Duke never suspected

THE EPISTLE.

vfyng thaduife and helpe of godly learned men, both in reducing the fame
to the trueth of the Greke texte (appoyntyng out alfo the diuerfitie wher
it happeneth) and alfo in the kepyng of the true ortographie of wordes,
as it fhall manifeftly appeare vnto them that wyll diligently and without
affection conferre this with the other that went foorth before. I haue (as
becommeth a true obedient fubiecte, done all that in me dyd lye, to fatif-
fie your graces mofte godly zeale and commaundement : and with fuche
fubmiffion, as it becommeth a fubiect to his moft drad foueraigne Lorde,
do nowe prefent it vnto your Maieftie, in moft humble wyfe defiring the
fame, accordyng to your princely clemencie, to accepte my good en-
deuour. The geuer of all power, whiche is kyng of all kynges,
and prince of all princes, vouchfafe of his goodnes to pre-
ferue your Maieftie, and in all your royall affaires fo
to affift your gracious hyghneffe with his holy
fpirite, that whatfoeuer your grace fhall
thynke or do, may be to Gods glory,
the continuall floryfhyng of
your hyghneffe ho-
nour, and the
common
wealth of your
fubiectes.
Amen.
(∴)

*Farewell good dyx, your fervys hathe bene fo faythefull vnto me
as I ame forye that I came not make profe off my good wyll to
the recompenfe yt. I truft my deathe fhall not make no change
in you towardes myne, but that you wyll faythefullye performe
the traft that I haue repofyd in you, forgyft me, and remeafer
me in myne. Forgett not the plannes to counfell et and advyfe
phylyps and Nannes vnexperyenced yeares, the reft off the brothers
and fyfters well doyng reftyth muche apon thir vertuous and
confyderat dealyngs god grant them hys grace wyche ys able
to worke better in them than my naturall well meanyng hurte can
wyche vnto them. Amen and fo hopyng off your honeftye and
faythefulnes when I am deade I byd you thys my laft farewell
the 10. off febru. 1571. T H.*

The 4th Duke of Norfolk's *New Testament* with his last message of farewell to his steward William Dyx
written while in the Tower awaiting execution.

Burghley's part in his downfall. He went to the scaffold believing that Mary's advisers, especially Ross, and his own servants had lured him to his death: 'I am betrayed and undone by mine own, whilst I knew not how to mistrust, which is the strength of wisdom.'[14] For Burghley the outcome of the whole affair was a brilliant success. His opponents were disarmed. The Queen of Scots was discredited and his own position beside his mistress was more secure than ever.

Nothing became the Duke like his manner of leaving the world. His last few months in the Tower under sentence of death were spent in settling his affairs, securing the proper education of his children, tying up for them such of his wives' patrimony as might escape his own attainder, especially the Audley, Dacre and Fitzalan estates, and above all in preparing to meet his Maker. His last letters to the Queen, to his children and to his loyal steward William Dyx are full of Protestant piety. They are signed simply Thomas Howard, for the dukedom was already attainted and all his honours stripped. Garter King of Arms had presided over the awesome ceremony of degradation from the Order of the Garter in St. George's Chapel, Windsor, the ultimate ostracism; his banner, helm and crest had been kicked out of the chapel into the castle ditch, and his stall plate removed.

The Queen signed his death-warrant on 6 February,[15] but perhaps she had doubts for she kept postponing the execution. Five months elapsed during which the Duke lingered on, ill and sad, as a prisoner of state before the sentence was finally carried out on 2 June 1572. He was attended on the scaffold by Dean Nowell of St. Paul's and John Foxe, his old tutor. In his last speech he declared his innocence once more, saying of Ridolfi: 'I never saw his face but once; a stranger, a naughty man with whom I never dealt but once, and that once touching a recognizance between him and me as the world knoweth.' He also made a profession of his Protestant faith: 'I take God to witness, I am not, nor never was, a papist since I knew what religion meant.' He was buried in the chapel of St. Peter ad Vincula in the Tower. His epitaph should perhaps be his last message to his steward written in his New Testament ('Farewell Good Dyx') with its reference to the twenty-first verse of the sixteenth chapter of Job: 'Naked I came out of my mother's womb, and naked I shall return thither. The Lord gave and the Lord hath taken away. Blessed be the name of the Lord.'

The death and attainder of the 4th Duke of Norfolk was a blow to the Norfolk family fortunes which it took half a century to restore. It also marked the beginning of the retreat from Norfolk, their county of origin which, apart from their conformity to Catholicism, is the most remarkable feature of the later Howard history. The death of the 4th Duke of Norfolk saw the third confiscation of the Howard estates and the dissolution of the Duke of Norfolk's liberty. Though James I in 1604 restored the estates and the liberty, this was not to the senior branch of the Howards. Instead he divided them between different members of the family, especially the Earls of Northampton and Suffolk. There were some half-hearted later attempts to retrieve the situation. The 4th Duke's grandson, the Collector Earl, made an effort to redeem his ancestral estates. His grandson the 6th Duke rebuilt the palace in Norwich as his country seat but owing to Titus Oates' Plot it was never finished or inhabited, and the 8th Duke of Norfolk finally demolished it in the early eighteenth century. Kenninghall was largely destroyed in the mid-seventeenth century; the 7th Duke sold Castle Rising in the late seventeenth century to pay some debts. The lordship of the manor of Kenninghall was sold by the executors of the young 15th Duke of Norfolk in 1872 without any awareness of its historical importance. Further land in Norfolk was disposed of in the nineteenth and twentieth centuries so that today all the Duke of Norfolk holds in East Anglia is an historical shadow of what once was: a few manors and common rights, and the one remaining wing of Kenninghall, while Arundel Castle in Sussex, inherited from the Fitzalans, has now been the principal ducal seat for two centuries. It is a very English and rather depressing story of pragmatic muddled recessional, not dissimilar, on a smaller scale, to the British withdrawal from Empire in the twentieth century.

6

St. Philip Howard, Earl of Arundel

THE eldest son of the 4th Duke of Norfolk has the unusual distinction in an English aristocratic family of being a canonized saint. Few English ducal houses, it can confidently be said, are descended directly in the male line from a saint. Philip, Earl of Arundel (the title he inherited through his mother from his Fitzalan grandfather and so not affected by his father's attainder) died of dysentery aged thirty-eight in 1595, a prisoner of conscience, having lost everything: his titles, his estates, his houses, all his worldly possessions; having never seen his son and having been forcibly separated from his wife for over ten years. 'Wonderfull it is how much he lost, and with what quietness of mind he endured all adversities' quoted his anonymous contemporary biographer, a Jesuit chaplain in Lady Arundel's household.[1]

Such an end would have been difficult to predict from the manner of his coming into the world. He was born at noon on 28 June 1557, the eldest son of the only English duke, and was baptized a few days later in the Chapel Royal at Whitehall with a pomp and circumstance rarely the lot of a commoner. The service was performed by Nicholas Heath, Archbishop of York and Lord Chancellor of England, in the presence of Queen Mary and all the principal members of the court. The font was of gold 'made of purpose and kept in the Treasury only for the Christening of the children of the Princes of the Realm'.[2] His godfather was Philip II of Spain, after whom he was named; it was the last public ceremony in England in which King Philip took part, before leaving his wife and returning to the Continent.

The Duchess of Norfolk did not recover from the birth of her son and died shortly afterwards from a puerperal fever, 'to the incredible grief of the Earl her father, the Duke her husband, and all their friends'. Philip's two step-mothers also died in rapid succession so that his upbringing was left in the hands of strangers, to an exceptional degree by sixteenth-century standards, although his father naturally took great care to ensure the best for his eldest son and heir. The

Attributed to George Gower. St. Philip Howard, Earl of Arundel, at the age of eighteen, 1575. A portrait once in the collection of Lord Lumley, his uncle.

Duke appointed a 'grave and ancient gentlewoman' to nurse him in infancy and give him the first rudiments of learning. His later education was entrusted to Gregory Martin, a fellow of St. John's College, Oxford, and a noted scholar of Greek and Hebrew, who had considerable influence over his young charge, sowing the seeds of Philip's later interest in religion, literature and history. Martin, though not yet openly a member of the Church of Rome was 'wholy Catholick in his judgement and affection' and this must have coloured the way he presented his subjects to the young Earl. He soon found the increasingly Protestant character of the Duke's household at odds with his own deepening Catholic convictions and shortly afterwards quitted the ducal service for the Continent. There he was ordained a priest and devoted himself to religion and scholarship, his principal achievement being the Douai translation of the Bible.

At the age of twelve Philip, as part of his father's ambitious programme for the further glorification of the dukedom, was betrothed to Anne Dacre, the eldest daughter and eventual co-heiress of Lord Dacre of Gilsland, whose widow had become the third wife of the Duke of Norfolk but had died two years previously.

When he was fourteen, the age of full consent, Philip and Anne (or Nan) were married. By that time the Duke himself was in the Tower and doomed, but even under the shadow of the executioner's axe he still concerned himself with the dynastic well-being of his children, and with planning their future. His last letters to them survive, full of good advice dictated by his own tragic experience and which in the long run Philip was to take to heart:

Oh Philip! Serve and fear God above all things. I find the fault in myself, that I have (God forgive me) been too negligent in this point. Love and make much of your wife . . . Show yourself loving and natural to your brothers and sister, and sister-in-law. Though you be very young in years, yet you must strive with consideration to become a man; . . . Marry! the world is greedy and covetous . . . Help to strengthen your young and raw years with good counsel . . . I wish you, for the present, to make your chief abode at Cambridge, which is the fittest place for you to promote your learning in . . . Beware of the court, except it be to do your prince service, and that, as near as you can in the lowest degree, for that place hath no certainty . . . Thus I have advised you as my troubled memory can at present suffer me. Beware of pride, stubbornness, taunting, and sullenness, which vices nature doth somewhat kindle in you, and therefore you must with reason and discretion make a new nature in yourself. Give not your mind too much and too greatly to gaming, make a pastime of it and no toil . . . When I am gone forget my condemning and forgive, I charge you, my false accusers, as I protest to God I do, but have nothing to do with them if they live . . . And now, dear Philip, farewell. Read this my letter sometimes over; it may chance make you remember yourself the better; and by the same, when your father is dead and rotten, you may see what counsel I would give you if I were alive. If you follow these admonitions, there is no doubt but God will bless you; and I, your earthly father, do give you God's blessing and mine, with my humble prayers to Almighty God that it will please Him to bless you and your good Nan; that you may both, if it be His will, see your children's children, to the comfort of you both; and afterwards that you may be partakers of the heavenly kingdom; Amen. Amen. Written by the hand of your loving father, T. H.[3]

Philip went up to Cambridge in 1572, the year of his father's execution, and he spent two years there, receiving the degree of MA. His tutor, George Laughton, wrote to Lord Burghley (whom the Duke had asked to act as his son's guardian) describing Philip's progress, his diligent reading of Plato and Demosthenes, and of Latin, Italian and French authors. This confirmed his love of 'polite literature' but in other ways Cambridge did him considerable harm. He fell in with unsuitable friends who set him a bad example. Still worse was the flattery of the dons, 'so palpable sometimes that his Lady has often told me she was ashamed to hear it', which had a demoralizing effect on his character.

At the age of eighteen he went to Court, where he quickly forgot his father's advice and, being witty, of good mind and 'comely countenance', threw himself wholeheartedly into a life of beguiling extravagance and 'wanton conversation'. He fell for 'the allurements of corrupted immodest young women wherewith the Court in those days did much abound' and rapidly became a dissipated, selfish spendthrift. The sad aspect of this was his ill-treatment of his wife, whom he more or less abandoned, widely confessing that he did not know whether he were married or not, in his attempt to court the favour of the Queen, who preferred her more good-looking young courtiers to be unencumbered with spouses and seems, in any case, to have had a special dislike for Anne Dacre.

Philip's selfish behaviour deeply upset his elderly grandfather, the Earl of Arundel, and his aunt, Lady Lumley, who as a result partly disinherited him. He also spent large sums of money in 'Tiltings and Tourneys' and in costly entertainments of the Queen and Court. As a result he got seriously into debt and was forced to sell some of his remaining land. He inherited the Earldom of Arundel, Arundel House in the Strand, and Arundel Castle in Sussex on the death of his Fitzalan grandfather in 1580, and this increase of responsibility may have been one of the factors which sobered him.

A more immediate cause was the religious disputation in the Tower between the condemned Jesuit Edmund Campion and a group of distinguished Anglican Divines, which made a profound impression on all who heard it and, according to the Earl's biographer, helped him to perceive 'on which side the truth, and true Religion was'. This perhaps rekindled the memory of the early influence of Gregory Martin and, combined with his increasing debts and a growing revulsion against the aimless frivolity of his Court life, together with his learned interest in the historical past, and wide reading, led him to ponder his destiny and to think seriously about religion. He made his decision one day while pacing the long gallery at Arundel Castle, a room which still survives, refitted, as the library. 'After a long and great conflict within himself', he determined to become a practising Catholic. He was received back into the Church by the Jesuit Fr. William Weston, but at first kept his conversion secret.

His wife, his favourite sister Lady Sackville, his aunt Lady Lumley and his uncle Henry (later Earl of Northampton) had already become Catholics; his younger brother Lord William Howard shortly afterwards embraced the same faith. They all formed part of the first stage of the English Counter-Reformation, as Cardinal Allen's grand plan for the reconversion of England began to bear fruit with the dispatch to their homeland of missionary priests, many of them Jesuits, from the English Colleges at Douai and Rome to minister to the remnants of the ancient Church and to win back lost souls. These were the heroic years of English recusancy; the period of priests in hiding, covert masses, the music of Byrd, secret printing-presses and Jesuit literature, the escapes, captures, triumphs and tragedies, which even now, after four centuries, shed a certain romantic glamour over the English Catholics.

Burghley and the government were not unnaturally deeply exercised by the increasing threat to the Elizabethan Settlement which they regarded as the essential foundation of the political independence, stability and prosperity of the

State. The defection, as they saw it, of the premier Earl at that moment could not but be regarded as a serious threat to the status quo, and not something that could be overlooked. The increasingly belligerent foreign policy of Spain (partly stimulated by English piracy) helped to undermine the relatively tolerant line hitherto taken by the English government towards recusants, who now came to be regarded not just as an irritating religious anomaly but as a potential third party within the State.

The Earl was aware of the dangers inherent in his decision and resolved to escape from the country and to live quietly abroad where he could practise his religion and follow his antiquarian studies in peace. His secretary, John Momford, was sent to Hull in Yorkshire to enquire about engaging a ship for Flanders. But before Momford could get a passage, he was arrested and brought back to London where he was interviewed by the authorities in the presence of Norton, the rackmaster, but without result. At this moment the Queen invited herself to Arundel House. Philip provided a sumptuous banquet, at the end of which the Queen declared her satisfaction, 'gave him many thanks for her entertainment there and informed him that he was imprisoned in his own house'.[4] The next day he was interrogated by the Privy Council on the matter of his religious beliefs 'whereto in all things he answer'd so wise and warily' that he was released.

The change in the Earl's manner however could not but draw the curiosity and suspicions of the court. The witty, frivolous exterior which he had formerly presented to the world gave way to sober restraint and high seriousness. At religious services in the royal palaces he either feigned some excuse to be absent, or lingered in the aisles. Once more he decided to escape to the Continent. Fr. Weston tried to dissuade him, but the Earl had written to Cardinal Allen for his advice and had received a reply strongly urging him to flee the country. It has been suggested that his letter to Allen was intercepted by Walsingham's secret service and that the reply was forged. This has not yet been proved, but it would be consistent with what is known of Walsingham's methods. Whatever the exact means, the Earl was certainly betrayed, probably by 'Fr.' Grately, alias Bridges, one of Walsingham's spies who posed as a Catholic priest and at the Earl's trial was stated to have been the go-between who carried Cardinal Allen's and the Earl's letters to each other.

Having made up his mind, the Earl wrote a long letter explaining his decision and motives which he entrusted to his sister, Lady Sackville, to give to the Queen once he had arrived safely on the Continent. It was never delivered. The Earl then caused a ship to be secretly hired at Littlehampton, the port which belonged to him at the mouth of the River Arun. On the appointed day he slipped out of Arundel Castle, taking with him only two servants, and embarked. To his disappointment he was informed that the ship could not sail immediately because of contrary winds, 'but more probable it is, that was but an excuse framed by the master of the ship or some others by whom he was betrayed to cause delay until all things were in readiness for his takeing'.[5]

The boat at last sailed, after a two-day delay. They were soon under way and making good progress out into the channel. He was free. He had escaped. What must have been his sense of relief after the suspense of the previous days? But when darkness fell, the master of the ship hung a lantern on the mast and shortly afterwards they were stopped and boarded by Captain Keloway, the commander of a little ship of war, who pretended to be a pirate until, having ascertained the identity of the unsuspecting Earl, he arrested him on the orders of the Privy Council and carried him back to land. As the Earl sarcastically pointed out later, he had no reason to suspect that Keloway was anything but a pirate, because his reputation was so notorious that nobody could have imagined him to be 'employed by publick authority'. Secret services, however, cannot afford to be scrupulous about the people in their pay. This terrible blow to his hopes, after imagining that he had got safely away, might have been expected to bring the Earl to his knees, but, according to his biographer, 'the Earl was nothing at all daunted with so unexpected an accident, and not only with great patience and courage did endure it, but moreover carry'd it with a joyfull and merry countenance' in the certainty that he had committed no treason, but had merely tried to leave the country without permission, a comparatively trivial offence.

He was committed to the Tower on 25 April 1585, and the now familiar Tudor machinery for judicial murder was set up and began to clank into operation. He was three times interrogated by the Privy Council, chiefly about his correspondence with Allen. The usual trick of a forged letter was resorted to, '3 sides of paper at the least' being waved in his face and withdrawn before he could read more than the melodramatic opening lines which ran, 'Sir, this letter containeth such matter as is fitter for the fire to consume, than to be laid up in your study.' He was told that the writing was his own, the content treason, and that he should be arraigned for it, but when he asked some pertinent questions about the provenance of the letter, Walsingham rapidly withdrew it and it was not mentioned at subsequent interrogations, though a version of it may have been used again at the trial in Westminster Hall. His accusers were obviously disappointed by the meagre results of this preliminary investigation and allowed twelve months to elapse before calling him to the Star Chamber on 15 May 1586. He was arraigned there on three specific points: that he had attempted to leave the realm without licence of the Queen, that he had been reconciled to the Church of Rome, that he was plotting with foreign powers in order to be restored as Duke of Norfolk. To the latter accusation, he replied 'that he never so much as heared thereof until the present time'. No evidence was produced and that charge was let drop. He did not deny the first two charges, but they were not treason and 'he gave such sufficient answers to every thing that was objected against him, and behaved himself so discreetly' that the attempt to condemn him for treason was abandoned. Instead he was fined £10,000 and imprisoned during the 'Queen's pleasure', which turned out to be a life sentence.[6]

The long tedious years in the Tower were made more than ordinarily unpleasant by three additional horrors: his cell in the Beauchamp Tower was rendered so noisome by the exhalations from an adjoining vault that even his gaolers were loath to enter it; he was extraordinarily strictly confined, and allowed no exercise, apart from a short walk in the afternoon in the gallery or the Queen's garden; and the Lieutenant of the Tower, Sir Michael Blount, resorted to every kind of petty persecution in his dealings with his prisoner. The Earl wrote: 'His injuries to me both by himself and his trusty Roger are intollerable, infinite, dayly multiply'd, and to those who know them not, incredible: and the most that you can imagin, will be far inferior, I think, to the truth when you shall hear it.' All this together with his own austerities made him physically ill, but as he wrote in Latin on the wall of his cell: 'The more suffering for Christ in this world, so much the more glory with Christ in the next.' He retained his sanity by a regular routine of prayers and contemplation, as if he were a priest, reciting the appointed offices of the day from a breviary which his wife had had smuggled to him; such was the intensity of his concentration that his knees became black and misshapen from kneeling on the flagstones of the floor.

Various attempts were made to trap him into some treasonable admission. One of the more friendly gaolers would engage him in easy conversation, during the course of which the question would arise as to what effect the Pope's excommunication of the Queen had on his allegiance to her. The Earl noticed from his window that immediately after these seemingly innocuous discussions, a messenger would be dispatched to some unknown destination.

Three years after his committal the Spanish Armada sailed against England in 1588. By a coincidence, the Earl was suddenly allowed more liberty and enabled to make contact with three other Catholic prisoners in the Tower, Fr. William Bennet, 'an old priest of Queen Mary's days', Sir Thomas Gerard, a Lancashire landowner who had been implicated with Mary Queen of Scots, and Mr. Shelly, 'a Sussex gentleman'. At Philip's instigation, Fr. Bennet said mass for them occasionally in his cell. The Council 'having got intelligence thereof, took occasion to conceive all that prayer to be made and meant by him for the good Success of the Spanish fleet, and afterwards induced both Mr. Shelly and Sir Thomas Gerard either through fear or promises to testifie against him, as also Mr. Bennet to confess how he had entreated him to say a Mass of the Holy Ghost to the same effect'.

The Earl was once more questioned by Burghley and some others of the Council. He was accused of asking Bennet to say a Mass for the success of the Spanish and of praying for twenty-four hours to the same end; to both of which charges he answered negatively. Bennet and Gerard were brought in to testify against him and swiftly removed before he could answer them back. The questioning went on, but the Earl kept his head and replied calmly and carefully until at last the Lord Chamberlain 'entering into a passion called the Earl beast and traytor, and said rather than he should not be hanged within four dayes, that he himself would hang him'. To which the Earl quietly answered 'the sooner the better if it please God'. Burghley more reasonably pointed out that it was 'no marvell he was so settled in religion, because he did read nothing to the contrary'. Philip replied that 'he neither did nor would do by his Lordship's favour'.

The trial took place in Westminster Hall on 14 April 1589 and the Earl of Derby was appointed to preside as Lord High Steward. Philip when he was brought in, though still young, tall and upright in his bearing, was seen to bear the marks of his suffering in his sallow complexion and sunken eyes. He was, like his father and grandfather before him, smartly dressed for the occasion in a 'wrought velvet gown, furred with martins, laid about with gold lace, and buttoned with gold buttons, a black sattin doublet, a pair of velvet hose and a high black hat on his head'.[7]

The indictment was read out and comprised two principal charges, the first that he had adopted Catholicism and had attempted to leave the country without permission; the second that he had offered up prayers and a Mass of the Holy Ghost for the success of the Spanish Armada. The case for the prosecution consisted of the usual groundless accusations, arguments and suppositions. The Earl in his defence remarked that there are those 'who, like the spider, can suck venom out of the sweetest flowers, and find materials for poison, where others would obtain matter only of a wholesome or harmless description'. He also pointed out that being a recent convert, he had never even heard of a 'Mass of the Holy Ghost'. Then came the Government's *pièce de résistance*, the calling of the witnesses Gerard and Bennet. (Shelly had been abandoned for some reason.) Gerard appeared first and was taken aback when Philip solemnly adjured him in the name of God to remember the last judgement and not to utter false witness. The flustered witness was floored by this, 'spake to very little purpose' and was rapidly withdrawn. Next came Fr. Bennet, and again the Earl was able to demolish his evidence with a dramatic flourish, for the priest had in the interval between examination by the Privy Council and the trial itself, undergone an attack of conscience and had written to the Earl to acknowledge that the charges he had uttered against him were false and had been extorted by 'fear of the Tower, torments and death'. To sensational effect the Earl was able to produce this letter in court. The witness however had now undergone a further reversal of conscience and stuck to his original accusation, claiming that the letter had not been written by him but by a fellow prisoner called Randal. Randal, however, was not called to substantiate this, and some of the peers murmured that Bennet was a 'fals man and no lawful witness'. Nevertheless the desired verdict was forthcoming and, to the astonishment of some of the observers, the Earl was condemned to death. He heard the verdict without emotion and merely said 'Sic voluntas Dei', 'God's will be done'.

He subsequently wrote to his wife:

Wherefore, for the satisfaction of all men, and discharge of my conscience before God I here protest before His Divine Majesty, and all the holy court of heaven, that I have committed no treason, and that the Catholic and Roman faith, which I hold, is the only cause (as far as I can any way imagine) why either I have been this long imprisoned, or for which I am now to be executed.

It is, incidentally, the only case in English legal history where somebody has been condemned as a traitor for *praying* for something to come about.

Lord Derby who had to preside over the trial, retired immediately to Lancashire 'much troubled with sorrow and melancholy'. According to Godfrey Goodman, Bishop of Gloucester, he called all his servants into his chamber at Lathom and told them that

he had been more beholden to Queen Elizabeth than any of his predecessors had been to any prince; . . . but this one thing did grieve him more than all the favours that he had received from her, that she had made him her high steward to condemn the Earl of Arundel, who was condemned upon a letter which, as he thought, was not sufficiently proved, but may be very well counterfeited, 'and this lies heavy upon my conscience'.[8]

Such was the general revulsion against the Earl's condemnation that Elizabeth did not sign his death-warrant and spared his life, but he was not informed of this decision. For six more years he lingered in the Tower under constant threat of death. 'Not a bell that sounded, but it might be his knell; not a footstep was heard, but it might be the messenger of death. Each morning, as he rose, he knew not but that, before night, he might be a headless corpse; each night, as he lay his head upon his pillow, he was uncertain whether the morning might not summon him to another world.'[9]

Gradually his health declined and in August 1595 after eating a roasted teal for dinner, he was immediately taken ill and after some violent retching he 'entered into a disentery which could never be stay'd till his very death, which gave occasion unto many to suspect he was poisoned'.[10] His weakened constitution, however, would have been cause enough for his illness. In the following week he rapidly declined and was confined to his bed. He gave up his reading and more strenuous prayers and betook 'himself only to his beads and some other devotions whereto by vow he had obliged himself'. When his physicians came to see him, he told them not to trouble themselves, his case being beyond their skills.

Sir Michael Blount, repenting of his previous harshness, came to see the dying man and kneeling beside the bed asked for his forgiveness. The Earl replied:

Do you ask forgiveness Mr. Lieutenant? Why then I forgive you in the same sort as I desire my self to be forgiven at the hands of God. And then kissing his hand, offered it in a most charitable and kind manner to him . . . You must think Mr. Lieutenant that when a prisoner comes hither to this Tower, that he bringeth sorrow with him. Oh then do not add affliction to affliction . . . It is a very inhuman part to tread on him whom misfortune hath cast down . . . There is no calamity that men are subject unto but you may also taste as well as any other man.

The Lieutenant then weeping took his leave. A few months later he was dismissed from his post and himself imprisoned in the Tower.

Philip asked to see his brother William and his uncle Henry, but this was refused. The Queen had 'made a kind of promise to some of his friends' that before his death he should be allowed to see his wife and children, Elizabeth and Thomas. He had never seen his son Thomas, who had been born after his committal to the Tower. Indeed at first he had not been told that he had a son and heir, but given to believe that the baby was another daughter. He now wrote to the Queen making this one last request. She sent back a verbal message: Yes – on condition that he renounced his faith. If he would attend the Established Church, not only could he see his wife and children, but would be restored to all his honours and his fortune. His reply is well-known: 'On such condition I cannot accept her majesty's offers, and, if that be the cause in which I am to perish, sorry am I that I have but one life to lose.'[12]

The last night of his life he spent in prayer, 'sometimes saying his beads sometimes such psalms and prayers as he knew by heart. And sometimes used these holy aspirations: "O Lord into thy hands I commend my spirit. Lord thou art my hope.'" He died at twelve noon on Sunday 19 October 1595. 'His long, lean, consumed arms' crossed over his chest, 'turning his head a little aside, as one falling into a pleasant sleep', he left this world, his servants in tears round his bed. 'Thus lived, thus suffered, and thus perished Philip Howard, Earl of Arundel, the idol of those who knew him, the admiration of Europe, and the object of the sympathies of the world.'[13]

Most governments are prepared to sacrifice the innocent individual if this is considered essential for the good of the State. To Burghley and Elizabeth the maintenance of the new Establishment was more important than the life of one man. It is rather unpleasant, of course, if you happen to be that one man, but by the standards of contemporary Europe Elizabeth and her ministers were not cruel or intolerant, rather the reverse. A blind eye was turned to the religious recusancy of many of her subjects. Philip's uncle Lord Lumley, for instance, was left more or less in peace at Nonsuch to practise his faith with all the pomp of the tridentine liturgy, even down to such details as six candles on the altar of his private chapel, and with a choir to sing masses specially written by Byrd, which are among the finest achievements in English Church music.

The persecution of the Earl of Arundel was, however, not just impersonally political; there was a horrible element in it of calculated vindictiveness. The rejection of the Court and all it stood for by the premier Earl, Burghley's ward and Elizabeth's cousin, was taken by them as a personal slight and this must explain the implacable hatred with which Philip and his long-suffering wife were pursued. Even his corpse was not 'sacred from the profanation' of the Queen's revenge. 'The most beautiful and most affecting service of religion was prostituted by her minister, to the heartless purpose of heaping insults on the grave of her victim: "Wee are not come to honour this man's religion; we publickly professe, and here openly protest otherwyse to be saved: nor to honour his offence; the lawe hath judged him, we leave him to the Lord, he is gone to his place. Thus we fynd it trewe wch is written, and is here sett downe in our booke: 'Man that is born of woman,' etc. Thus God hath layd this man's honour in the dust."'[14]

Lady Arundel was treated throughout with unnecessary callousness. On her husband's attainder the royal agents descended on Arundel House stripping it bare, taking her jewels, her carriage, and all the furniture except some of the beds. She was allowed to stay as a lodger of the Crown in the empty rooms with a pittance on which to live, but whenever the Court came to Somerset House she was ordered to the country lest the nearness of her presence might disturb the Queen. It is even recorded that Elizabeth, on visiting Arundel House in the absence of Lady Arundel and finding an inscription in a window on the theme of the sadness of life in this world and hopes for a better in the future, scratched an unpleasant message underneath 'expressing much passion and disdain . . . on purpose to grieve and afflict the poor Lady'. Lady Arundel outlived her husband by thirty-five years. She never married again, but devoted her life to good works and austere devotions, and is perhaps best remembered as the foundress and chief benefactor of the English Jesuit house at Ghent. She died at Shifnal in Shropshire in 1630 aged seventy-four.

She and her son Thomas had the last word. They successfully petitioned King James in 1624 to remove the Earl's remains from the chapel of St. Peter ad Vincula in the Tower and to rebury them in the Fitzalan Chapel at Arundel. There the coffin was placed in a newly constructed vault and a plate was fixed to it with a Latin inscription recording that the Earl had been 'wickedly sentenced to death' under Elizabeth for 'profession of the Catholic Faith', had been imprisoned in the Tower and there had led 'a most holy life for ten years and six months' and that his death had not been 'without suspicion of poison'. He is now enshrined in Arundel Cathedral, having been canonized by Pope Paul VI in 1970.

Philip's religious conversion, his imprisonment, his resolution, integrity and premature death are the main aspects of his life. But he was also noted in his day for his studious and antiquarian interests, interests which he shared with his uncle Lord Lumley and his brother Lord William Howard, the three of them foreshadowing the great antiquarian scholars and collectors of the seventeenth century. Like many historians, Philip had an exceptional, almost photographic, memory. To test it he once memorized all the hanging signs in Fleet Street while walking back from near St. Paul's in the City to Arundel House opposite St. Clement Dane's, in the Strand. There were several hundred and when he reached home he called a servant and dictated them in order; they were checked and found to be accurate.

Lord Lumley's antiquarianism took the form of collecting portraits or erecting monuments to his ancestors and those families with which he was connected. The portrait of the 1st Duke of Norfolk, now at Arundel, was almost certainly painted for him in the late sixteenth century. It was the distinctive Lumley *cartellino* in one corner, as indeed has Philip's own portrait. Several pictures from the Lumley collection later passed to Philip's son Thomas, the Collector Earl. Lord Lumley also erected the tomb (on the model of a medieval chantry) in the Fitzalan Chapel, to the last three Fitzalan Earls of Arundel. Lord William Howard's antiquarian and historical tastes were perhaps even more enterprising for, in between war-like operations against the Scots on the Borders, he excavated the Roman remains on his Cumberland estates, rescued some important medieval carved and painted ceilings from Kirkoswald Castle when it was demolished, and formed an interesting library some of which is now at Durham University. The Earl of Arundel too, had an exceptionally fine library and, according to Richard Gough, he was considered 'the greatest antiquary in Europe except Ferdinand de Medici . . . Among the celebrated libraries of the age in this kingdom, his was the compleatest in the antiquarian way.'[15] It is probable that the historical interest of these three noblemen in the Middle Ages was one of the circumstances which made them embrace Catholicism.

Thus, in the late sixteenth century there began that remarkable cult of the past which is such a strong and consistent feature of the Howard family history. The execution and attainder of the 4th Duke of Norfolk and the saintly hiatus of his son's brief life and tragic death marked the end of an era. Their successors would always look back with nostalgia and reverence to the departed glories of the first four Howard dukes, to the Mowbrays, the Brothertons, the Staffords, the de Veres, the Fitzalans and the whole host of the medieval baronage, a lost world of ancient Catholic piety and aristocratic privilege, in contrast to the decadence and mediocrity of the present. The urge to revive, to relive, or to commemorate adequately, that lost baronial and Catholic past would be a powerful force determining the behaviour to a greater or lesser degree of all the future heads of the family, even into the late twentieth century.

The Howard Earldoms

'WHAT has not the house of Howard suffered for my sake', lamented Mary Queen of Scots at the end of her tragic life. Her son was aware of this, and on his accession to the English throne in 1603 attempted to make suitable restitution, as a result of which the early seventeenth century saw a renewal of the Howard role in political life with the spectacular advance of the representatives of the four principal cadet lines of the Howard family, each of whom was to be the recipient or progenitor of an independent earldom in addition to the main ducal line. Such a rapid restoration to power is all the more astonishing in the light of the disfavour in which nearly the whole Howard clan had been held in the latter part of Elizabeth's reign because of the taint of recusancy, Lord Henry Howard, the younger brother and Lord William Howard, the younger son of the 4th Duke, having been viewed with special suspicion by the authorities and having spent much of their time in prison. Only Lord Howard of Effingham escaped this general aura of disfavour as a result of his naval abilities, mild manner and predominantly Protestant outlook, and he was the only one to be raised to an earldom before James came to the throne.

His father, the founder of the Effingham branch of the Howards, was Lord William Howard, son of the 2nd Duke of Norfolk by his second wife, a respectable but not brilliant man. Chapuys, the Spanish ambassador, described him as stupid and indiscreet. He occupied a series of official posts, more because of his birth and uncontroversial outlook than because of any outstanding personal qualities. He took part in the French campaigns of 1544 and 1546, becoming Lord Deputy and Governor of Calais. In 1553 he was placed on the Privy Council and appointed Lord Admiral, a not inappropriate post in view of his seafaring concerns which included sponsoring Richard Chancellor's journey round the North Cape to Archangel. The following year he was made a Knight of the Garter and created Baron Howard of Effingham as a reward for his loyalty to Mary during Wyatt's rebellion, when he took the lead in preventing the rebels entering the City through Ludgate. 'They won't come in here', he shouted as he barred the gates. In the last year of Mary's reign he was made Lord Chamberlain, and under Elizabeth, to whom he had wisely shown much deference and courtesy before she came to the throne, he was appointed Lord Privy Seal. After an impeccably correct and moderately distinguished career holding high office under four monarchs he died in January 1573 and was buried in the Effingham vault at Reigate in Surrey.

His son who succeeded him was a man of different calibre, *the* Lord Howard of Effingham, famous as the conqueror of the Spanish Armada, and the last member of the Howard family to fill the office of Lord High Admiral of England, an appointment he held for thirty-four years from 1585 till his retirement in 1619. A humane and honourable man with considerable administrative ability, his great opportunity came when he was fifty-two years old; it was his careful preparation and steadfast opposition to Elizabeth's spasmodic cheese-paring which ensured that there was a well-equipped English fleet to meet the Spanish when the long-awaited Armada finally sailed in 1588. On one occasion when Elizabeth had ordered four of his largest ships to be put out of commission he had replied that rather than that he would prefer to pay for their maintenance himself. Howard's determination and administrative flair ensured that the fleet was ready to fight but the detailed plans of action were Drake's, and the Lord Admiral made it clear that he was prepared to bow to the other man's superior seamanship when making decisions. He appointed Drake his Vice-Admiral and second-in-command and freely admitted Drake's better judgment of naval strategy:

The opinion of Sir Francis Drake, Mr. Frobisher and others that be men of the greatest judgment and experience is that the surest way to meet with the Spanish fleet is upon their coast, or in harbour of their own, and there to defeat them . . . I confess my error at that time, which was otherwise, but I did, and will, yield ever to them of greater experience.

His preparations were finally put to the test when the Armada set sail at the end of May, and Effingham leading in the Ark Royal took the main English battle fleet from the Thames to Plymouth. There with tact and firmness he was able in the intervening weeks to weld the disparate English seamen into a co-operative band under a single directing command, 'the gallantest company of captains, soldiers and mariners that I think was ever seen in England'.

On Friday 19 July, the Armada was sighted off the Lizard and a messenger sped with the news to Plymouth where he arrived at four in the afternoon to find the Lord Admiral on the Hoe playing bowls with Drake. The beacons were lit that night to warn that the Armada had at last arrived and the following morning, 20 July, the English fleet set sail. The commander of the Armada, the Duke of Medina Sidonia, had firm instructions from Philip II to sail straight up the Channel to Flanders to meet the Duke of Parma and embark the army prepared for the invasion of England, so he sailed majestically on his way in crescent formation ignoring the little English ships which swept down on his flanks firing

Daniel Mytens. The 2nd Lord Howard of Effingham, Lord H
Admiral of England and victor of the Spanish Armada.

Henry, Earl of Northampton (1540–1614). The effigy by
Nicholas Stone on his monument now at Trinity Hospital,
Greenwich, but originally in the chapel at Dover Castle.

salvoes of shots which failed in the course of three engagements to sink a single Spanish ship. At first the English were outnumbered two to one but gradually the entire royal navy assembled under the Lord Admiral's command forming a concentration of ships equal in numbers but not in size to the Spanish.

It was essential for the English to break the Spanish formation before the Armada reached Dunkirk and embarked Parma's troops. It was decided, off Calais, to resort to fireships in the night and this proved successful in scattering the Spanish ships, enabling the English, in the engagement off Gravelines on 29 July, to inflict considerable damage on them. Over half the crew of Medina Sidonia's flagship was killed, twelve Spanish ships were knocked out entirely and the remaining one hundred and twenty so winded that they decided not to make contact with Parma but fled to the North and round the top of the British Isles, where the weather and then the barbaric population of Ireland took their toll of much of the remainder, only twenty-four rotten hulks eventually returning to Spain.

Effingham's fleet followed the Spanish up the east coast as far as Newcastle, though they were entirely out of ammunition and victuals: 'we set on a brag countenance and gave them chase as though we wanted nothing'. The fleet then dribbled back in detachments and in sorry condition to be treated with characteristic lack of generosity by Elizabeth. Neither Effingham nor any of the other commanders received any peerage honours in recognition of the great victory, and the sailors, short of food and riddled with disease, were left to rot. Effingham complained: 'It would grieve any man's heart to see them that have served so valiantly die so miserably.' He did his best for them. 'It is a most pitiful sight to see how the men, having no place to receive them into here, die in the streets. I am driven myself, of force, to come a-land to see them bestowed in some lodging. And the best I can get is barns and outhouses.' He himself advanced half the cash needed to pay the wages of the discharged men.[1]

Effingham's other principal naval engagement was the attack on Cadiz in 1596 where he held the joint command with the Earl of Essex of the English expeditionary force. Essex took precedence on land and Effingham at sea, but despite this arrangement, specially calculated one might think to cause maximum ill-feeling and inefficiency, the expedition was a success and the Spanish fleet lying in Cadiz harbour was destroyed. Effingham now received his belated reward. On 22 October 1597 he was created Earl of Nottingham, the patent containing the following clause: 'That by the Victory obtained anno 1588, he had secured the Kingdom of England from the invasion of Spain and other impending dangers; and did also in conjunction with our dear cousin Robert, Earl of Essex, seize by force the isle and strongly fortified city of Cadiz, in the farthest part of Spain; and did likewise rout and defeat another fleet of the King of Spain, prepared in that part against this Kingdom'.

For the remainder of his life he was deferred to in all defence matters and in 1599 was appointed 'Lord Lieutenant General of All England' commanding both the fleet and the army, an office which has never existed before or since. Like his Howard cousins he came down firmly on the side of James I as Elizabeth's successor and he placed a naval squadron in the Channel over the period of the succession just in case. At the coronation he was Lord High Constable. James bestowed on him several Howard properties and Arundel House in the Strand. The old Earl continued to serve on various commissions and embassies till his retirement at the age of eighty-three in January 1619. He died in 1624 and was buried at Reigate. The Nottingham title became extinct in 1681 on the death of both his sons without issue.[2]

In his support for James I in 1603 the Lord Admiral was no doubt influenced by his cousin Henry Howard, the younger son of the Poet Earl of Surrey and brother of the 4th Duke of Norfolk. Henry Howard was the brain behind the Howard restoration in the early seventeenth century and his manoeuvrings behind the scenes were responsible for carrying the family back to power and fortune. His support for Cecil and James I was recognized by his being created Lord Marnhull and Earl of Northampton on 13 March 1604 and by the grant of half the attainted ducal estates in East Anglia and Shropshire.

This sinister bachelor don is among the most fascinating members of the Howard family, though his true character remains an impenetrable enigma. He was a master of slander and intrigue, almost certainly an agnostic, a cynic with an eye for the main chance whose subtlety of mind was matched by his lack of scruple. Estimates of his complex and contradictory personality have varied, but nearly everybody is agreed that he was very clever and not very nice. Sir Anthony Weldon wrote of his 'venemous and cankred disposition' and summed him up as 'a great clerk, yet not a wise man, but the grossest Flatterer of the World'.

Hasted was even more damning and later described Northampton as 'composed of singular contradictions. With the talents, tastes and accomplishments of his father; amiable and refined in his manners; apparently pious; extensively charitable; he was nevertheless a monster of wickedness and hypocrisy; leagued in the murder of Overbury, the letters in proof of which displayed such a mixture of ferocity and obscenity that the Chief Justice could not read them entire in court; endowing almshouses, and writing on devotional subjects, he nevertheless appears to have had no religious principle.'[3]

Sinister slander was his forte and he was able to undermine the reputations of his enemies so successfully that their total destruction usually followed easily, as in the case of Lord Cobham and Sir Walter Raleigh at both of whose state trials he sat as a commissioner. His innuendos against Edward de Vere, 17th Earl of Oxford, who was an old enemy partly responsible for his imprisonment in 1582, included accusations of chronic drunkenness, attempted murder, pederasty and bestiality.

His twisted personality may have been the result of the frustrations of his early life. Born in 1540 he had been educated at King's College, Cambridge, taking the degree of MA in 1564. He subsequently entered Trinity Hall and as a young man earned the reputation of being a scholar of exceptional attainments; he lectured on Rhetoric and Civil Law at Cambridge for his livelihood and his discourses, in Latin, were said to be 'very brilliant'.

In the 1570s he fell under the shadow of his brother's 'treason' and was himself accused of dealing with Mary Queen of Scots, being interrogated in 1571, 1574, 1582 and 1583 and being imprisoned several times, though on each occasion he was able to talk his way out of his predicament. This was despite the fact that he was in constant correspondence with Mary Queen of Scots, to whom he despatched long flowery letters bedecked with elaborate quotations from the classics and giving up-to-date news of the goings-on at Court. In view of his brother's execution for more or less the same offence this showed rashness to the point of arrogance.

Elizabeth suspected but could do nothing. The Earl of Oxford pleasantly informed Howard that the Queen hated him 'and sought his head more than that of any person living'. She remained blind and deaf to Howard's flattery, such as his *Dutiful Defence of the Lawful Regiment of Women*, and he spent the last twenty years of her reign in poverty, enlivened now and then by sparks of trouble, such as that caused by his *Preservative Against the Poison of Supposed Prophecies* (1583), a learned attack on astrology which was deemed treason and led to a spell in the Fleet Prison 'suffering the utmost misery'. He was refused permission to serve against the Spanish Armada. This could not have been a result of his furnishing Mendoza the Spanish ambassador with 'confidential and minute accounts twice a week' of all that went on at Elizabeth's Court in return for an annual salary of 1,000 crowns, because it is unlikely that Elizabeth and her advisers knew of this.

At the end of the reign his love of underhand plotting proved his salvation, for he began a secret correspondence with James concerning the latter's succession to the English throne, and he sided with Robert Cecil against Essex and the younger element at Court. Having backed the right side, and with James I's accession smoothly accomplished he at last received the honours, power and riches to which he had always considered himself entitled by his birth and genius. As the 'learnedest counsellor in the Kingdom' he was appointed to the Privy Council in 1603, made Lord Warden of the Cinque Ports in 1604, Lord Lieutenant of Hertfordshire and Norfolk and a Knight of the Garter in 1605, Lord Privy Seal in 1608, Steward of Oxford in 1609, Chancellor of Cambridge in 1612 and Keeper of Greenwich Park in 1613. Following the death of Cecil he was the most powerful person in the Government and from 1612 till his own death in 1614 he was First

Commissioner of the Treasury. James was especially susceptible to North-ampton's flattery and lapped it up, though he was heard to complain that the Earl's long grandiloquent letters were 'asiatic and endless volumes'.

One result of Northampton's success at the Stuart Court was that for the first time he had the means to indulge his passion for architecture; he built and richly furnished for himself a house overlooking Greenwich Park and also erected, at Charing Cross, Northampton House, a large quadrangular mansion with four corner towers and a fantastic columned frontispiece designed by Bernard Jannsen.[4] He bequeathed the Greenwich house to his grand-nephew the Earl of Arundel, and Northampton House to his nephew the Earl of Suffolk whose own country house, Audley End, was built under Northampton's direction, the surveyor being again Bernard Jannsen. Northampton was unmarried and had no children; his various architectural enterprises represented for him some of the satisfaction which other people derive from their offspring.

He died at Northampton House of gangrene in his thigh on 16 June 1614 aged seventy-four. His handsome tomb with a kneeling effigy by Nicholas Stone was erected by his grand-nephew the Collector Earl of Arundel and was originally in the chapel at Dover Castle, but was removed to Trinity Hospital, Greenwich, by the Mercers' Company in the late seventeenth century when the Dover chapel fell into ruin. Northampton himself had taken a special interest in the erection of tombs. He was one of those responsible for the magnificent marble memorial to Mary Queen of Scots erected in Henry VII's Chapel, Westminster, by Cornelius Cure, and also commissioned a tomb of painted and gilded alabaster, probably by William Cure II, to his father, the Poet Earl, at Framlingham, having obtained permission to transfer his body there from London as a mark of filial respect.

The most revealing aspect of Northampton's character was his attitude to religion. He was formally a Catholic yet trimmed his beliefs to accommodate his political ambitions and probably believed in nothing much. As a commissioner at the trial of the Jesuit Fr. Garnett in 1606 he made a long and ostentatiously brilliant speech against the papal supremacy which so pleased James I that he ordered it to be translated into French, Latin and Italian.[5] Lady Bacon, who had Northampton's measure, warned her son against him as a 'dangerous intel-ligencing man and no doubt a subtle papist inwardly'. Following Northampton's death, John Chamberlain wrote to tell Dudley Carleton that several Popish ceremonies were observed at his funeral and that he received extreme unction. In his will dated 14 June 1614 Northampton wrote 'I dye . . . a member of the Catholicke and Apostolicke Churche saying with Saint Jerome "In qua fide puer natus fui in eadem senex morior."'[*6] In the will he set up a symbolic benefaction of three almshouses (or hospitals) for the poor, each dedicated to the Holy Trinity,

---

* 'I will die as an old man in the same faith in which I was born as a child.'

The arms of Henry, Earl of Northampton. A stained-glass panel in a window of his almshouses at Castle Rising, Norfolk.

Trinity Alms Houses, Castle Rising, Norfolk. One of a symbolic benefaction of three almshouses or hospitals dedicated to the Holy Trinity and erected on his estates under the terms of the will of Henry, Earl of Northampton.

Thomas, 1st Earl of Suffolk (1561–1626), second son of the 4th Duke of Norfolk and Lord Treasurer of England, dismissed for corruption.

at Castle Rising (Norfolk), Clun (Shropshire) and Greenwich as a thanksgiving for deliverance from the wiles of his enemies. Such deliverance was a marginal scrape at the end, for by dying at that moment before the revelation of the Overbury murder and the peculations of his nephew and protégé, Thomas Howard Earl of Suffolk, he avoided certain implication. The revelations brought about Suffolk's ruin and would have brought about Northampton's too, had he lived another year.

Thomas Howard, son of the 4th Duke of Norfolk by his second wife Margaret Audley, was born in 1561 and educated at St. John's College, Cambridge, though unlike Northampton he never pretended to be an intellectual or a scholar. Indeed when James I appointed him Lord Treasurer in 1614 he emphasized that 'he had made choice of him not for his learning in Greek and Latin, or for that he could make epigrams and orations, but for his approved fidelity and integrity, etcetera'.[7] His character nevertheless remains something of a puzzle. He presented himself as 'a plain honest man' yet he surrounded himself with a following of 'dishonest scoundrels' and was strongly influenced by his scheming old uncle Northampton, not to mention his over-ambitious and corrupt wife Katherine.

Because of his father's attainder and the wreck of much of the family fortune, he had to make his own way to the top using his own abilities and the weaknesses of the system, not that he started out totally penniless. Though his first marriage to Mary Dacre proved abortive because she had died young and he had not therefore inherited any of the Dacre property, he nevertheless inherited through his mother the Audley estate, including Audley End in Essex, from which he derived an income of £1,000 per annum. His second marriage to Katherine, daughter and co-heiress of Sir Henry Knyvett, brought him the Charlton estate in Wiltshire, worth about £2,000 per annum. Though substantial, neither of these two inheritances was enough in itself to support an extravagant life at Court, and he therefore pursued his ambitions in adventure at sea.

He was restored in blood in 1584 and soon after was allowed to serve under Lord Howard of Effingham against the Armada, where he was captain of the Golden Lion, and on the Azores expedition in 1591, where he assured Sir Richard Grenville 'Fore God I am no coward', and in the campaign against Cadiz in 1596. He so distinguished himself in the latter that he was created Lord Howard of Walden and a Knight of the Garter in 1597. His attempt to supplement his income with Spanish loot was a failure, however, and in the 1590s he came very near to bankruptcy, Elizabeth not showing the slightest inclination to release any of the attainted Howard estates.

Like his uncle Northampton, he too was saved by backing Cecil against Essex and supporting the succession of James Stuart to the throne of England. The rewards were immediate and enormous. In 1603 he was created Earl of Suffolk, made Lord Chamberlain (one of the most important and profitable Court offices), appointed to the Privy Council and granted the other half of the old Howard estates, the liberty of the Duke of Norfolk being revived and shared between him and Lord Northampton. This added about £4,000 to his income. But direct grants of land formed only a part of the fruits of success. Equally profitable were the farm of the customs, and the imposition on currants which he received in the same year and exploited for all they were worth with the help of dishonest henchmen like Sir John Bingley and Sir Arthur Ingram. By 1612 it was said that he was receiving £5,000 a year from these and other equally shady public sources.[8]

From 1603 to 1618 his political career 'pursued a consistently upward path'. Following the death of Cecil in 1612 the Howards, Northampton and Suffolk, enjoyed complete control of the government and two years later Suffolk received the richest office of all, the Lord Treasurership. 1615 saw him at the height of his power but that year was also a turning-point, for it saw the introduction to Court, by another political faction, of a handsome young man called George Villiers, soon to be Marquess of Buckingham. The Howards made a frantic last-ditch attempt to maintain their influence over James. Just as the 3rd Duke of Norfolk had introduced his pretty nieces Anne Boleyn and Katherine Howard to Court in order to engage the attentions of Henry VIII, so Suffolk and his colleagues attempted to supply James with an alternative to Villiers, picking out a good-looking youth, William Monson, whom they 'tooke great paines in tricking and prancking up' and to maintain his fine complexion, washed 'his face every day with posset-curd'[9] – but to no avail. James thought him 'forward', took against him, and Villiers was soon immovably established as the King's chief favourite in place of Robert Carr, Earl of Somerset.

The sudden and dramatic fall of Somerset was brought about by the disclosure of his complicity in a cold-blooded murder. One of Suffolk's daughters, Lady Frances Howard, had been married at the age of seventeen to the immature fifteen-year-old 3rd Earl of Essex, who shortly afterwards had departed on a Continental Grand Tour in order to 'grow up' before living with his wife. In the absence of her young husband Frances became enamoured of Robert Carr, who had come to Court from Scotland in 1605 and had rapidly advanced in James I's affections, being created successively Viscount Rochester and Earl of Somerset. In 1613 Frances, having been inspected by 'some ancient ladies and midwives expert in those matters' who declared her to be 'a pure virgin; which some doctors think a strange asseveration', secured a divorce from Essex 'on a completely false' and humiliating charge of impotence. She was immediately married to Somerset in the face of contrary advice from the latter's friend Sir Thomas Overbury, a man of sound judgement as well as literary ability, whose attempt to stop the marriage aroused the fury and hatred of Frances and her family. The Earls of Suffolk and Northampton devised a plan for getting Overbury out of the way by offering him a foreign embassy. When he declined to accept this, they used his refusal as a pretext for having him placed in the Tower and while there he was poisoned at the instigation of Lady Frances, aided and abetted by Lord Northampton.

Sir William Wade, the Lieutenant of the Tower, a man of inconvenient probity, was removed and Sir Gervase Helwys, who could be trusted not to notice anything, was substituted at Northampton's instigation, and a ruffian called Weston was put in as assistant keeper. Frances supplied the prisoner with confectionery which she warned the Lieutenant against using in his own household. Overbury died on 15 September 1613 and was hurriedly buried by the Lieutenant on the written instructions of the Earl of Northampton, who put about the convenient rumour that the 'foulness of the corpse' was due to 'the pox or somewhat worse'.[10]

This sordid scandal came out in 1615 when Weston confessed his guilt. He, Sir Gervase Helwys, an assistant called Mrs Turner and an apothecary called

Audley End, Essex. (Partly demolished.) The great mansion built by the 1st Earl of Suffolk out of the irregular proceeds of his offices, to the design of Bernard Jannsen and the Earl of Northampton. From an engraving by John Britten.

Franklin were all condemned and executed for murder. The Earl and Countess of Somerset were also condemned to death, but reprieved and after six years in the Tower were banished to Somerset where they passed the remainder of their lives in miserable obscurity.

The final blow fell in 1618 when Suffolk was tried before the Star Chamber for gross corruption in office. He and his wife had been involved in a whole series of shady deals and had enforced a ruthless system of bribes from underlings in return for political favours. Case after case was cited of Crown creditors not getting satisfaction until they had paid a ten per cent bribe to Lady Suffolk. The Treasurer at War in Ireland had been paying the Suffolks £1,000 per annum in order to 'facilitate' payment of the monies allocated to him. The Suffolks had also received no less than £11,000 from the Spanish for information about English policy. Following the example of Cecil before him, Suffolk had exploited a corrupt system for all he could get, but he had exceeded even the lax standards of public life at the early Stuart Court. He was dismissed from all his offices and fined £30,000, though in the event this was commuted to £7,000, and in his later years he was restored to royal favour, though not to power.[11]

Suffolk has generally been thought to have been pushed into large-scale corruption by his wife, but his own extravagance was also a spur to rapacity. Though he and his son Theophilus, who had inherited the large Dorset estates of Viscount Bindon, were among the richest peers in England, with a combined income totalling about £15,000 per annum, this was not enough to meet the cost of life at Court, Suffolk's over-generous provision for his six sons and three daughters, and his fantastic building activity.[12] He rebuilt his principal seat at Audley End, Essex, on a scale that was barely credible and made it by far the largest private house in England. The present house at Audley End, which seems large enough, is in fact a much reduced eighteenth-century reconstruction; the original house, built between 1603 and 1616 under the supervision of Lord Northampton and Bernard Jannsen, was a gigantic edifice at least three times as big, with two immense courtyards covering a total of five acres. It cost upwards of £80,000. Suffolk himself told James I that, with its furniture and fittings, it cost him £200,000. James is supposed to have replied that it was too large for a king but would do very well for a Lord Treasurer, foreshadowing Louis XIV's quip to the unfortunate Fouquet at Vaux le Vicomte. 'Just as Hatfield House imposed corruption on the Earl of Salisbury, so Audley End imposed corruption on the Earl of Suffolk.' The house was, despite its dubious financing, a magnificent architectural achievement and of great importance in the development of English architecture as one of the first buildings to display the Anglo–Flemish style of the early seventeenth century, coarse, vigorous and romantic.

Despite his dramatic career which had taken him to the very top of the greasy pole of political power and had made him one of the richest peers in England,

Suffolk left his descendants saddled with huge debts and a house so big that no private family could afford to keep it up. Under his son Theophilus, 2nd Earl, an 'able-bodied nonentity' and a spendthrift, matters got steadily worse and he was forced to sell several family estates including Framlingham in 1635. But there were still debts of £132,000 when he died and his son James, 3rd Earl, had no option but to sell more land including the whole of the Bindon estate in Dorset, the northern estates and the house at Charing Cross, which the 1st Earl had inherited from Lord Northampton, to the Earl of Northumberland. Between 1633 and 1641 he and his father disposed of half the Suffolk patrimony.

This decline continued into the second half of the seventeenth century. Audley End itself was sold to Charles II, but in 1701 it reverted to the Suffolks who, as they could not afford to live in it, demolished over half in 1721. A series of childless marriages finally brought the main line of the Suffolks to an end in 1745 with the death of the 10th Earl. The last seven Earls had been undistinguished, though the wife of one was Horace Walpole's *sympatico* friend, the attractive though plain mistress of George II who built Marble Hill at Twickenham; and two younger sons 'Ned' and Sir Robert were popular playwrights in the Restoration period although Sir Walter Scott dismissed the latter's poetry as 'freezingly mediocre'.

The second son of the 1st Earl of Suffolk, Thomas, who inherited his mother's property at Charlton (Wiltshire), was Master of the Horse for a time to Charles I and was created Earl of Berkshire in 1625, though Clarendon thought 'his interest and reputation less than anything but his understanding'. His great-grandson Henry Bowes Howard, 4th Earl of Berkshire, became 11th Earl of Suffolk in 1745 and the late eighteenth century saw the Suffolks undergo a revival. The 12th Earl had a moderately distinguished political career, becoming Lord Privy Seal, and internally remodelled Charlton in elegant neo-classical taste to the design of the younger Matthew Brettingham, while the 16th Earl was a distinguished art collector, owning among other works, the Leonardo da Vinci 'Madonna of the Rocks' now in the National Gallery. The Suffolks have continued at Charlton down to the present time. The 19th Earl was killed in action in the First World War and the 20th Earl in the Second World War, being posthumously awarded the George Cross for conspicuous bravery. He was an important figure in the history of bomb disposal, the director of the Scientific Research Experimental Unit set up at the beginning of the war to investigate and make trials of methods required to defuse new types of unexploded bombs. He met his death on 12 May 1941 while working on an unexploded bomb in the Erith Marshes.

To turn from the 1st Earl of Suffolk to his younger brother Lord William Howard, founder of the Carlisle branch of the Howard family, is to exchange the shady but glittering scenes of the Jacobean Court for the bracing wilds of Cumberland, and the flashy corruption of the Court nobility for the solid virtue of

Naworth Castle, Cumberland. The seat of Lord William Howard, ancestor of the Earls of Carlisle, inherited from the Dacres through his wife Elizabeth.

Castle Howard, Yorkshire. It was designed by Sir John Vanbrugh and Nicholas Hawksmoor and begun in 1700.

the rural nobility. Lord William Howard who is remembered for sternly enforcing law and order in the anarchic Border region was also a reader, scholar and collector of books and manuscripts whom Camden called 'a singular lover of valuable antiquity and learned withal' and whom Sir Walter Scott inflated into the legendary hero 'Belted Will' in the *Lay of the Last Minstrel.*

Through his wife, Elizabeth Dacre, he inherited the Dacre estate at Naworth in Cumberland, and Henderskelfe (later Castle Howard) in Yorkshire, but during the reign of Elizabeth he was debarred from holding them because of his religion. Like his eldest brother Philip he had become a practising Catholic, and as a result had drawn down the full force of Elizabeth's displeasure. He was three times imprisoned in the Tower but on the accession of James I he benefited from the general restoration of the Howards and, having secured his wife's estates, he promptly left for the North where he took up his abode at Naworth Castle which he restored in a conservative Gothic style introducing genuine carved and painted medieval ceilings from nearby Kirkoswald Castle.[13] He devoted his days to reforming the administration of the 'middle shires' and controlling the 'moss troopers', freebooting raiders like the Grahams, who flourished in the no man's land between England and Scotland. His leisure he spent in such scholarly work as editing the *Chronicle of Florence of Worcester.* His household books survive and show that he and his wife lived at Naworth all the year round, surrounded by their married sons and their families. A party of officers from Norwich who visited them while making a survey of the North in 1634 gave an endearing portrait of the elderly couple: 'the noble twaine (as it pleased themselves to tell us themselves) could not make above 25 years together when first they marry'd but now could make above 140 years and are hearty well and merry'.[14]

'Belted Will' died in 1640. His great-grandson Charles, born in 1629, was created 1st Earl of Carlisle at the Restoration, despite the fact that during the Civil War he had joined the parliamentary side and was one of the two peers created by Cromwell when in 1657 he was called to the House of Lords as Viscount Howard of Morpeth. He served in several official capacities: special Ambassador to the Tsar of Russia in 1663 and to Sweden and Denmark in 1664, finally becoming Governor of Jamaica. He was an Anglican and was buried in York Minster where the epitaph on his monument draws attention to his 'courage, justice, generosity and a public spirit'. He set the pattern for later generations of the Carlisles who were the archetypal great Whig family: enlightened landowners, serious politicians, holding high office from generation to generation providing, for instance, two of the best Viceroys of Ireland, but above all the creators of Castle Howard which many would consider the finest house in England. The Carlisle Howards are the most distinguished of the later Howards and have played a remarkably consistent role in national life, Whigs in politics and unusually discerning patrons of artists, from Vanbrugh and Hawksmoor to the Pre-Raphaelites and Philip Webb. Unfortunately in this book, which is devoted primarily to the main ducal line of the Howards, it is not possible to follow their later history in any more detail here, except to note that in 1921 the estates were divided, Naworth Castle in Cumberland remaining with the Earl of Carlisle and Castle Howard and the Yorkshire estate descending to a younger son, now owned by Mr George Howard, Chairman of the Governing Body of the BBC.

The Collector Earl

THOMAS, Earl of Arundel, the only son of St. Philip Howard, was the greatest of the early English private collectors and patrons. Rubens described him as 'uno delli quatro evangelisti e suportator del nostro arte', and Horace Walpole called him the 'father of vertu' in England. He had a collection of over seven hundred pictures, while his antique marbles, gems, prints and drawings were unequalled. As a connoisseur he was of European stature, a rival to Italian cardinals and Spanish courtiers, not just an English figure. He was the most significant as well as the most serious and influential of the patrons whose taste developed in the reigns of James I and Charles I. In the twentieth century he has been studied and written about more than any other member of the Howard family, a fact which would have given him great pleasure could he have known it. As he intended, his 'love and reverence to Antiquities and all thinges of Art' has ensured him immortality in the magnificent series of portraits by Mytens, Van Dyck, Rubens, Jan Lievens, Dieussart and Hollar, less ephemeral than his political achievements or diplomatic triumphs.

His collections, the patronage of artists and scholars, his cult of the past, all formed part of a single-minded attempt to restore the glory and honour of his family; and in this he was largely successful. For, though the dukedom itself remained under attainder throughout his lifetime, he was able to secure to his line several other titles, to win back many of the lost estates and to play a significant role in political and diplomatic affairs, as well as embellishing the family honour with all the glory which discerning patronage of the arts and scholarship could bestow. The extent of his achievement can be judged by measuring it against the seemingly hopeless ruin of the family at the time of his birth, an event which occurred at the nadir of the Howard fortunes: his father imprisoned in the Tower under threat of death for treason; his grandfather, the 4th Duke of Norfolk, executed for treason and the dukedom attainted; the earldoms of Arundel and Surrey and the various baronies also lost by his father's

Daniel Mytens. The Collector Earl with part of his collection of Antique Sculpture, painted in 1617. Many of the statues can still be identified among the Arundel Marbles in the Ashmolean Museum at Oxford.

Daniel Mytens. Aletheia Talbot, 1617, wife of the Collector Earl and eventual sole heiress of her father Gilbert, 7th Earl of Shrewsbury; she was Bess of Hardwick's grand-daughter, and brought Sheffield and Worksop to the Howard family. The IHS pendant which she wears in all her portraits was left to her by her mother-in-law Anne Dacre, widow of St. Philip Howard.

attainder; all the family estates, houses and possessions confiscated by the Crown.

He was born penniless in a cottage at Romford in Essex and brought up in straitened circumstances by his austere and pious mother whose rigorous supervision of his studies of the classics and mathematics was important for the early training of his mind, though his somewhat bleak introduction to religion seems to have discouraged him for life. His precocious intelligence and the austere circumstances of his youth led the Earl of Essex to refer to him as 'the winter pear'. His later education was entrusted to a private tutor, probably the chaplain in his mother's household, and there is no truth in the old myth that he was educated at Westminster and Trinity College, Cambridge. Had he gone to Cambridge it would almost certainly have been to St. John's, the preferred Howard college. In a letter of 25 June 1624 recommending his son to the Master of St. John's he mentions that his father and uncles had been educated there; he would not have omitted himself had he been there too. His intellectual stimulus came not from a university but from within his own family, from his great-uncles Northampton and Lumley and his uncle Lord William Howard, with their knowledge of the classics, history and antiquities, their respect for scholarship and their lively interest in the arts.

I ke them Thomas was fascinated by the story of the Howards and 'thought no other part of History so considerable, as what related to his own Family; in which no doubt, there had been some very memorable people'.[1] For this reason Holbein was among his favourite artists; he formed the greatest collection of this master's works ever assembled including forty-four oil paintings and the well-known portrait drawings now in the Royal Library at Windsor. Not only was Holbein one of the greatest geniuses of portraiture, but he had immortalized the Howards and their world in what seemed in retrospect their golden age of power, riches and glory.

Much of Arundel's own achievement, the repair and recording of ancient tombs, the erection of monuments to his relations, the commissioning of paintings of his ancestors and events in family history, his patronage of historical scholarship, was a tribute to and commemoration of the history of the Howards. In his will he desired that a history might be written of 'his noble ancestors, whereby their good memory may be preserved, and those that shall succeede may be invited to be virtuous, or at least ashamed to be vitious'.[2] His ambition developed out of his ancestor worship and family pride. His ancestors had been distinguished for their role in the affairs of the State and in their patronage of scholarship and the arts. He intended to renew that pattern in his own life; he was therefore consciously following family tradition in almost everything he did.

The late sixteenth century had seen the eclipse of the Howard fortunes, but the accession of James I had ushered in a new phase of Howard supremacy with the advance of Northampton, Nottingham and Suffolk, as has been seen already. Thomas Howard, the head of the family, also benefited from Stuart favour, though being younger he was not influential at Court and so unable to press his own claims with the power of his uncles. As a result many of the properties which should have been his were granted to older relations: Framlingham to Lord Suffolk, Arundel House to Lord Nottingham and other estates to Lord North- ampton. The Earl of Suffolk's lands were never reclaimed by the senior branch, but Thomas was able to retrieve much of the remainder. He bought back Arundel House for £4,000 in 1607 from Lord Nottingham, the memory of which transac- tion left him feeling bitter for the rest of his life: 'if the Admirall were not damned for makinge me pay four thousand pounde for this house . . .' he exclaimed. Lord Northampton on his death in 1614 left his nephew the majority of his estates in East Anglia together with his richly appointed house at Greenwich (burnt in 1617). The ill-feeling caused by this redistribution of the Howard estates was not entirely without benefit, for it caused a coolness between Thomas and his uncles which later worked to his political advantage. When Suffolk was disgraced in 1618 he was able to stand aside, and to continue unaffected along the path to political power.

Though some of his land was lost, Thomas was restored in blood as Earl of Arundel and Surrey in 1604, and granted Arundel Castle and the remaining Norfolk estates. He was introduced to Court in 1605 and the following year married Aletheia, third daughter and eventually sole heiress of Gilbert, 7th Earl of Shrewsbury. Her inheritance not only transformed Arundel's financial position but that of the family as a whole. She brought to the Howards vast estates across South Yorkshire, Derbyshire and Nottinghamshire, estates rich in minerals, lead, coal and iron, and with a great house at Worksop which was to become the principal ducal seat in the eighteenth century, while the industrial town of Sheffield has formed the backbone of the family fortune ever since. This influx of new land was to transform the balance of the family's territorial power. The Sheffield ('northern') estate and the Arundel (Sussex) estate were in the course of the seventeenth century to replace the dwindling East Anglian estates as the real basis of the family's influence, a trend which was to be completed by events in the eighteenth and nineteenth centuries. Even in the early seventeenth century when the industries of Sheffield (nurtured by the 7th Earl of Shrewsbury, a remarkable proto-tycoon) were still in their infancy, Aletheia's income was estimated at 60,000 crowns a year.

With some of his titles and part of his ancestral estates restored and with the prospect of his wife's inheritance, Arundel embarked on his programme for the reconstruction of his political position as head of the senior branch of the Howard family. Well understanding the value of appearances in building up a political connection, he took pains to look the part, as well as to play the part, of a great nobleman. As can be seen in the succession of his portraits, the callow, gawky youth gradually gave way to the majestic, serious, bearded appearance of his maturity.

It cannot be denied that he had in his person, in his aspect, and countenance, the appearance of a great man, which he preserv'd in gate, and motion. He wore and affected a Habit very differente from that of the time, such as men only beheld in the Pictures of the most considerable men; all which drew the eyes of most, and the reverence of many towards him as the Image and Representative of the Primitive Nobility, and Native Gravity of the Nobles when they had been most Venerable.[3]

He soon became a prominent figure at Court, frequently taking part in masques and tilts, such as 'Prince Henry's Barriers' on Twelfth Night 1610 in which he was one of the six supporters of the Prince.[4] He became intimate with Prince Henry and his circle, sharing their passion for art, books and collecting. Many friends in this group, such as John Holles (Earl of Clare) were to be his political allies in later years. Arundel rapidly advanced in the King's favour and was created a Knight of the Garter in 1611. The following year the Venetian Ambassador succinctly summed up his potential in a report to the Doge, describing him as 'the premier Earl of this Kingdom, in which there are no Dukes save the King's sons . . . nor Marquises save Winchester who does not come to Court. Arundel will be, through his wife, a daughter of the Earl of Shrewsbury, heir to sixty thousand crowns a year; he is nephew of Northampton who has no children and is very powerful in the government.'[5]

Only his religion stood in the way of his advance and in 1616, the year of his father-in-law's death when Aletheia came into her share of the Shrewsbury inheritance, he conformed by receiving communion in the Chapel Royal at Whitehall and was immediately appointed to the Privy Council. The following year he was one of the noblemen who accompanied James on the Progress to Scotland and at that time he wrote his first will. He was probably involved with his brother-in-law the Earl of Pembroke and the Earl of Southampton in the machinations that led to the fall of Robert Carr, Earl of Somerset, for unlike his uncles, he was not tainted by suspicion of involvement in the Overbury murder. The fall of Carr and disgrace of Suffolk opened the way for Arundel as the natural successor to his uncle's office and influence, but this was not to be. When Suffolk was removed from office in 1618 the post of Lord Treasurer for which Arundel was hoping went instead, at Buckingham's suggestion, to Henry Montagu and when Nottingham retired in 1619 Buckingham himself obtained the office of Lord High Admiral.[6]

At this stage Arundel threw in his lot with the favourite who, though of comparatively lowly birth, was 'of handsome presence, amiable and courteous manners' (characteristics which had won the King's heart), and moreover shared an interest in art and supported the policy for a Spanish marriage for Prince

Charles in which Arundel also believed. In the parliament of 1621, where Arundel played a major role on various committees including that for customs, orders and privileges, he stood out in the Lords as a supporter of Buckingham and was adamant in his condemnation of Sir Henry Yelverton's speech in the Commons against the favourite. Lord Spencer, who moved on 8 May that Yelverton be given a personal hearing, reminded Arundel that several of his Howard ancestors had been condemned for treason without proper defence. Arundel was stung to retort that his ancestors had suffered 'and it may be for doinge the Kinge and country good service, and in such time as perhapps the Lord's auncestors that spake last kept sheepe'.[7] This was adjudged an affront to the dignity of the House and he was committed to the Tower where he remained for several weeks because he refused at first to apologize to Spencer, though Prince Charles was able to bring about a reconciliation between the two peers, and Arundel was then released.

The incident did him no harm, and on 29 August 1621 he was created Earl Marshal, a post which he particularly coveted because it had been held by his ancestors for centuries, though it only became hereditary in the Howard family in 1672. The Earl Marshalship brought with it a pension of £2,000 a year, and was a major factor in the restoration of Arundel's political power and his eventual emergence as a leader of the group opposed to Buckingham. Antiquarian friends like Sir Robert Cotton were able to produce historical precedents for various ways of strengthening the power of the Earl Marshalship which James accepted and which gave Arundel an enhanced political standing. The Earl Marshal's claim to the role of Constable when there was no Constable of the Realm, for instance, made him the senior Privy Councillor. In May 1623 it was rumoured that he was to be made a duke, but he refused anything except the restoration of the Norfolk dukedom and, as this would have given him precedence over Buckingham, James was not prepared to acquiesce. Arundel had to make do therefore with the Lord Lieutenancy of Norfolk. The decision to advance Buckingham to a dukedom and the position of senior English nobleman, thereby usurping Arundel's hereditary right, greatly offended the Earl. This incident was probably the chief reason why he moved into opposition against Buckingham and for a time became 'a great strainger at the Court', using the death of his eldest son James Lord Maltravers from smallpox as an excuse for leaving the country and resuming his Continental travels.

The death of James I, to many people's surprise, did not affect Buckingham's position as royal favourite and the animosity towards him increased. Arundel came to be regarded by Buckingham as an inveterate enemy and the leader of the opposition to him. When Arundel's eldest surviving son Henry Frederick married in February 1626 without royal consent the Duke of Lennox's daughter, whom Charles intended to marry Lord Lorne, Buckingham was able to use the incident to remove Arundel from the political arena, on the grounds that he must have encouraged the marriage. He was arrested, imprisoned in the Tower and fined a large sum (which worsened his already precarious finances). Arundel's arbitrary arrest while Parliament was sitting raised the matter of parliamentary privilege. The Lords demanded his release, voting on 2 June to conduct no further business in his absence. He returned to his place on 8 June but remained barred from Court. Almost against his wishes therefore he found himself at the head of the mixed bag of Buckingham's opponents. In 1628 it was thought that he and Lord Bristol might begin impeachment proceedings, though in the event this move was forestalled by Buckingham's assassination. The favourite's death removed the great obstacle from Arundel's course and it was noted soon afterwards that he had 'grown into great grace with the King'. He now emerged as a leading figure on the Privy Council, retaining his influence throughout the 1630s and being employed on two important diplomatic missions, for which he was especially well-suited with his Italianate manners, dignified bearing, command of foreign languages and wide-ranging interest in Continental culture.[8]

Both these special embassies were connected with the affairs of Princess Elizabeth, Charles I's sister whom the Arundels had accompanied to Heidelberg in 1612 following her wedding to Frederick, Prince Palatine of the Rhine. Frederick's ill-considered acceptance, as leader of the German Protestants, of the crown of Bohemia had brought about his ruin by rousing the 'undying resentment' of the Imperial Catholic party. Frederick and Elizabeth sat on the throne of Bohemia for only one winter before their army was defeated by the Emperor and they had to flee to the Hague where they spent much of the rest of their lives in exile. The loss of the Palatinate and the long wars which followed reduced Frederick to penury, and finally in November 1632 while on campaign he succumbed to an attack of plague leaving his wife a widow. Charles I suggested that she return to England and sent Arundel to persuade her to leave Holland. The Earl Marshal reached the Hague in January 1633 with a retinue of a hundred and fifty people. Elizabeth however was adamant that her return to England at that stage would look like a retreat and would jeopardize the prospects of her sons Prince Charles Louis and Prince Rupert. Arundel conducted the embassy with considerable ability and reported Elizabeth's decision back to Charles who accepted the sense of it. Altogether the embassy to Holland enhanced Arundel's reputation as a statesman and gained him the King's good opinion. On his return he was chosen to accompany the sovereign to Scotland for the coronation in Edinburgh.

Four years later he was appointed special ambassador by Charles I to the Emperor to press Charles Louis's claim to the Palatinate at the Diet of Ratisbon. This embassy is especially well-documented as two of the gentlemen in Arundel's retinue, Edward Walker and William Crowne, wrote accounts of it, while Wenceslas Hollar, an artist of Bohemian origin whom Arundel met in Cologne,

After Peter Paul Rubens. The Collector Earl,
engraved by J. L. Krafft. The Rubens portrait
was intended as part of a larger group to
celebrate the Earl's acquisition of the
Pirkheimer Library while in Nuremberg in
1636.

A contemporary German cartoon showing
the return of the Collector Earl from his
embassy to the Holy Roman Emperor in 1636,
unsuccessful but not empty-handed.

made a series of water-colour views of the towns and landscapes along the route: Cologne, Mayence, Frankfurt, Wurzburg, Nuremberg, Ratisbon and Linz, where Arundel had his first interview with the Emperor in June 1636.

Eighteen years of the Thirty Years War had now elapsed and everywhere Arundel's party met with terrible scenes of war, famine, brigandage and plague. The battlefield of the White Mountain was still littered with unburied bones and most shocking of all, two of his trumpeters were horribly murdered, their mutilated corpses nailed to trees. Nevertheless the Earl pursued his passion for art, avidly visiting places of interest and purchasing objects for his collection. His principal coup was the acquisition in Nuremberg of the Pirkheimer library *en bloc*. During a pause in proceedings he took the opportunity to visit Vienna and Prague. In the latter city the celebrated collection of Rudolph II was still *in situ*. A possibly more moving sight were the English portraits in the Royal Castle, a memento of the brief reign of Frederick and Elizabeth. Wallenstein's palace also made an impression with its fantastic grotto and stables with thirty-eight columns of red marble.

After a further sight-seeing trip to Augsburg, Arundel was back in Ratisbon for the state entry of the Emperor and the opening of the Diet. It rapidly became clear however that the Emperor had no intention of reinstating Charles Louis. The Palatine had been granted to the Catholic Duke of Bavaria and, as his vote was essential to the election of the Emperor's son as King of the Romans, the main business of the Diet and the preliminary for securing the succession to the imperial crown, the Emperor was not prepared to dislodge the new possessor. So Arundel returned with his mission unaccomplished, though not empty-handed. The Emperor, aware of the Earl's taste for art, gave him eleven volumes of 'exquisite drawings'. Further works of art were acquired on the homeward journey, the star among which was a painting of the Madonna by Dürer given to Arundel by the Bishop of Würzburg. The English were somewhat surprised to find the Bishop dressed in secular clothes just like any other country gentleman with only a cross on a black ribbon round his neck to denote his episcopal rank. The Earl valued this Dürer so highly that he carried it with him in his own carriage, rather than placing it with the rest of the baggage. He arrived back in England on 27 December 1636. Notwithstanding the failure to achieve the objects desired, both Elizabeth of Bohemia and Charles I showed satisfaction with the Earl Marshal's firm conduct of affairs and refusal to compromise: 'The Earl Marshal has carried himself very nobly, and like a right English Earl.' Arundel had made some lasting friendships in the imperial entourage including one with Count Leslie, and his collection had benefited enormously. Indeed a contemporary German cartoon shows Arundel returning not with his mission achieved but carrying a basket of trinkets.[9]

Arundel had first visited the Continent in pursuit of art in the summer of

1612. After a spell at Spa in the Low Countries, recommended by his doctors for his health, he had gone south to Venice and stayed for several months at Padua, overcome with the powerful enchantments of Italian civilization; 'it was there that he either took or improved his natural disposition of being the great Master and Favourer of the Arts'.[10] The death of Prince Henry brought him back to England to take part in the obsequies; but the following year he returned to the Continent as part of the delegation that accompanied Princess Elizabeth to Heidelberg. As soon as the official business was over, Arundel and his wife went back to Italy taking with them Inigo Jones who had been employed on the progress to supervise the masques and similar ceremonial events.

The Italian visit of 1613 was the crucial episode in Arundel's emergence as a patron of a type not seen in England before, a patron on the Continental model, though with that strong atavistic streak which is such a fascinating facet of his patronage. In September 1613, he wrote from Venice to Sir Robert Cotton asking him to recommend a suitable subject from Howard history for a Venetian artist to paint.[11] After a time in Venice where he was splendidly received by the Doge who treated him almost as if he was of vice-regal status and gave him a state banquet in the Arsenal, the Earl and Inigo Jones left Lady Arundel behind at the Padua villa, and went on to Vicenza to look at the architecture of Palladio. After that they visited Florence and then Siena, where the Countess rejoined them at the Monasterio delle Grazie for the winter.

Immediately after Christmas they moved to Rome for six months, ignoring the official ban on Englishmen visiting the seat of the Papacy.[12] Arundel stayed in the palace of Vincenzo, Marchese Giustiniani, whose excellent picture gallery much influenced Arundel's taste, introducing him to the work of Caravaggio and followers. He excavated in the forum, discovering several full-length portrait statues. Though it has been suggested that some of these marbles were specially planted for his benefit, this does not alter the significance of Arundel's enterprise as the first archaeological excavation conducted by an Englishman on foreign soil. He also commissioned Egidio Moretti to carve four statues all 'antica. Moretti was a second-rate artist about whom little is known except that he was employed by Carlo Maderna on the façade of St. Peter's. Nevertheless this patronage was an epoch-making act, for Arundel was the first Englishman to commission works of art from a contemporary sculptor in Rome. He bought many other antiques and copies of famous statues, including a bronze cast of the Laocoön, and, as well as sculpture, he acquired paintings and books.

After eighteen months in Italy he returned to London in winter 1614, a transformed man, determined to become a cultural patron in the Italian mould: 'he was the first great subject of the Northern parts who by his conversation and great collection set a value upon that country'.[13] He had bought a house in Highgate from Sir William Cornwallis in 1610, which he now transformed into an

Italianate villa with a casino or banqueting house in the garden. There the Arundels gave a famous feast 'in the Italian manner' in 1617, such as had never been seen in London before.[14] Later in life Arundel sold Highgate and developed Albury in Surrey, 'o[u]r poore cottage', as his villa instead, creating another Italian garden with a grotto and other architectural features in the 1630s.

At Arundel House in the Strand, the Earl embarked on an ambitious programme of rebuilding, intended to transform the rambling Tudor building into a formal palace on the Italian model. The project was never completed because of shortage of money; Hollar's engravings, for instance, show a half-built classical range in the outer courtyard. Arundel's principal additions however were on the river side of the house. There he added a projecting wing with galleries for his paintings and statues, the exterior of which is recorded in an engraving by Hollar. The architect was probably his 'good friend' Inigo Jones. The portrait of the Poet Earl of Surrey, commissioned by the Collector Earl, is set in a *trompe l'oeil* architectural framework almost certainly designed by Inigo Jones and probably forming part of the decoration of a lost room with ancestral portraits and heraldry. A similar portrait of Arundel between supporters bearing arms, but made in *pietra dura*, was ordered through 'Antonio Trasie' (Anthony Tracy) in Florence, and some matching table tops of *pietra dura* decorated with heraldry may have formed part of the same scheme. Arundel remodelled the garden, partly as a setting for some of his sculpture, which was disposed along the walls and colonnades in the manner of a Roman villa. The 'Roman Bath' which still survives in Surrey Street is a remnant of this garden. It has been suggested that he may also have made a larger garden on the opposite side of the Thames with vistas to the 'colossi', an antique column of Egyptian granite (now at Wilton) and an obelisk or 'guglia' from Rome.[15] Arundel's interest in the architectural appearance of London extended beyond the confines of Arundel House. He was a member of Charles I's Building Commission for London which, among other improvements, determined the layout and design of Lincoln's Inn Fields and the recasing of Old St. Paul's Cathedral under the supervision of Inigo Jones. Jones also designed the offices in Lothbury for a wholesale fish company set up by the Howards in 1637.[16]

1616 was Arundel's *annus mirabilis* as a collector, and that year saw a dramatic expansion due to gifts, good fortune, timely deaths and the work of excellent agents. On the death of Lady Lumley in October he was able to acquire many family portraits as well as half a dozen Holbeins including that of the Duchess of Milan (now in the National Gallery). About half the paintings in his collection were by 'modern' Flemish artists such as Rubens and Honthorst. Arundel was one of the principal backers of Mytens who came to England in 1617 and painted in that year the famous pair of portraits of the Earl and Countess in the sculpture and Holbein galleries at Arundel House, as well as a double portrait of them, also now at Arundel Castle but originally intended for their friend, the

British Minister first at. Venice then the Hague, Sir Dudley Carleton (Viscount Dorchester), and a portrait of their son Henry Frederick.

Shortly afterwards Arundel was able to secure the services for England of a much greater Flemish painter, Van Dyck, who came to London for the first time in the winter of 1620–1 before going on to Italy to join Lady Arundel at Venice and accompany her to Turin, Mantua and Genoa, an artistic pilgrimage that had an important effect on his artistic development. As well as portraits including his earliest of Arundel (now in a private collection in Washington) Van Dyck also painted in England a large canvas of the 'Continence of Scipio' which Arundel presented to Buckingham during their short-lived 'friendship' and which incidentally incorporated in the foreground a fragment of a classical marble frieze, which was excavated on the Arundel House site in 1972.[17]

It came from Asia Minor as did many of the finest pieces in the sculpture collection. They were acquired for Arundel by his brilliant agent, the Revd William Petty, a fellow of Jesus College, Cambridge, who, often at great risk to himself, excavated and 'liberated' the remains of classical art from the clutches of the Turks. As a result, the Arundel marbles were distinguished for their authenticity. His antique marbles, to a greater degree than any other aspect of his collection, revealed the seriousness of the Earl's 'sedulous knowledgeable' connoisseurship. Unlike many later English collections of classical sculpture, Arundel's did not consist just of prettily restored statues and modern copies, but contained many archaeologically important fragments, such as a torso from the Pergamon frieze, and the inscribed tablets of more interest to the scholar than the aesthete. Arundel was a 'lover of Antiquitie' and bought his marbles as much because they were clues to the thought and aspirations of the ancient world as for their artistry.

The Earl was a self-conscious personification of the classical virtues of 'gravitas' and 'dignitas', and his general philosophy was more neo-Stoic than Christian; for instance, he had seven editions of Seneca in his library, as well as a bust. His outlook is a refreshing contrast to the religious fanaticism of the time. Art was his religion, and he could not have cared less about the minutiae of contemporary religious politics. George Conn, who hoped to enlist his support for a scheme for reconciling the Church of England to Rome was disappointed, and astonished, by the Earl's lack of interest and refusal to talk about anything except Art: 'With the authority he has, he could no doubt do something, but he is as far removed from these negotiations as he is given up to pictures and statues, around which he would like us to pass all our time.'[18] Clarendon wrote of Arundel's religion, or lack of it, that he 'was rather thought not to be much concerned for Religion, than to incline to this or that Party . . . and died in Italy under the same doubtful character of religion in which he liv'd'.[19] The philosophy of the Ancient World or the authority of Art meant more to him than the Bible.

He saw his house as a museum and encouraged scholars and artists to visit his collections. In his 1617 will he stated 'my desire is that all gentlemen of vertue or Artistes wch are honest men may allways be used with curtesy & humanity when they shall come to see them'.[20] Clarendon, who was prejudiced against Arundel because of his opposition to Buckingham (Clarendon's uncle Sir Nicholas Hyde being Buckingham's lawyer), wrote: 'He was willing to be thought a scholar, and to understand the most mysterious parts of Antiquity, because he made a wonderful and costly Purchase of excellent statues . . . [but] as to all parts of learning he was allmost illiterate.'[21] This has generally been considered unjust. While no doubt Arundel was intelligent rather than intellectual, and valued gentle birth and military prowess, he nevertheless respected the mind and valued learning above most things. He understood, even if he did not create himself, and he sustained for twenty-five years a remarkable 'Academie' of scholars, heralds, genealogists, painters, engravers and sculptors in his London house.

He was the first nobleman in northern Europe to establish a workshop for the restoration of antique sculpture, under the direction of a Roman called Coltreci, and he commissioned Selden to write a scholarly catalogue of his marbles, *Marmora Arundelliana*, which came out in 1628. His librarian Francis Junius was of European renown, the greatest of the early students of the Old English and Germanic languages. He was Dutch by birth and something of an eccentric. Like later ducal librarians he worked excessively and ate a lot, but less like them, he slept little and got up at four in the morning to go 'jogging'. Other scholars in Arundel's circle included William Oughtred the mathematician, whose *De Classis Mathematica* is the most important English mathematical treatise, and Henry Peacham, whose *Compleat Gentleman* was a statement of the Renaissance humanist ideals of the Arundel House circle. There were also the heralds to be expected in the Earl Marshal's household, including Edward Norgate, Windsor Herald, employed by Arundel to do heraldic painting, and Henry Lilly, Rouge Dragon, who was commissioned to paint a series of miniatures of Howard memorials on vellum, bound magnificently in red velvet with silver gilt mounts.[22] Apart from his employees, Arundel had a wide circle of scholarly and aesthetic friends: James Ussher, Bishop of Armagh and author among other works of *Britannicarum Ecclesiarum Antiquitates* (the copy in the library at Arundel was a present from the author to the Collector Earl), Edward Alleyn, the art collector and founder of Dulwich College, Sir Francis Crane, director of the Mortlake tapestry factory, Dr William Harvey, discoverer of the circulation of blood,[23] and Sir Robert Cotton, the famous antiquary.

The library at Arundel House was not the least of its attractions; furnished with globes and marble busts of Greek and Roman philosophers, it contained an impressive accumulation of books and manuscripts from different sources. Some were inherited from other members of the family, from Lord Northampton, from

Bookbinding from the library of the Collector Earl showing his arms on the back. The book is *Amphitheatrum Honoris* by Clarus Bonarschius (1605).

Memorial tablet in the Fitzalan Chapel at Arundel to Robert Spyller, steward to Anne Dacre and the Collector Earl, probably designed by Inigo Jones.

the 4th Duke of Norfolk, from Lord Lumley.* Then there were the books bought by Arundel himself, especially the Pirkheimer Library. There were also prints, especially historic sets of Dürer woodcuts, and Italian topographical and architectural engravings. Arundel himself employed four engravers: 'Cornelius van Dalen, Giovanni Waldor, Hendrick van der Borcht II (whom Arundel sent to train in Italy) and, the most famous, Wenceslas Hollar, whom he brought back from Germany in 1636 to engrave the works of art in the collection and who married a lady-in-waiting to the Countess of Arundel, Mistress Tracy. After the Restoration he became Scenographer Royal to Charles II. The residue of Arundel's print collection sold at the Stafford sale in 1720 amounted to 6,282 items.

By the 1630s Old Master drawings had succeeded sculpture as Arundel's chief enthusiasm, and he was the first connoisseur of this art in England, setting a fashion which was copied by the other Whitehall collectors and the King. His collection of drawings was reputed the finest in Europe. No one owned more Leonardos, or more Holbeins, or more Dürers. He paid (when he did pay) vast sums for drawings. Raphael's 'Massacre of the Innocents' in black chalk, for instance, cost him £100. Parmigianino was perhaps his favourite draughtsman. Following the dispersal of his collection his drawings found their way into other collections. His Leonardos and Holbeins are now in the Royal Library at Windsor, while several of his Raphaels and Parmigianinos were given by the 6th Duke of Norfolk to Lely, and are now among the Devonshire drawings at Chatsworth.

Another field in which his collection was pre-eminent was antique gems. He bought the Nys collection in its entirety for the staggering sum of £10,000. It was considered that the Arundel gems were not surpassed by those of any prince in Europe. The 6th Duke of Norfolk left them at his death to his second wife Jane Bickerton who sold them to the Earl of Peterborough. They later passed into the Marlborough Collection at Blenheim but were sold and tragically dispersed in the late nineteenth century and are now divided between museums all over England, Europe and America.

The Earl's extravagance in collecting led him to the verge of bankruptcy. 'His expenses were without any measure, and allways exceeded very much his Revenue.' By 1640 his debts amounted to £103,234 3s. 11d.[24] Part of this resulted from the sums borrowed to redeem his estates. An attempt to pay off these debts came to nothing when the money raised by selling land and felling timber was directed into paying the fine for his son's marriage in 1626. At one stage he toyed with the idea of going to Madagascar to escape his creditors and taking his collection there. The double portrait by Van Dyck shows him seated by a globe and pointing to Madagascar. He had various conferences with merchants who had visited the island but the project was abandoned when he discovered that

---

* Most of Lord Lumley's library was bought by Prince Henry and passed to Charles I.

Madagascar was infested with fleas. He had an interest in islands and remote places. He tried to buy Lundy as well as being involved in various schemes to improve the barbaric wastes of Ireland, which he had visited in 1617 and where he attempted to reclaim the 4th Duke's estates.[25]

In the end he turned for advice to the Jacobean financier, Lionel Cranfield, who had advised his uncle Northampton on financial matters and whose suggestion for funding his three sets of almshouses has secured their economic survival down to the present. Even Cranfield could not do much with debts of Arundel's magnitude and they remained a problem for his successors to solve. There is no doubt that in his own lifetime it was Lady Arundel's money which kept him solvent.

Arundel's relations with his wife are not entirely clear. They shared an interest in art and collecting, Lady Arundel being the first to be painted by Rubens, in Antwerp in 1620, and while in Venice in 1622 her house was a resort of many artists and men of learning including Van Dyck. Tizianelo, for instance, dedicated his life of Titian to her. Several letters from the Earl to his wife survive and are affectionate in tone, all beginning 'Dearest Harte'. Yet at times there was considerable independence between them. On her 1622 visit to Venice to see her sons at Padua University, the Countess, who rented the Palazzo Barberigo on the Grand Canal, became involved with Foscarini, though whether this was a love affair or a platonic friendship cannot, of course, now be guessed. When Foscarini was wrongly condemned and secretly strangled for suspected treason the fact of his having been so much at her house gave rise to the suspicion that the Countess might be a spy. She was on the point of being ordered out of Venice, but on being warned of her position by Sir Henry Wotton the English Minister, she went straight to the Doge and defended herself with such ability and strength of mind that the Venetians not only denied any intention of expelling her, but regarded her with much increased respect. In 1638 the Countess built her own London house, Tart Hall, Buckingham Gate, near St. James's Park, which was designed by Nicholas Stone and where she had her own independent household as a place to entertain her more overtly Catholic friends and following, without embarrassing the Earl. At the end of his life, in Padua, Arundel told Evelyn that he was upset that his wife was not with him but had stayed behind in Antwerp. All this suggests that while the couple had much in common and conducted their lives on affectionate terms with each other, nevertheless they maintained a degree of mutual independence.

The 1630s were the high point of Arundel's career, a period in which he enjoyed the increasing favour of his sovereign and in which his collections reached their greatest extent and splendour. His appearance at this time is recorded in Van Dyck's magnificent portraits, that of 1635 showing Arundel with his grandson 'little Tom' (later 5th Duke of Norfolk) and intended as a model for

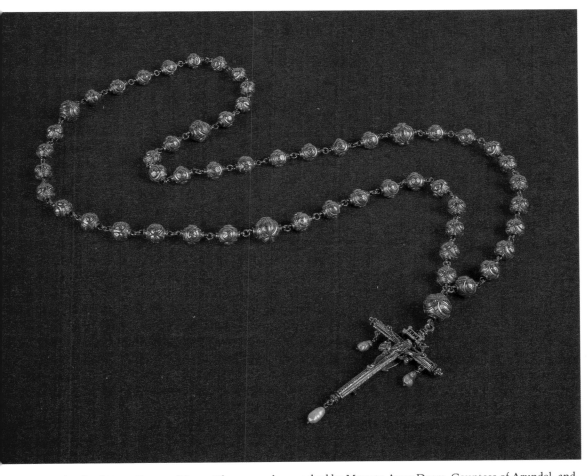

The rosary beads of Mary Queen of Scots. These were bequeathed by Mary to Anne Dacre, Countess of Arundel, and have been an heirloom in the Howard family ever since.

The Tournament Shield decorated with scenes of Roman history by Pordenone and one of the few items from the collection of the Collector Earl to have descended in the possession of the Dukes of Norfolk.

Bernini to make a marble relief, and that of 1639, 'the Madagascar portrait' showing the Arundels in the full panoply of peers' robes, the Earl Marshal's baton, and objects from the collection including the Arundel 'Homer', a Hellenistic bronze bust now in the British Museum, richly strewn around them. At the end of the decade he received the appointment of Captain General of the English armies against the Scottish Covenanters. Clarendon wrote 'The King chose to make the Earl of Arundel his General, a man who was thought to be made choice of for his negative qualities. He did not love the Scots; he did not love the Puritans; which qualifications were allayed by another negative – he did not much love anybody else. But he was fit to keep the state of it, and his rank was such that no man would decline the serving under him.'[26]

This appointment did not, as it turned out, involve any active military service, but the Earl saw himself as literally stepping into the armour of his ancestors, the 2nd Duke, the 3rd Duke, the Poet Earl, the 4th Duke, who had occupied similar commands before him. He commissioned Van Dyck to paint a vast group portrait to commemorate the event, showing himself and his wife sitting under a canopy of state surrounded by their children holding the 'Flodden' helmet and sword and the Florentine tournament shield, relics redolent of the martial triumphs of his ancestors.[27] This magnificent composition, probably inspired by Mantegna's fresco of the Gonzaga family at Mantua, did not materialize and is recorded only in a miniature by Fruytiers.

Other official appointments fell fast and thick. In March 1641 the Earl of Strafford was condemned and executed; Arundel was appointed High Steward for the trial in Westminster Hall, over which he presided in a just and dignified manner. The following year he accompanied the Queen Mother, Marie de Medici, from England to the Continent, and shortly afterwards performed the same service with Henrietta Maria and Princess Mary when they went to Holland for Princess Mary's marriage to Prince William of Orange.

He did not return to England. When his official business was over, as once before in happier circumstances, he headed south to his beloved Venice and as the clouds of Civil War gathered at home, established himself in a villa at Padua, where he spent the last four years of his life. Conflict between King and Parliament was now inevitable and, as an old man, he felt he had no part to play. He contented himself with contributing generously to the royalist coffers and leaving his son, Henry Frederick, to fight in the royalist army. He had already delegated all the Norfolk estate business to his son, and he now left him to do the best he could to maintain the family hegemony in the ruinous years ahead.

Before leaving England the Earl petitioned Charles I for the restoration of the Dukedom of Norfolk. This had no immediate result, but in 1644 by patent dated from Oxford on 6 June the King created Arundel Earl of Norfolk, thereby ensuring that the Norfolk title remained in the Howard family and was not granted out to

Anthony Van Dyck. The Collector Earl of Arundel and his grandson 'little Tom', later 5th Duke of Norfolk, who went mad as a result of a fever contracted while at Padua.

P. Fruytiers. A miniature of the proposal by Van Dyck for a large family group commemorating the Collector Earl's appointment as Captain General of Charles I's army against the Scots in 1640; he is being handed symbolic military trophies by his children. The two Holbeins in the background are of the Poet Earl of Surrey and the 3rd Duke of Norfolk.

strangers in the way that many other ancient titles had been by the Stuarts. Arundel himself had already benefited from a similar grant when the Stafford title was bestowed on his younger son William, a pleasant but not very clever youth, rather than on the rightful heir, the penurious Roger Stafford, on the grounds that the latter had not the economic resources to maintain the dignity of a title. The Collector's greatest achievement, however, was to entail the Earldom of Arundel in the Howard family. It had come to his father through the female line as a title in fee, but by Act of Parliament of 1627 the Collector altered the character of the title and made it an entailed earldom restricted to the male descendants of the 4th Duke of Norfolk (but excluding the Suffolks).[28] If it had not been for this entail the Arundel earldom would have parted from the entailed dukedom in the late eighteenth century on the death of the 9th Duke of Norfolk, and passed again through the female line, like the Mowbray barony.

The Collector also entailed Arundel Castle and the Sussex estate, and Arundel House, London, by Act of Parliament and this unusual parliamentary entail survived until 1956 when it was repealed by a further Act of Parliament in response to the threat of death duties. The Collector also had the ancient territorial 'baronies' of Clun and Oswaldestre made into entailed titles of honour by the 1627 Act of Parliament, as a result of an historical error in assessing their origin. It is not clear whether this *was* a deliberate error or not. So though he did not manage to pull the dukedom itself out of attainder, the Collector was able to gild the family with a whole galaxy of lesser coronets, a substantial portion of the ten titles held by modern Dukes of Norfolk.

This solid and lasting achievement should not be forgotten in contemplating the tragic last act. Evelyn, for whom the Collector wrote out in his own hand a list of things to visit in Italy, gives a touching picture of the sad end of the old Earl's life in exile: 'I took my leave of him in bed, where I left that great and excellent man in teares on some private discourse of crosses that had befallen his illustrious family . . . and the misery of his country now embroiled in Civil War.' Arundel Castle was besieged and reduced to ruins. Arundel House was occupied by troops and many of the marbles broken and ill-treated. The tomb with a bronze statue of the Earl by Francesco Fanelli was never erected. The collections, never entailed, were largely dispersed over the following half century. The King was executed, while Lord Lichfield (Arundel's son-in-law) and many other friends and relations were killed in the fighting. The whole fragile hot-house civilization of the Stuart Court was broken into fragments, Henrietta Maria's Rubens altarpiece at Somerset House thrown into the Thames. The Earl's body was brought back to England and buried in the Fitzalan Chapel (which had been desecrated by parliamentarian troops) but his heart and entrails were left at Padua in St. Anthony's basilica under a slab of black marble: 'Hic iacent interiora Tomae Hovvardi Ill[mi] Et ecc[mi]Comitis Et Dni Arundeliae et Surriae Magni Mariscali Angliae.' The collections may be dispersed; the architecture may be destroyed and 'the once magnificent Arundel House, with terraces to the river, and its statuary, be represented by one commonplace street, but their name will be for ever associated with art in its widest acceptation and its noblest forms'.[29]

9

Restoration

WHEN the Collector Earl died at Padua in 1646 he was succeeded as Earl of Arundel, Surrey and Norfolk by his eldest surviving son Henry Frederick, named after the Prince of Wales. Born in 1608, Henry Frederick had been styled Lord Maltravers from 1624 till 1640 when he was summoned to Parliament under his father's barony of Mowbray. As a young man, he seems to have behaved in an exemplary manner, accompanying his mother on her Continental travels in the 1620s, later playing the parts of a good husband and accomplished courtier, and on the outbreak of the Civil War becoming a zealous Royalist; but when his father died he made a most unworthy attempt to set aside the terms of his will and was responsible for the regrettable ill-treatment of his mother, Aletheia, the aged Countess of Arundel.

Henry Frederick had been brought up a Catholic and educated abroad at the University of Padua, where he was sent at the age of eleven with his brother James in 1619 under the care of Thomas Coke and a tutor Mr Tunstall,[1] though later he probably conformed to the Established Church. At least he was one of those who signed the 'Protestation' in 1641 by which he bound himself to 'maintain and defend the Protestant religion expressed in the doctrine of the Church of England'. He had been created a Knight of the Bath at the age of eight, sat in the lower house in the Parliament of 1628–9 and was sworn of the Privy Council on 10 August 1634. This easy assimilation of conventional honours had received a jolt when, as already seen, he temporarily forfeited royal favour by marrying without the King's consent Elizabeth, daughter of Esme Stuart, 3rd Duke of Lennox, on 7 March 1626. Despite this inauspicious beginning it seems to have been a happy enough marriage and it was the large family which Elizabeth bore him, nine sons and three daughters, which secured the future of the family, for on each occasion that the male line later failed there was a cadet line descended from Henry Frederick on which to fall back.

On the outbreak of the Civil War Henry Frederick threw in his lot with the King. He took part in the Battle of Edgehill and was with the Court at Oxford,

Daniel Mytens. Henry
Frederick, Earl of Arundel
(1608–52), as a boy.

being created Hon. MA after the capture of Banbury. He left England for a period
round about 1646 and was present at his father's deathbed. Two years later he was
fined £6,000 by Parliament for his support of the Royalist cause, but he was
allowed to compound for his estates. His father's debts were still unpaid, added to
which Arundel Castle had been reduced to ruins by Sir William Waller in the
siege and subsequent slighting of 1643–4 and so his affairs generally must have
been in a parlous state which perhaps explains, but does not excuse, his treatment
of his mother after his father's death; 'he hathe used all meanes to take my due
from mee, not suffering mee quietly to possesse any thing that he conceaves may
any way be disputable, though it be my inheritance'.[2]

The Collector Earl in his will, written at Dover before he left England for the
last time in 1641, gave detailed directions for the erection of his monument with a
bronze statue by Francesco Fanelli, for the preservation of his great collection as a
family heirloom, and for the disposal of his estates and revenues. Not one
sentence of this document was complied with, largely because of Henry
Frederick's decision to contest it. The Collector had left most of the revenues and

the enjoyment of his collection for life to his widow Aletheia, with the final decision left to her whether to entail the chattels as heirlooms on her death or not. This was only fair as the Norfolk estates had been redeemed and the collections formed largely out of the Shrewsbury inheritance, estimated at £30,000, which Aletheia had brought into the family.

Henry Frederick tried every means to get the will declared invalid and to disinherit his mother, behaving in the most undutiful way, harassing and robbing her, encouraging her servants to neglect and speak ill of her and writing unpleasant letters accusing her of frittering away the family fortune on such unnecessary expenses as going to Rome 'to kiss the Pope's big toe'. But after three years of litigation the will was declared to be valid and Henry Frederick, much to the satisfaction of Victorian moralists, predeceased his mother on 17 April 1652. Aletheia lived for another two years 'praying God to forgive him for his unnaturall carriage towards her'. In view of her eldest son's behaviour, it is not surprising that Aletheia decided not to entail the collection but left as much as possible to her favourite younger son, William, Viscount Stafford. Much remained *in situ* at Tart Hall, Westminster (renamed Stafford House) till the great sale in 1720 when it was dispersed. So was lost one of the greatest glories of the house of Howard.

Of Henry Frederick's sons, Thomas and Henry succeeded him, Philip became a priest, and Charles and Bernard, the fourth and eighth sons, were the ancestors of the Greystoke and Glossop lines, each of which in turn was later to inherit the dukedom. Thomas, the eldest son, was born on 9 March 1627 at Arundel House and though, like his brothers, he was enrolled at St. John's College, Cambridge in 1640, was chiefly educated at Utrecht university. He left England with his grandfather on the outbreak of the Civil War and never returned, for at his grandfather's house in Padua in 1645 he succumbed to a fever which damaged his brain causing him to sink into irredeemable lunacy; he was confined at Padua for the rest of his life under the care of the English physician and scholar, Dr. Henry Yerbury, formerly a fellow of Magdalen College, Oxford, who became Professor of Medicine at Padua University. The household at Padua was run by an Italian, Carlo Theobaldi, and the accounts are preserved in the muniment room at Arundel.

The management of family affairs after the death of Henry Frederick therefore passed into the hands of his able, amiable second son Henry. It was rumoured at first that Henry kept his elder brother out of the country and locked up in Padua, pretending he was mad, in order to enjoy the family's possessions himself. The Venetian Resident in London, however, was able to deny this. The rumour was due, he said, 'to the pure malignity of an uncle', William, Viscount Stafford. 'The Earl is living at Padua to the entire satisfaction of his mother and relations and is maintained there by his brother here with great generosity and splendour.' The Podesta and Captain of Padua reported him to be 'unapproachable . . . an

Anthony Van Dyck. Henry
Frederick, Earl of Arundel.

After Anthony Van Dyck. William,
Viscount Stafford (1614–80).

incurable maniac'. Sir John Reresby, who had seen him while travelling in Italy, reported that he displayed 'all the marks imaginable of lunacy'.

It was at Henry Howard's instigation that within months of Charles II's restoration to the throne a petition in the form of a Bill was presented by ninety-one peers, including all the Howard Earls, for the restoration of the insane Thomas Howard as 5th Duke of Norfolk. The Bill was introduced on 30 August and received the Royal Assent on 29 December 1660. The Act was more precisely defined by a second one passed on 29 December 1661. After being under attainder for nearly a hundred years the dukedom was restored with the original precedence and the Collector Earl's life's ambition achieved fourteen years after his death.

For Henry Howard of Norfolk (as he usually signed himself) in 1660–1 the world must have seemed extremely promising. The dukedom had been restored and, as his mad brother was unmarried, it was only a matter of time before he inherited it. He himself was happily married to Lady Anne Somerset, daughter of the great royalist 2nd Marquess of Worcester.[3] There was the prospect of a substantial degree of toleration for his co-religionists from the new King as a mark of gratitude for their loyalty to the Crown during the Civil War. A meeting of Catholics was convened at Arundel House in 1660 to discuss terms for toleration but this came to nothing, largely because of disagreement between the moderates, who included Henry Howard, and who 'desired nothing but the exercise of their religion with the greatest secrecy and caution' and the extremists, Jesuit-led, among the Catholic party who wanted to hold out for an unreasonable amount. The moderates had the mortification of seeing their hopes blighted by 'the folly and vanity of some of their friends'. This internal split between the moderates and extremists in the Catholic party was as much responsible as external hostility for the failure of all proposals for some degree of Catholic toleration in England in the late seventeenth and eighteenth centuries. Despite the breakdown of these talks there were still sufficient grounds for hope that Charles II would not forget his Catholic supporters and there was not yet sufficient cause to cloud the optimism of the early Restoration years.[4]

As great an achievement as the restoration of the dukedom was Henry Howard's payment of his grandfather's enormous debts in the ten years following his father's death in 1652, during which he had control of the family finances. Evelyn recorded in June 1662, 'I went to Albury to visit Mr. Hen. Howard soone after he had procur'd ye dukedom to be restor'd. This gentleman had now compounded a debt of £200,000 contracted by his grandfather.'[5] So he faced the future with a clean slate, the dukedom restored and general grounds for hope and optimism. One sign of this was his proposal for rebuilding the various family seats on palatial lines. During the Commonwealth he had lived quietly at his grandfather's villa at Albury in Surrey which he had improved and embellished, especially the garden, over a number of years with Evelyn's help. Evelyn designed

Adrian Hanneman. Henry, 6th Duke of Norfolk. Painted in Holland in 1660 on the eve of the Restoration of the English monarchy and the Dukedom of Norfolk.

Michael Wright. Lady Anne Somerset (d. 1662), first wife of the 6th Duke of Norfolk.

the 'Great Room', the canal and a grotto or 'crypta thro' the mountaine in the park' and supervised the laying out of a vineyard.

Evelyn recorded as early as 1655, 'I went to Alburie to visit Mr. Howard who had begun to build and alter ye gardens much. He shew'd me many rare pictures, particularly the Moore on horseback, Erasmus as big as the life by Holbein, a Madonna in miniature by Oliver; but above all the skull carv'd in wood by Albert Dürer, for which his father was offered £100; also Albert's head by himselfe, with divers rare achates, intalias and other curiosities.'[6] In 1659 Evelyn visited Henry Howard at Arundel House in London and was shown 'his designe of a Palace there'.[7] This scheme developed in the 1660s – Henry's intention at Arundel House was to pull down the old building and to lay out a development of streets on that part of the site next to the Strand, and to build a new house of detached 'double pile' plan with a hipped roof on the garden overlooking the river to the design of Robert Hooke, a scientist, gentleman-architect and fellow-member of the Royal Society. The best statues from his grandfather's collection would be reused in the new house, but the inscribed tablets and fragments, which were of more scholarly than aesthetic interest and had been somewhat damaged during the Civil War (one of them had been used as a hearthstone), would on Evelyn's advice be given to the University of Oxford. This was implemented in 1668 and in return Henry was created a Doctor of Civil Law by the grateful university, which also set up an inscribed marble tablet to record his noble generosity for posterity.

One of the weaknesses of Henry's character, if it was a weakness, was an impulsive generosity. He could not resist giving things away. He allowed Lely to have some of the Raphael drawings at the time he was painting his portrait. He allowed priests and visiting scholars to help themselves to books from the library if they wanted them. He let Elias Ashmole have his grandfather's George. He gave away antique carved gems from his grandfather's collection as if he was handing out sweetmeats. Evelyn himself was given an important gold-mounted sardonyx from the collection, but nevertheless noted bitterly in his diary the gifts to 'priests, painters and panders' who hung around the house. Evelyn unfortunately decided to counter this by imposing on Henry's good nature and generosity to the extent of giving away whole chunks of his patrimony to various learned bodies. The gift of the antique inscriptions to Oxford was perhaps justifiable, but Evelyn's next suggestion, that the great library of the Howard family to which the Collector had added so magnificently should be given to the Royal Society, was a disaster. The odd book or manuscript given to priests and panders would have been far preferable to the wholesale dispersal which this caused. The books were of much more family and antiquarian interest than practical use to ordinary scholars and the Royal Society never paid much attention to the gift. As Tierney remarked, 'the conduct of the Society was somewhat extraordinary'.[8] It did not bother to catalogue the books for fourteen years and in 1677 Henry Howard felt constrained to send a message to the council of the Society asking that 'the library given by him to the Royal Society, might be better looked after'. Finally in the nineteenth century, without consulting the donor's family, the Royal Society *sold* the whole library as irrelevant to its immediate purposes. This contrasts with the exemplary treatment of the collection of heraldic manuscripts given to the College of Arms at the same time.

The newly-founded Royal Society played an important part in the life of Henry Howard and his circle. Though not a bookish man, he was not a fool, nor uneducated; he had a good mind and a lively curiosity in practical matters. He encouraged scholars, frequently attended meetings of the Society and read them papers himself. One of these, given in 1677, was 'A Description of the Diamond-mines . . . (of) the Coast of Coromandel, with which I am acquainted, and having visited several of its mines, am able to say something thereof Experimentally'. This paper, as well as being published in *Philosophical Transactions*, was also found worthy of translation into French and printed with Barbo's *Metallurgie*.[9]

He almost certainly met Robert Hooke through the Royal Society and as a result employed him as the architect for his various building projects. When Gresham College, where the Society held its meetings, was destroyed in the Great Fire, Henry Howard offered the Society Arundel House as a meeting place instead and, as part of the redevelopment plans for the site, he considered providing a plot of ground to build a 'College' for the Royal Society.

Henry contributed notes to Evelyn for his *History of the Three late Imposters*, derived from 'the relation of Signor Pietro, as unpolished as the usual style of the Levanters'. Evelyn also dedicated his book *The Perfection of Painting* to him. He was a patron of music as well as architecture and practical scholarship. Evelyn, for instance, recorded an important musical evening in 1662. 'I dined at Arundel House where I heared excellent music performed by the ablest masters, both French and English, on theorba, viols, organs, and voices, as an exercise against the coming of the queen, purposely composed for her chapel.'[10] Pepys, who met him at the Royal Society, recorded that 'Mr. Henry Howard . . . is a very fine person, and understands and speekes well; and no rigid Papist neither, but one that would not have a Protestant servant leave his religion, which he was going to do, thinking to recommend himself to his master by it; saying that he had rather have an honest Protestant than a knavish Catholique.'[11]

He was extremely well travelled, probably the most widely travelled among his peers. Apart from long periods of his life spent in the Low Countries and Italy he also visited a number of more exotic countries. Nothing much is known about his visit to the diamond mines of Coromandel on the east coast of India, but two other long journeys are remarkably well-documented because they formed part of official embassies.

As a result of his grandfather's friendship with Count Leslie, chief minister to the Emperor, he was able to accompany Leslie on his special embassy in 1664–5 from the Holy Roman Emperor to Sultan Mahomet IV, following the imperial victory at St. Gothard, which secured a truce for twenty years between East and West. Howard spent Easter 1664 in Vienna where he attended the Holy Week ceremonies in the royal chapels and waited on the Emperor several times. The embassy then proceeded by boat down the Danube through Turkish-occupied Hungary and Bulgaria before going overland to Adrianople where the Sultan's Court was for the moment established. There Count Leslie and his suite, which included Henry Howard, made a splendid state entry dressed in cloth of gold and accompanied by halberdiers, trumpeters and kettle drummers; 'the pomp of this Embassy which rather represented the Glory and Triumph of the Emperor of the West than a salutation and an address to the Monarch of the East'.

At Adrianople they exchanged courtesies and gifts, Leslie and his suite being presented with caftans lined with sables. The Sultan asked them to proceed to Constantinople on their own, where he would join them after a maritime expedition to Gallipoli, to discuss the main business of the embassy. The travellers took a keen interest in the Turkish Empire and its customs, noting especially the general illiteracy, the cruelty of the Turks and the severe punishments imposed for trifling offences and the wretched conditions of the native villages: 'the cow-houses commonly in England (are) much sweeter and cleanlier'. But they were nevertheless impressed by the religious tolerance extended by the Turks to Christians and Jews; by the discipline of the Janissaries and by the cleanliness of the Turks themselves, who 'as they had occasion to urine, still kneel'd with one knee at the least on the Ground, and afterward wash'd their Hands, as they do still before and after eating'.

Constantinople was entered 'with all the usual Ceremonies of greatness' and there they were lodged in a garden house overlooking the Bosphorus. They admired the Seraglio which occupied the site of the ancient city and had beautiful gardens and a great piazza with two 'antick Pyramids' entwined with bronze serpents. Most of the town, though, they found ill-built with mean streets and not worthy of its magnificent position, but the 'moschees' copied from Santa Sophia they considered very noble structures. Leslie's business concluded, they all returned to Vienna by the same route, reaching it in March 1665. Howard then returned to London and John Burbury, whom he had taken with him, prepared a published account of the journey.[12]

In 1669, Henry Howard, who was created Lord Howard of Castle Rising for the occasion (until then though virtually head of the Howard family he had had no title of his own), was appointed Ambassador-Extraordinary from Charles II to Taffaletta 'Emperor' of Morocco to try to establish trading relations between England and Morocco. The dowry of Catherine of Braganza had included the port of Tangier. Charles II improved the harbour and fortifications (Christopher Wren turned down the job of supervising this work) and declared the town a free port with many trading privileges. The viability of this bold scheme, however, depended on the co-operation of 'the Moors'. Lord Howard was sent to negotiate a trading treaty. He was equipped with four trumpeters, a kettle drummer 'and a pavilion and tents'. The main tent consisted of two halls with a gallery and lodging for 'his excellency, the Lord Howard, ambassador extraordinary to the emperor of Morocco', and there were other smaller tents for his suite.

He embarked at Plymouth with a splendid retinue on 22 July 1669 attended by the fleet under the command of Sir Thomas Allen. They sailed by way of the Scilly Isles, Bay of Biscay, coast of Portugal and Cape St. Vincent to Tangier where Lord Howard stayed while Captain Warren was dispatched inland to Fez to announce the arrival of the embassy to the Emperor. Taffaletta, however, had disappeared with his army on a military expedition to the south. A message was sent after him with the news of 'the Honour our King hath done him, to send him a person so eminent in our Nation, and of that great Wisdom'. But the Emperor did not return, nor did he send any message in reply. After waiting in Tangier for the best part of a year the Ambassador-Extraordinary had no option but to return to London with nothing achieved. In the end Tangier was abandoned by the English in 1683 after a half-hearted defence, in which the Grenadier Guards gained their first battle honour; the fortifications and harbour were destroyed and the town razed, the ruins being left to fall into the hands of the Moors.

From Lord Howard's point of view the embassy was not a complete waste of time, because he had been entrusted by the Royal Society 'with certain inquiries concerning Barbary', and he and an assistant later gave a paper to the Society on the fruits of their research. As in the case of the journey to Constantinople, a description of the Moroccan embassy was published by one of the gentlemen who had travelled with him in his retinue.[13] He had also taken with him Wenceslas Hollar, now Scenographer Royal to Charles II, who made detailed drawings of the town and harbour.

An aspect of his plan for the restoration of the dukedom was an attempt to revive the Howard family interest in Norfolk. By the mid-seventeenth century Kenninghall had fallen into disrepair and most of it was demolished in the 1650s, the materials being used to repair other buildings on the estate. He decided to concentrate his efforts on the Duke's palace in Norwich. He revived the custom of annual visits to Norwich, establishing good relations with the Mayor and Corporation, dining in public with them and making rich presents of plate, one year a basin and ewer, another 'a noble mace of silver gilt' and his two sons were admitted Freemen of the City.

Christmas 1663 was spent in Norwich at the palace, on which occasion the entertainments were of considerable splendour and set the tone which the

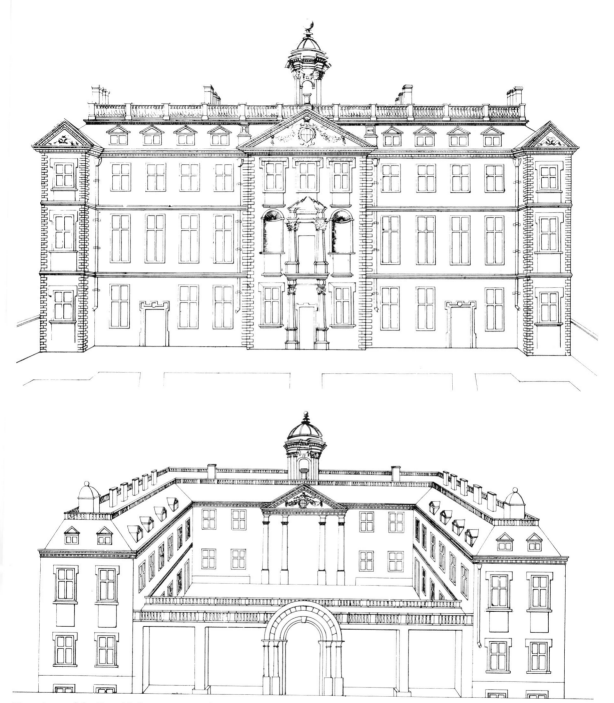

Two views of the Ducal Palace in Norwich, rebuilt by the 6th Duke in 1672, probably to the design of Sir Robert Hooke, and demolished in 1711.

Duke-to-be wished to establish. Edward Browne described the jollifications in his journal:

I was at Mr. Howard's, brother to the Duke of Norfolk, who kept his Christmas this year at the Duke's palace in Norwich, so magnificently that the like hath scarce been seen. They had dancing every night, and gave entertainments to all that would come; he built up a room on purpose to dance in, very large, and hung with the bravest hangings I ever saw; his candlesticks, snuffers, tongues, fire-shovel and andirons were silver; a banquet was given every night after dancing . . . I have seen his pictures, which are admirable; he hath prints and draughts, done by most of the great masters' own hands. Stones and jewels, as onyxes, sardonyxes, jacinths, jaspers, amethysts etc., more and better than any prince in Europe . . . These things were most of them collected by the old Earl of Arundel.[14]

Evelyn saw the Arundel gems at Albury and it is likely that Henry Howard carried his plate, jewels and old master drawings with him from house to house, to set the appropriate note of splendour. He stayed in Norwich after Christmas, celebrating his son's birthday there and entertaining the Portuguese ambassador before returning to London in the middle of March.

Charles II lodged at the palace in September 1671 on his state visit to Norwich. For this event Henry had started to reconstruct the building, though much of the work was rushed to temporary completion for the King's stay and the fabric was not properly finished till the following year. Evelyn who visited Norwich with Henry Howard in October 1671, a month after the King's visit, was shown by Howard 'the contrivance he had made for the entertainment of their M'ties and the whole Court not long before, and which tho' much of it was but temporary, apparently fram'd boards only . . . he advised with me concerning a plot to rebuild his house, having already as he said erected a front next the streete, and a left wing, and now resolving to set up another wing and pavilion next ye garden'.[15]

The architect for this work was almost certainly Robert Hooke whom Howard knew through the Royal Society and had already consulted over proposals for the Arundel House site in London. The details of the Norwich design are just what might have been expected from Hooke with its combination of French planning and Dutch-inspired elevations, the *cour d'honneur* towards the street with arched gateway, the hipped roof and pedimented dormers and little central cupola.

In building such a large house in a provincial city, Henry, inspired by former Howard glories and anxious to restore the family position in full, was perpetuating an anachronistic anomaly, and in fact the house was never properly lived in. The site, hemmed in by a loop of the river and industrial premises, was not particularly suitable for such an architectural venture. Thomas Baskerville in 1681 referred to 'the Duke of Norfolk's palace, a sumptuous new-built house not yet finished within, but seated in a dunghole place, though it has cost the Duke already 30 thousand pounds in building, as the gentleman as shewed it told us, for

Anthony Van Dyck. 'The Madagascar Portrait' of the Collector Earl and his wife Aletheia, which commemorates his scheme for colonizing Madagascar. The bronze bust in the background, 'the Arundel Homer', is now in the British Museum.

Norffolke sonne of Phillip Earle of Arundell and Surrey And for default of such issue to the heires males of the body of Thomas late Earle of Suffolke deceased one other of the sonne of the said Thomas Duke of Norffolke And for default of such issue the heires males of the body of the lord William Howard of Naworth in the county of Cumberland deceased yongest sonne of the said Thomas Duke of Norffolke And for default of such issue Charles Earle of Nottingham whoe is lineally descended from Thomas Duke of Norffolke the sonne of John Duke of Norffolke and the heires males of the said Charles Earle of Nottingham shall and may from henceforth have holde and enioye and shall be and are hereby restored unto the honor dignitie state authoritie and title of Duke of Norffolke with all priviledges preeminences and preheminencies thereunto belonging as fully amply and honourably as the said Thomas Duke of Norffolke did or might att any tyme before the same the said Attainder or corruption of blood thereupon ensuing or any other matter or thing to the contrary notwithstanding Provided alwaies and be it enacted by the authoritie aforesaid that nothing in this Act shall extend or be construed to restore to the heires to any Mannors lands tenements or other hereditaments the said honor dignitie state authoritie and title of Duke of Norffolke with all priviledges preeminences and preheminencies thereunto belonging onely excepted or to invalide or make voide any grantes or grauntes made thereof or of any parte thereof./ Ego Johannes Browne Muniger Clericus &c.

Parliamentorum virtute Bris Sni Domini Regis de Certiorand mihi direct et hijs annexat certifico superius scriptum esse tenorem Actus Parliament supradict in cedie expss In huius rei testimonium sigillum meum apposui &c. huicmodi meum subscripsi dat vicesimo nono die Novembris Anno regni dni domini nostri Caroli secundi decima Nugito Henrie et Hibernie Regis fidei defensoris &c Duodecimo Annoq domini Millesimo sexcentesimo sexagesimo &c

Johannes Browne Clericus Parliamentorum Nos autem separales tenores predictos premissoq ad requisitionem dilecti &c

Howard filij &c nostri prenobilis Henrici Comitis Arundell Surrey et Norffolke defunct duximus exemplificand per presentes Testo me ipo apud Westminster &c &c &c die &c februarij Anno regni nostri tricesimo it hath but little room for garden and is pent on all sides both on this and the other side of the river, with tradesmen's and dyers' houses.'[16] It was pulled down in 1711 by the 8th Duke, who took advantage of an imagined slight on the part of the Mayor and Corporation to rid himself of an expensive white elephant.

One reason why the interior of the palace in Norwich was left unfinished was the gradual deterioration of the political scene for a family so closely connected with the Catholic party at Court. Disappointment and persecution, of a sort, had its effect on Henry's amiable, easy-going, generous, pleasure-loving character, and as he grew older he succumbed to bouts of melancholy and ennui. One by one the great projects were abandoned with a shrug and with the implied question 'does it really matter?' Norwich was left unfinished. The Arundel House scheme was abandoned before it was begun, the remaining statues on the site left to the mercies of the builders who now carved up the garden into streets too. Albury, where he had been so happy in the 1650s and 60s, gardening with Evelyn and planning the restoration of the dukedom and family fortunes, was sold to a Mr Finch. The castle at Arundel was allowed to moulder away as a heap of ruins. None of the great projects was fulfilled.

The years 1671–2, with the visit of the King to Norwich and Henry's subsequent creation as Earl of Norwich and hereditary Earl Marshal of England, together with the short-lived Declaration of Tolerance for Catholics, turned out to be an illusory high point. After that things seemed to turn steadily downhill. Optimism, hope and a keen interest in political and intellectual matters gave way to lassitude, disappointment and cynicism. It seemed that the lunatic Duke of Norfolk in Padua would linger on for ever and probably outlive him. The various attempts to secure the peaceful practice of their religion for Catholics since 1660 had all foundered and now a strongly Puritan Parliament and a wave of popular anti-Catholic feeling in the country at large was to lead to something much worse: Titus Oates' Popish Plot. Bit by bit the King had been forced to legislate against his erstwhile friends. In 1674 Papists were forbidden to come to Court. Henry and his two sons were proceeded against for recusancy but were able to claim the protection of Parliamentary privilege.

The melancholy and lassitude which were eventually to poison his life had made their initial appearance as early as 1662 after the death of his first wife. At that time he withdrew from England for a period to the Low Countries where he bought a small plot of ground adjoining the Franciscan convent of St. Elizabeth, at Prinzenhof near Bruges, where he built a little house. In this retreat he spent an increasingly large amount of succeeding years in quiet retirement. With reference to this self-imposed exile he remarked that he felt 'soe uselesse a drogne toe my owne countrye on account of the character of a papist . . . ever indealable in mee'.

Thomas, 5th Duke, finally died in December 1677 and Henry at last inherited the dukedom for which he had waited patiently for seventeen years. He took his

Sir Peter Lely. The 6th Duke of Norfolk, 1677.

Sir Peter Lely. Jane Bickerton, second wife of the 6th Duke of
Norfolk, 1677.

long-awaited seat as a duke in the House of Lords on 15 January 1678. At more or less the same time he publicly announced his second marriage, to Jane Bickerton, a daughter of Robert Bickerton, Gentleman of the King's Wine Cellar, and reputedly a lady of beauty and accomplishments but not considered his equal and who had been his mistress before their secret marriage. Evelyn was astonished by the news and confided to his Diary: 'The Duke had now newly declar'd his marriage to his concubine, whom he promis'd me he would never marry.' Jane Bickerton had a house of her own at Weybridge which the Duke adopted as his villa near London in place of Albury. Evelyn, who visited it in August 1678, admired the wainscotted and parquetried rooms and some good pictures but was generally unimpressed by the barren, sandy situation and summed up 'never in my life had I seene such expense to small purpose'.[17]

The new Duke only enjoyed his exalted state in Parliament for ten months before the Act of 30 November 1678 disabling Papists forced him to withdraw from the Lords. The House moved before his removal 'to take notice of the good service of the duke of Norfolk herein, before his withdrawing, which their lordships took very well of him, and asked that a memorandum thereof be entered in the journals, for the honor of his Grace'. He, together with his Duchess and young family, retreated from disappointment and persecution to his house at Prinzenhof. There he spent the next three years, returning briefly only in autumn 1680, when having been indicted for recusancy in his absence at the Norwich Assizes (being no longer protected by Parliamentary privilege), he appeared at Thetford to answer the charge on 14 October and left again for Flanders the next day. He had already, expecting the worst, vested all his estates in the hands of Anglican trustees, so that they would not be confiscated, and this arrangement lasted for the rest of his life and that of his son.[18]

The Duke returned to England in 1682 after the excesses of the 'Popish Plot' had subsided having destroyed amongst others his uncle, William Howard, Viscount Stafford, who had been condemned and executed as the Catholic peer least likely to be able to defend himself and discredit Titus Oates' disreputable witnesses at the trial. The Duke only lived two more years, dying on 13 January 1684 in London. He was buried at Arundel, but his heart, like that of his infant son John who had predeceased him, was embalmed and placed in a porphyry urn in the chapel at Prinzenhof where it remained till the French Revolution. After his death, the house at Prinzenhof became the conventual chaplain's quarters and at the French Revolution, when the convent was destroyed, it was converted into a public house but not called the 'Norfolk Arms'.

The 6th Duke, though himself amiable and benevolent, nevertheless seems to have been on poor terms with his uncle, Viscount Stafford, a well-meaning but weak character who had been responsible for the rumour that Thomas was not a lunatic but was kept abroad so that Henry could enjoy his goods. Henry also fell

The trial and execution of William, Viscount Stafford, uncle of the 6th Duke of Norfolk, an innocent victim of Titus Oates' Plot in 1680.

out over land with one of his younger brothers, Charles Howard of the Deepdene, a scholar-hermit. They had a lawsuit over the Greystoke estate in Cumberland, which the Duke thought ought to be part of the ducal patrimony, but which Charles won. Henry was however on the best of terms with his brother Philip, who was probably the most distinguished member of the family at that time, a Dominican friar who restored the English Dominican Province, was created a cardinal by Pope Clement X, and played an important role in Anglo–Roman relations in the reigns of Charles II and James II.

Born in 1629 his early education was entrusted to tutors and though, like his brothers he was enrolled at St. John's College, Cambridge in 1640, it is unlikely that he spent much time there before he accompanied his grandfather to the Continent in 1641. He decided to become a Dominican at the age of sixteen while travelling in Italy, probably as a result of meeting the eminent English Dominican Fr. John Baptist Hackett in Milan. He put on the habit at Cremona on 28 June 1645 and took as his name in religion Thomas after St. Thomas Aquinas.

His grandfather, the Collector Earl, was furious and moved heaven and earth to prevent his grandson joining the Order. The elderly Earl wrote to several Cardinals and used his influence to get the Pope to intervene, asserting that his grandson had been inveigled into the Order by Fr. John Baptist Hackett. The Pope instructed Caesar-Monti, Cardinal-Archbishop of Milan, to look into the matter and in July Bro. Thomas was taken to the Archbishop's Palace and interviewed several times but was found constant in his vocation. On the Archbishop's orders he was sent to the Dominican priory of Santa Maria delle Grazie in Milan but as a result of continuing family pressure he was soon removed to Rome.

All his family tried to dissuade him, Henry came to see him several times and even his pious Catholic grandmother Aletheia threw her influence in with her husband. This united family opposition was not so much religious as political. For an Englishman to join a religious order was legal death, he ceased to exist under English law and all his property could be confiscated. To the Earl of Arundel, who had spent his whole life trying to reinstate the Howard family to its rightful position, his grandson's choice was a potential disaster. Not only Philip, but the whole family could be disgraced by one of its members turning a friar. If the matter were to be taken up by Parliament, the Earl might have to suffer imprisonment and the forfeiture of his estate should he ever return to England.

Such a prospect does not seem to have deterred Philip and in Rome he completed his novitiate with the Oratorians (the first Howard contact with an Order whose later connection with the family was to have an important impact on English history), and only after being interviewed personally by Pope Innocent X, who was convinced that the young man's vocation was genuine, was he admitted to the Order. He made his Solemn Profession of Vows on 19 October

1646 and after further study in Naples and Rennes, was ordained priest in 1652 at the early age of twenty-three.

Three years later he left Italy for Brussels with the intention of founding an English Dominican house in Flanders. He raised £1,600 of his own money for this purpose and acquired an old castle at Bornhem from the Baron of Bornhem in 1657. He converted the building into a priory, fitting up the cells for friars and forming a library, to which he gave some books from the family library including a splendid illuminated Book of Hours of 1475, and adorning the church under the direction of Sebastian Reynaets, an architect from Brussels. There he gathered round him all the scattered English Dominicans in the Low Countries and was appointed first prior in 1658. Subsequently he started a college for educating English Catholic youths and two years later he was joined at Bornhem by his younger brother Francis who took the name of Brother Dominic, but who was never ordained a priest because of ill-health. He also founded a convent at Vilvorde for English Dominican nuns.

While in Brussels, he came into contact with the exiled Charles II and became closely involved in negotiations for the restoration of the monarchy. He was sent to England in September 1658 by Charles II with a secret letter to the Royalists but was betrayed by Fr. Richard Rookwood and had to escape back to the Continent disguised in the entourage of the Polish Ambassador, who was fortunately leaving England for France at that moment. On the Restoration of Charles II in May 1660, Philip accompanied the King to England and was involved in Charles's marriage negotiations in between visits to Bornhem. He was the only English witness to Charles's marriage to Catherine of Braganza, which was performed by his uncle Lord Aubigny, Grand Almoner.[19] He was subsequently appointed first chaplain to the Queen and from that time he resided permanently at the English Court, succeeding his uncle as Grand Almoner in 1665. He was entrusted with the supervision of the royal oratory, Inigo Jones's handsome chapel at St. James's originally prepared for Henrietta Maria but which had been rehallowed for Catherine of Braganza. The post of Grand Almoner brought with it a salary of £500 per annum with a further £500 for the expenses of his table and a state apartment at Whitehall. Pepys, who was shown round it, noticed the fashionable dummy windows with panes of looking glass and 'the deske which he hath, made to remove, and is fastened to one of the arms of his chayre'. Pepys also gives a picture of Philip Howard's good-humoured and sweet-tempered character which is corroborated by other contemporaries. 'The almoner seemed a good-natured gentleman. He discussed much of the goodness of the musique in Rome; and of the great buildings which the Pope (whom in mirth to us, he calls Anti-Christ) hath done in his time.'

The Almoner was the only person in England who was allowed to appear in public dressed as a Catholic priest; he chose the soutane of a French abbé. As well as his religious duties he was employed on a number of diplomatic missions and in 1667, for instance, he accompanied the English Ambassador-Extraordinary to assist at the Congress in Holland which re-established peace between England and Holland. But more interesting than his official duties was his unofficial role as chief representative of the Catholic party at Court and it was this which was responsible for his increasing unpopularity in the 1670s. He had a strong hand in drawing up the royal Declaration of Toleration for liberty of conscience which Charles published in March 1672, and which gave to Catholics and non-conformists some degree of freedom of religion before Charles was forced almost immediately by parliamentary and popular pressure to revoke it. Two years later the Almoner was driven to leave England and he never returned, though he kept up a close correspondence (partly in cypher) with his brother Henry and various other friends and supporters.

The immediate cause of his exile was the threat of impeachment by the Dean of Windsor for a book which had appeared in 1669 entitled *The Method of saying the Rosary . . . as it is said in Her Majesty's Chappel at S. James*, which included quotations from a papal bull of Indulgence relating to the rosary when technically it was treason to publish papal bulls in England. He was appointed Vicar-Apostolic of All England by the Pope on 26 April 1672 and on 16 May Bishop of Helenopolis, but because of the unexpectedly violent reaction to the Declaration of Indulgence it was deemed inopportune to publish the briefs and he never took up the appointment, and it is possible that he never knew of his abortive promotion.

At this time of mounting crisis he played a decisive role in the marriage of James, Duke of York, to Princess Mary Beatrice of Modena. Only days before the marriage was due to take place in Modena after years of tortuous negotiations and the princess's reluctant decision to give up her intention of becoming a nun and instead to marry an unknown man twenty years her senior for the good of the Church in England, the papal dispensation for the marriage was not forthcoming because of justified doubts about the effectiveness of the English guarantee that the Princess would be allowed freedom of religion. Mary was waiting, the guests had been invited, Modena Cathedral had been prepared for the nuptial mass. But at this point the Bishop of Modena refused to conduct the marriage without the necessary papal dispensation and cancelled the cathedral ceremony. Philip Howard, however, had foreseen some such last-minute hitch and had sent Fr. Thomas White, a fellow Dominican, to be on hand in the event of a crisis 'with full instructions to employ all his little wits' as the need arose, and so it was he who was responsible for celebrating the nuptial mass privately in the palace chapel and the Pope had no option but to give his consent after all.[20]

The Almoner left England in 1674 under a cloud and returned to Bornhem, of which he was still the prior, though he had only been able to pay fleeting visits in recent years. One reason for his unpopularity in London had been his conversion of Raymond Greene, an Anglican canon at Windsor, and this young man now joined the Dominican Order at Bornhem. The Compline Book which Brother Raymond wrote out for the prior's niece, Sister Dominica Howard, is still preserved in the library at Arundel. Sister Dominica was a member of the convent which Philip Howard had founded at Vilvorde in 1660 but which had moved into Brussels in 1668 as a precaution against the dangers of war, always a real threat in the Low Countries. Several Howard nieces and cousins had taken the veil there including Antonia, Frances and Catherine, as well as Mary Delphina the daughter of Viscount Stafford, and Mary (Sister Rose) and Elizabeth (Sister Dominica) daughters of Bernard Howard of Glossop. Sister Dominica became sub-prioress of the Covent at Spellekens. She was an accomplished musician and miniature painter and was no doubt responsible for the pretty table of Founder's Kin from the chapel at Bornhem now at Arundel.

Philip Howard was only to spend a year in the peace of his own foundation. On 9 June 1675 an unexpected messenger arrived at the little priory to announce that on 27 May Pope Clement X had made Fr. Howard a cardinal as a reward for his zeal in forwarding the interests of the Church in England and as a recompense for exile. The recipient of the honour was so amazed that he burst into tears. He was the first English cardinal since Cardinal Allen, the founder of the English College at Douai, a hundred years before.

The cardinal's biretta was publicly placed on his head by the Archbishop in a ceremony at Antwerp Cathedral and he then took his leave of his brethren and set out for Rome, where he was to spend the rest of his life. He broke his journey at Padua where he stayed for a few days at the house where the Duke of Norfolk was confined. His brother Henry had written congratulating him on his elevation and with characteristic generosity offering money and plate for his state entry into Rome: 'I believe Dr. Yerbury has . . . (a) good store of silver plate, and some very good moveables in Padova. I freely offer all that . . . to your present service, to go to Rome for a yeare, two or three, till your owne condition may be better and do consent, if you please, to put out the armes, if any were now graven upon such plate, and put yours in the place.'[21]

The new cardinal made his entry into Rome accompanied by his uncle Viscount Stafford, his nephew Lord Thomas Howard of Worksop and the president of the English College at Douai, Dr. John Leyburn, to receive the cardinal's hat from the Pope. He took his title from the church of Santa Cecilia trans Tiberina, though he shortly changed it to that of Santa Maria Sopra Minerva (the Dominican church near the Pantheon), and assumed the name of Cardinal of Norfolk in common with the seventeenth-century practice whereby cardinals used their family title rather than their surname. Henry wrote: '[I] also agree and like extreemly the name of Card. of Norfolke as Vendosme and others did'.[22]

In England public affairs were shortly disturbed by the shameful episode of Titus Oates' 'Popish Plot', which engulfed several of Cardinal Norfolk's Dominican brethren as well as his uncle Stafford. He himself was named by Oates as the intended Archbishop of Canterbury if 'the Plot' had succeeded. In the circumstances it was just as well that he was safely out of London. He succeeded Cardinal Francesco Barberini as Cardinal Protector of England in 1679 thanks to the recommendation of Charles II. This was no sinecure as it involved overall supervision of English Catholic affairs, granting faculties to priests in the English mission, answering all questions relating to England raised by the Roman Congregations and general control of the English Colleges on the Continent, which numbered over thirty. This latter involved dealing with complaints from the students such as this one of 1693 directed at the Spanish Jesuits who ran the English College in Seville:

They give no clothes to the students but let them go naked with rags like beggars. I have worn a shirt nine months together and a pair of sheets twelvemonth without changing. They give us nothing but few olives, granades and oranges with water for our diet, but they themselves eat flesh even on fridays and fastdays, besides the provision of jocolate and sweetmeats in their chambers.[23]

He used every effort to forward the affairs of the Church in England; it was at his suggestion for instance that the feast of St. Edward the Confessor, hitherto a localized English feastday, was extended to the universal Church. This was of more significance than perhaps it seems, because Edward the Confessor was supposed to have prophesied on his deathbed that England would break with the Holy See but would eventually be reconciled again. He also rebuilt the Venerable English College in Rome to incorporate his own palace to the design of Legenda and Carlo Fontana. The work was completed in 1685 and is a rare reflection of the brief mood of English Catholic triumphalism at the opening of the reign of James II, a mood that was rapidly nipped in the bud so that Andrea Pozzo's splendid design for an oval church was never executed, though he did design the frescoed decorations of Cardinal Norfolk's chapel.[24]

As well as his state apartments at the English College, he also had a suite of rooms in the Vatican and a pension of ten thousand scudi from the Pope, but most of the time he chose the simple cloistered life in the Dominican priory of Santa Sabine, eating communally in the refectory with the other friars. In general he wore his black and white Dominican habit with just a scarlet scull-cap to denote his cardinal's rank, and certainly considered himself as much a friar as a cardinal. He restored the Basilica of SS. John and Paul on the Coelian Hill, where the facade had been built by the English Pope Adrian IV, as an English Dominican priory, and

devoted much effort to founding the English Dominican college of St. Thomas at Louvain in Flanders.

There was a constant coming and going of English visitors at his palace including the three sons of John Dryden the poet (the youngest of whom, Thomas, entered the Dominican order) James Earl of Salisbury (another Catholic convert) and Gilbert Burnet, later Bishop of Salisbury, who visited Rome in 1685 and recorded his impressions of Cardinal Norfolk, noting the 'soft temper of that good natured man' and the

many obliging marks of his goodness for myself as went far beyond common civility . . . He used me in such manner that it was much observed by many others. So two French Gentlemen desired a note from me to introduce them to him. Their design was to be furnished with Reliques; for he was then the Cardinal that looked after that matter. One evening I came in to him as he was very busy in giving them some Reliques. So I called in to see them. And I whispered to him, that it was somewhat odd, that a Priest of the Church of England should be at Rome, helping them off with the ware of Babylon. He was so pleased with this, that he repeated it to the others in French; and told the Frenchmen, that they should tell their countrymen, how bold the hereticks, and how mild the Cardinals were at Rome.[25]

In Macaulay's words, Cardinal Norfolk was now 'the chief counsellor of the Holy See in matters relating to his Country'. He was definitely a 'gradualist', and both he and Pope Innocent XI were against the new King James II's headstrong and tactless policies in England. He had always recommended patience, moderation and respect for the prejudices of the English people when dealing with Catholic matters. At his suggestion Innocent XI on 30 June 1688 divided England into four districts with episcopal vicars-apostolic to minister to the Catholics; this arrangement, which survived until the restoration of the Catholic Hierarchy in 1851, was intended to stall James II's rumoured intention of appointing Catholics to vacant Anglican Bishoprics. Burnet recorded:

Cardinal Howard showed me all his letters from England, by which I saw, that those who wrote to him reckoned, that their designs were so well laid that they could not miscarry. They thought they should certainly carry everything in the next parliament. There was a high strain of insolence in their letters . . . The Romans and Italians were much troubled at all this . . . The Cardinal told me, that all the advices carried over from thence to England were for slow, calm and moderate courses.[26]

The Cardinal himself was able to judge at first hand the tactlessness and exacerbatory qualities of James's religious policies when Lord Castlemaine arrived in Rome in 1686 as James's special ambassador to press various ill-considered petitions at the papal court. The choice of man was disastrous, for a start. Castlemaine was pompous, arrogant and hectoring; his only claim to prominence was that he was the husband of one of Charles II's mistresses, not,

left. Italian School. Philip Howard, Cardinal Norfolk (1629–94).
right. Fame preparing a monument to Cardinal Norfolk.
om. The roast ox stuffed with lambs and fowls provided by Cardinal Norfolk for the *lace* of Rome to celebrate the birth of a son to James II and Mary of Modena in 1688.

one would have thought, the highest recommendation for a supplicant at the Court of Innocent XI. It had been arranged that Castlemaine should be Cardinal Norfolk's guest at his palace in the English College, but this arrangement only lasted four days and provoked a row between the Cardinal and the interfering Fr. William Morgan, Jesuit Rector of the College, in which the Cardinal gave vent to an uncharacteristic outburst, 'which expression from so meek a gentleman and clothed with the purple was not without very great provocation', and led to Morgan's dismissal and replacement as Rector by Fr. Charles Campion. Castlemaine was rehoused elsewhere.[27]

One of Castlemaine's briefs from James II was to secure a cardinal's hat for the Queen's uncle, Rinaldo d'Este of Modena. This secured, against the Pope's better judgement, the King next attempted to get Rinaldo d'Este made joint Cardinal Protector of England. Despite this, Cardinal Norfolk did his best to serve the ungrateful king and to moderate his unrealistic policies. On the birth of an heir to the throne in 1688 he gave a feast in Rome at which 'an ox roasted whole, stuffed with lambs, fowls and other provisions of all kinds stirred up the wonder and gladdened the hearts of the common people of the city'. There is an engraving in the library at Arundel showing the ox being roasted in the open air with the heads of the lambs and fowls poking out through its sides while servers in Cardinal Norfolk's livery offer round loaves of bread and wine to the crowds. The jollity was short-lived, for almost immediately James fled the country in the face of the revolution which he had provoked, deserted by his ministers and supplanted by his own daughter, leaving the Catholic cause in England in ruins.

Cardinal Norfolk, however, had the benefit of seeing his life's ambition realized when the English Dominican Province was revived in 1694 with himself as first Vicar-General. He died three weeks later on 17 June 1694 aged sixty-four. In his will he left his Raphael Holy Family (possibly from his grandfather's collection) to the Pope and several English clocks to fellow cardinals, but most of his property he left to the Dominicans, especially funds for the endowment of St. Thomas's College at Louvain. The English College which he had partially rebuilt at the College's expense and where he had had his state apartments was disappointed of the legacy it had been expecting, and even had to struggle to get the Dominicans to accept that Cardinal Norfolk's palace was not included in his bequest to them. The Cardinal was buried in the choir of his titular church, Santa Maria Sopra Minerva, where his simple grave is marked with a white marble slab with his arms and a Latin epitaph.

In 1793-4 French Revolutionary soldiers sacked the convent in Brussels and the nuns fled to England; Bornhem was also confiscated by the French at the same time and the friars removed to England. The nuns, after various vicissitudes were eventually established in a convent on the Isle of Wight and the friars founded a new house at Hinckley, moving later to Laxton Hall (Northamptonshire).

Cardinal Norfolk's cope of cloth of gold with the Howard arms on the orphreys (a cardinal's privilege) is preserved in the sacristy at Arundel Cathedral and the arms have recently been restored after being cut off by a vandal in the nineteenth century.

Though the two brothers, Henry and Philip Thomas, saw in their own lifetime the ruin of much that they had attempted to bring about, and the eclipse of their political and religious party within the State, nevertheless they each left behind them solid achievements. In both cases their two principal and most longed for objectives, the one secular and the other spiritual, were not only attained but have survived the vicissitudes of the intervening three centuries. The restored Dukedom of Norfolk has flourished and is still an integral part of English life. The same is also true of the revived English Dominican Province.

Whigs and Tories

THE political and religious troubles of the late seventeenth century could easily have wrecked the family; that they did not is largely due to Henry, 7th Duke of Norfolk, who was successful in staving off disaster not so much because of any noble personal qualities or great abilities as the absence of any such dangerous encumbrances. In the circumstances a more virtuous, more rigidly upright, less time-serving man might easily have ruined the dukedom. Instead by complying with the prevailing trends, conforming to the Established Church at the time of Titus Oates' Plot in 1679, seeming to support James II during his brief reign, promptly going over to William III in 1688, he ensured that he floated above the upheavals of the times. The most memorable and best-documented aspect of the 7th Duke's life is his long-drawn-out divorce of his wife for adultery, a proceeding not stimulated by any moral scruple but by shortage of money.

Born on 11 January 1655, Henry Howard was educated at Magdalen College, Oxford and received the degree of MA at the age of thirteen in 1668 when his father was created DCL in gratitude for the gift of the Arundel Marbles. He was styled Earl of Arundel from 1677 but was called to the House of Lords as Lord Mowbray on 14 January 1678. On the enforcement of the Oath of Allegiance in 1679 he withdrew from Parliament, but seeing which way events were developing changed his mind, conformed to the Established Church by publicly receiving the Sacrament, took the Oath of Allegiance (with its recognition of the sovereign's position as Head of the Church of England) and was back in his seat in the Lords in the same month. He was rewarded by being created Lord Lieutenant of Berkshire, and Surrey and Governor and Constable of Windsor Castle, positions which had become vacant on the death of Prince Rupert in 1682. Two years later he succeeded his father as Duke of Norfolk on 13 January 1684.

He was the third head of the family to conform to the Established Church, but it is doubtful whether his change of religion was directed by any sincere convictions. As the *Complete Peerage* puts it, 'The temptation to conform was at this date so strong for Roman Catholics that conformity by itself is no guide to

...on Verelst. Henry, 7th Duke of Norfolk (1655–1701). It
...s while Verelst was painting a pendant to this portrait, of
... Duchess of Norfolk, that her liaison with Sir John Germain
...1e to light, leading to a scandalous divorce.

Sir Joshua Reynolds. Posthumous portrait of Lord Thomas
Howard of Worksop (1659–89), father of the 8th and 9th Dukes
of Norfolk; he was drowned in the sinking of *La Tempête*
while returning to France from Ireland in the service of the
deposed King James II.

religious views.' He maintained the arrangements set up by his father whereby his estates were vested in the hands of Anglican trustees, just to be on the safe side.[1]

The accession to the dukedom brought further honours and in the same year he was created DCL by Oxford, and Lord Lieutenant of Norfolk, High Steward of Lynn, and High Steward of Norwich Cathedral. His change of religion did him no harm on the accession of the overtly Catholic James II, on the contrary the new King was eager to woo the chief of a clan notorious for its general Catholic sympathies. He acted as Earl Marshal and Chief Butler at the coronation, receiving the traditional perquisite of a gold cup and cover weighing thirty-two ounces. The Duchess, who had not followed her husband into the Anglican fold, bore Her Majesty's train and was appointed Lady of the Bedchamber to Queen Mary of Modena, a post worth £500 a year. The following month the Duke received the Garter, being the first nominated by the new King on 6 May 1686; he was installed on 22 July. James II was keen that the Duke should play an active role as Earl Marshal and it was by the King's orders that he held regular Marshal's courts in 1687, 1688 and 1689 'to hear causes, abuses having gone unreformed by discontinuance of the court ever since the horrid Rebellion'.[2]

The Duke seems to have remained outwardly Protestant throughout the reign, as is suggested by Bishop Burnet's amusing but apocryphal story of the Duke's supposed retort to James II over the Sword of State: 'One day the King gave the Duke of Norfolk the Sword of State to carry before him to the Chapel, and he stood at the door, upon which the King said to him, "My Lord, your father would have gone further", to which the Duke answered, "Your Majesty's father was the better man, and he would not have gone so far."'[3] This cannot be true as it was the correct etiquette for the person carrying the Sword of State to remain outside the chapel door and there are in any case numerous examples of genuinely Anglican peers attending Catholic services in the chapel at Whitehall. Nevertheless, that such a piece of gossip had contemporary currency implies that the Duke had maintained his Protestant stance; which was just as well as things turned out.

The Duke's private views of the political situation under James II are preserved in a letter written by him to his cousin and trustee the 5th Lord Howard of Effingham, Governor of Virginia, in September 1687:

I cannot help telling you that you never could have found a more seasonable time to bee where you are, and that if your owne conveniency, and inclinations will allow of it, a yeare or two where you are may not bee for your disserve.[4]

It has been stated on various occasions that the Duke of Norfolk was one of those who signed the written invitation to William of Orange dated 30 June 1688 to accept the English throne, but this is not so. When on 28 November 1688 the proclamation was issued that a Parliament should meet the following January to deal with the kingdom's ills the Duke, as Lord Lieutenant, hurried to Norfolk and called an assembly in Norwich, attended by the Mayor and Corporation. He advised acceptance of the proclamation and support for James II, trusting to Parliament to remedy the country's difficulties. In the words of the Editor of the *Complete Peerage,* 'He seems to have sat the fence with masterly firmness, and so long as hopes were held out by James II that a Parliament would be summoned the forces of the county were engaged to maintain the existing regime.' With James II's flight, however, and the arrival of William of Orange the Duke changed sides at just the right moment and called out the county militia in defence of William III.

He acted as Earl Marshal and Chief Butler at the coronation of William and Mary and received once again the customary gift of a gold cup and cover. He was further rewarded for his timely support by retaining all the honours granted to him by the exiled James II as well as being made a Gentleman of the Bedchamber and a Lord of the Privy Council on 14 February 1689. In March the following year he was granted a pension of £3,000 per annum 'for good and acceptable services' and he remained one of William's trusted supporters till his death. He acted as Captain General of the Artillery during William's absence in Holland in June 1690 for example, and the following January was one of those chosen to accompany the King to Holland.

Despite the salaries of his various official positions and his landed revenue (estimated at £25,000 per annum) the Duke found it difficult to keep afloat financially. But it is probable that he never received all his official salaries. According to Charles Howard's *Anecdotes of the Howard Family,*[5] the Duke was owed the sum of £12,000 at the time of his death, arrears of his salary as Governor of Windsor Castle which was never paid. Whatever the reasons, the Duke found himself increasingly short of money as the century drew to a close. In 1695 he sold to his cousin Thomas Howard (6th son of the Earl of Suffolk, and Teller of the Exchequer) the manor, castle and estate of Castle Rising in Norfolk which had been granted to the 3rd Duke by Henry VIII. It was his financial straits which caused the Duke to attempt to divorce his wife, because several manors which he wished to sell were encumbered with a life interest to the Duchess under their marriage settlement. So if the Duke wished to free these, he first had to get rid of her.

He had married Lady Mary Mordaunt, daughter of the last Earl of Peterborough, in 1677. Shortly after the coronation of James II there had unfolded round the Duchess a scandal with a scenario not unworthy of a French farce. She succumbed 'to the ogles of the invincible Germyn', that is (Sir) John Germain, described by Evelyn as 'a Dutch gamester of mean extraction, who had got much by gaming'[6] and who was generally regarded as William of Orange's illegitimate half-brother. The Duchess's liaison with Germain was discovered while Simon

Verelst was painting her portrait, as a pair to a full length of the Duke.[7] At the end of a painting session in the Duchess's room at Windsor Castle, Verelst put his canvas and brushes in a cupboard where were discovered some articles of men's clothing, not the Duke's. Shortly afterwards Germain came to Verelst and offered him money to say that the clothes were his own. Unfortunately for Germain their conversation was overheard by Mrs Verelst who spread the news. The painter later admitted, somewhat ruefully, 'I should not have been here to give this evidence had not my wife overheard the conversation with Germain and the proposals that were made.'

The Duke separated from the Duchess and took her away from Court, placing her in a convent in Paris, surely rather an odd retreat for a man who posed as a Protestant to choose for his wife? There the Duchess spent thirteen months but, finding it 'not congenial to her taste' as Tierney put it with delicious understatement, eventually petitioned the Duke to allow her back to England, a request with which the Duke complied on the Duchess signing away her life interest in various manors. It was not long however before she was up to her old tricks with Germain. The Duke seems to have ignored her behaviour for a couple of years but in January 1692 he introduced his first bill for divorce into the House of Lords. He met with opposition at every stage over precedent and form. The Duchess herself was called in witness to the bar at the House of Lords and denied the allegations, not only 'adhering to her protestations of innocence' but submitting 'that by the laws of the land, a husband suing for a divorce for the adultery of a wife, ought not to obtain a sentence of divorce, if he be found guilty of the same; and she is ready to aver that the Duke, her husband, is guilty of adultery, and hath continued in the same for ten years past, and doth so continue'.[8]

On 23 January no fewer than twenty-eight witnesses were sworn against the Duchess. By this time the trial had become something of a fashionable entertainment. The King himself went incognito to hear the evidence in the Lords on 26 January. There was much debate of the pros and cons of the case, though in general sympathy was with the Duchess, 'a Papist, and a busy Jacobite'. According to Bishop Burnet, 'All who favoured the Jacobites, and who were thought engaged in lewd practices espoused the concern of the duchess with a zeal that did themselves little honour.'[9]

It would perhaps be fairer to attribute the support for the Duchess to the general knowledge that the Duke himself was in no position to point an accusing finger at his wife. The Earl of Dartmouth said that the Duke was 'notoriously a very vicious man; and besides his own example, had been the original introducer of all the bad company she kept to her own acquaintance'. On another occasion Dean Prideaux described how the Duke had given a ball with his mistress, Mrs Lane, and was displeased that 'no one with any regard to their reputations would accept his invitations'.[10]

The upshot was that the House of Lords declared that the Duchess could not be divorced until the Duke had got proof in Common Law against her. As a result the Duke took out an action in the Court of King's Bench, Westminster, on 24 November 1692 claiming £100,000 damages from Germain 'for lying with the Duchess'. 'It is a very melancholy thing', intoned Attorney-General Somers, 'for the first duke in England, installed Knight of the Garter, lord high Marshal of England, and one of the lords of his Majesty's Privy Council, to be thus abused: and it was not kept secret; all the world did ring of it.'[11]

That may have been the lawyer's view of the affair but the popular one was that the Duke himself had turned a 'scandal of quiet endurance' into a matter of public shame. He was abused by the audience at the Playhouse, which led the Lord Chamberlain to suspend the acting for the offence to the dignity of the Peerage. Worse, a 'wretched scribbler' inspired by the evidence which was being paraded before the world, produced an alleged correspondence, 'The Secret Letters of Amour between the duchess and mynheer', for the entertainment of the Capital.[12] The events under discussion had taken place six years earlier, in 1686, so that many of the witnesses had difficulty remembering the exact facts. Eventually the jury found for the Duke but showed their sympathy for the Duchess by only awarding damages of a hundred marks. For this they were rebuked by the Chief Justice who owned that 'he was a little surprised at the verdict, when he considered that 'twas not long since a Surrey jury gave a commoner £5,000 damages in the like cause: that the sin of adultery was of so high a nature that it well deserved their consideration, especially if they had any sense of the *ability* of the person that committed the crime, and the *greatness* of the peer that sustained the damage.'[13]

The Duke now brought a second bill of divorce before the House of Lords but it was thrown out by six votes, according to Evelyn, because the Duke 'manag'd it very indiscreetly'.[14] The Duke and Duchess agreed in any case to live apart, she going back to her own house, Drayton in Northamptonshire, where she lived with Germain (whom she eventually married). The Duke bided his time and in February 1700 introduced yet another bill which this time was passed, though he was ordered to repay the £10,000 dowry which the Duchess had brought him. This he never did; nor did he marry again, for only a year later he died of an apoplexy in London, aged forty-six. He left no children so that he was succeeded by his nephew Thomas, son of Lord Thomas Howard of Worksop, a young man of very different stamp from his uncle, a devout Catholic, a man of sincere convictions, a Tory and a Jacobite. Evelyn described the new Duke and his younger brothers as 'Papists indeede, but very hopeful and virtuous gentlemen, as was their father'.[15]

The new Duke's father, Lord Thomas Howard, had been drowned at sea off Brest in 1689 *en route* from Ireland to France in the service of James II, a tragic but not inappropriate end to a career distinguished for its consistent loyalty to the doomed monarch. Lord Thomas, like his elder brother the 7th Duke, had been educated at Magdalen College, Oxford and after leaving the university had obtained a military commission as a Lieutenant, probably in the King's Life Guards, 'a place of refuge for and retreat for papists and men popishly inclined', but had been forced to resign because of the build-up of anti-Catholic feeling in the 1670s.[16] Unlike his brother he did not conform (he had in any case less to lose), but went to the Continent where he accompanied his uncle Cardinal Norfolk on the latter's state entry into Rome in 1675. He stayed in Rome till 1678 when he returned to England, spending the last years of Charles II's reign quietly in retirement at Worksop in Nottinghamshire, and at Redhall upon Whinmore, his wife's house near Leeds. Worksop was part of the inheritance brought to the Howards by Aletheia, wife of the Collector Earl, and it included the great Elizabethan house built for her grandfather by Robert Smythson. The manor of Worksop carried with it the ancient right of providing a right-hand glove at the coronation and supporting the King's arm while he was holding the sceptre.

At the accession of James II Lord Thomas emerged from retirement to take his appointed part in the coronation ceremony. As a Catholic nobleman he immediately came to the King's notice as James was eager to promote his co-religionists. Lord Thomas became one of the new king's staunchest supporters and was rewarded by being made Master of the Robes in 1687 and Lord Lieutenant of the West Riding of Yorkshire, a county in which he had acquired an interest through his marriage to Mary Elizabeth Savile, heiress of the Roundhay estate near Leeds.

The following year he was appointed to succeed Lord Castlemaine as James II's special ambassador to Rome, entrusted with the task of bringing about the reconciliation of England, Ireland and Scotland with the Holy See. His appointment must have come as a considerable relief to his uncle Cardinal Norfolk, but he had little opportunity to exert his more tactful and accommodating character before the revolution of 1688 and the flight of the King on 23 December made his embassy redundant. Thomas Howard made his way to join the King at St. Germain to declare his continued loyalty, and subsequently went to Ireland to support the Jacobite cause in 1689. He returned on 5 December, embarking on 'La Tempête' at Kinsale, but never reached France, the boat going down in the channel with all on board.[17]

His wife, meanwhile, who was in London, had sent their four sons Thomas (Tom), Henry (Harry), Edward (Ned), and Richard (Dick) and their daughter Mary (Mall) to France for safety in the charge of their nurse. They were detained by the authorities at Faversham but managed to slip away on 30 January 1689. The children lived in Paris till 1693 when it was thought safe enough for them to return to England, though the boys subsequently returned to the Continent for their schooling at Douai. The children had their own little individually bound account books kept from birth until the age of sixteen; these still survive and show the sums of money each spent on clothes, toys, travel and nurses' wages.[18]

Two of the boys later became priests: Richard, afterwards a canon of St. Peter's in Rome with the title of Mgr. Howard de Norfolk, and Henry, who was appointed Bishop of Utica *in partibus infidelium* and co-adjutor to Dr Giffard, Vicar Apostolic of the London District, but died in 1720 before he was consecrated. His death was caused by a fever contracted while ministering to the poor in London. 'Such charity, such piety, has not been seen in our land for a long time', wrote Dr Giffard; he was buried at Arundel.

At the time of his succession the new Duke was only eighteen and his youth helped soften the disabilities of his position; his cousin the 3rd Earl of Carlisle acted as Deputy Earl Marshal at the coronation of Queen Anne as much because the Duke was a minor as that he was a Catholic. Shortly afterwards the Duke set out on his Grand Tour, in the course of which he visited Rome, the artistic as well as the religious capital of Europe, and was away till 1705. He returned in his twenty-second year 'to kiss her majesty's hand; and receive from another power the nominal appointment of chief of a faction opposed to the political and religious maintenance of her throne', as a Victorian historian somewhat fancifully put it.[19]

The Duke was certainly a zealous 'papist' and as a young man may have been a Jacobite. The story that he had taken an active part in the disturbances of 1690 and had submitted himself to the authorities after the defeat of the Jacobite army at Waterford, is unfounded; he was only seven at the time and in any case was resident in Paris. His father's active espousal of the Jacobite cause, however, would have been grounds enough for suspicion, and his marriage in 1709 to Maria Winifreda Francisca Shireburn of Stonyhurst, daughter of a prominent member of the 'popish gentry' of Lancashire, reinforced his position as head of the Catholic faction. His younger brother Edward, afterwards the 9th Duke, was directly involved in the Earl of Mar's rebellion and was taken in arms at Preston in 1715; he was tried for High Treason but was successfully acquitted because no witnesses came forward to give evidence against him.

It is said that this was because the Duke had gone to George I and promised that if his brother was not proceeded against, he would henceforth support the Hanoverian dynasty. There is no direct evidence that he did not keep his word though he was arrested in Bath on 29 October 1722 on suspicion of being involved in a Jacobite plot and was imprisoned in the Tower, the last Duke of Norfolk to be incarcerated there. His wife, who was refused permission to visit him, got the Earl of Carlisle to stand bail for the Duke and he was released after six months in May 1723.

There are a number of indirect pieces of evidence that the Duke was at heart a

Jacobite. There was a rumour that he melted down the ducal plate to support the Old Pretender. This may or may not be true, but there is certainly no old family plate of earlier than the eighteenth century in the Duke of Norfolk's possession now and the series of coronation cups begins with George II's. Another indication is that he was a freemason and succeeded the notorious Jacobite Duke of Wharton as Grand Master of the Grand Lodge of England in 1729 at a time when it has been suggested that the freemasons were partly a club of Jacobite supporters.

The Duke's real political views remain veiled and can only be guessed at. There is no secret however about his wife's. She was an out-and-out Jacobite. According to Henry Howard of Corby, who had the story from the 11th Duke of Norfolk, the Duchess never forgave her husband for 'truckling to the usurper' in 1715 and as a result they never lived together as man and wife again. As she was only fifteen when she married the Duke in 1709 their life together must have been very short and they had no children. The Duchess owned a villa of her own at Chiswick and a house in Arlington Street. At some stage she fell in love with Peregrine Widdrington, another Catholic Jacobite, and after the Duke's death lived openly with him at Stonyhurst (a house with a resident chaplain), though it is not clear whether she ever married him or not. Some authorities say she did; and some say that she ought to have done. In the epitaph on the monument which she erected to the memory of Peregrine Widdrington in the Shireburn Chapel at Mitton near Stonyhurst, she does not state that he was married to her. Henry Howard puts the matter tactfully: 'it was supposed and hoped she was privately married' and perhaps it should be left at that.[20]

In his religious views the Duke was a moderate sensible Catholic, certainly not bigoted, as Evelyn had noticed when he had met him as a youth. In 1719 George I's ministry made an attempt to alleviate the lot of his Catholic subjects on condition that the leading Catholic nobility and gentry should sign a letter to the Pope suggesting a concordat whereby, in return for a degree of tolerance and an acceptable form of the Oath of Allegiance, the Pope would withdraw from the English mission any priest hostile to the English Government and dismiss Cardinal Gualterio, the Pretender's agent, from the office of Cardinal-Protector of England. The chief advocate of this sensible compromise in England was Dr Strickland (afterwards created Bishop of Namur, as a result of George II's intercession as Elector of Hanover with the Holy Roman Emperor). The Duke supported Strickland and took a letter to the Papal Internuncio at Brussels with their proposals. But this constructive scheme came to nothing because the Catholic community as a whole would not support it as a result of the wrong-headedness of the extremists, apparently led by the Duke's cousin Henry Charles Howard of the Deepdene. Once again an initiative on the part of the English government proposing some degree of tolerance for Catholics came to nothing because of internal disagreement in the English Catholic body itself.[21]

R. Van Bleeck. Thomas, 8th Duke of Norfolk.

Maria Winifreda Francisca Shireburn, wife of the 8th Duke of Norfolk, heiress of Stonyhurst and an ardent Jacobite.

It is difficult not to feel sorry for the 8th Duke, a good, upright and honest man denied the public life which was his birthright and enmeshed in a web of conflicting loyalties and responsibilities: his religion, his rank, his wife, his relations, his duty as a subject all seeming to pull in different directions. His portrait by Van Bleeck (a Catholic artist who specialized in recusants) shows something of this tension in the slight melancholy of his expression and the contrast between the Duke's fashionable clothes and the little gold crucifix on his watch-chain.

His only solace, apart from the quiet practice of his religion, lay in the improvement of his estates and especially the embellishment of his houses and chapels. He acquired magnificent rococo altar plate from Charles Kandler in 1730 including an ormolu tabernacle now at Arundel Cathedral. His decisions over the various family seats dictated the future pattern of the ducal houses. He bought the freehold of Norfolk House in St. James's Square which was to remain the Norfolks' London house down to 1938. He disposed of the embarrassing white elephant of the incomplete ducal palace in Norwich as a retort to the mayor Thomas Haber's refusal to allow the Duke's players to perform in the city in 1710, perhaps from a fear that they might instigate a Jacobite disturbance. The Duke, in response, demolished most of the house in 1711 and let the remaining wing as a workhouse to the guardians of the Poor Law; it was the second Howard house to become a workhouse, that fate having already overtaken Framlingham Castle. The Duke must have received a certain world-weary satisfaction from the ironic inference.

As his principal seat he chose his father's house at Worksop, the magnificent castle-like pile built by the 6th Earl of Shrewsbury in the 1580s. It was of H plan and, even by the standards of Elizabethan 'prodigy houses', was extravagantly high, eighty or ninety feet from ground to parapet and above that there was a splendid array of domed turrets and tall chimneystacks on the skyline. He almost doubled the size of the house between 1700 and 1704 by adding a new centre to the north front, with a baroque doorcase and pediment and projecting wings. A formal *cour d'honneur* was formed in front, closed by iron railings between single-storey pavilions. The old mullions and transoms were removed from all the windows and replaced by sashes. The interior was splendidly redecorated in the baroque taste and the new grand staircase was painted by Jacques Parmentier, a pupil of Sébastien Bourdon, in the years 1709–10; Vertue thought this Parmentier's best work. Elaborate formal gardens were also laid out, on a vast scale extending to one thousand seven hundred acres with long straight avenues and rectangular canals. To one side of the house was built a new quadrangular office court with hipped roofs, slightly reminiscent of an early-eighteenth-century Cambridge college, and this of all the magnificence is the only building which still survives. The Duke's architect at this stage is not known, but many of the craftsmen are recorded and were of the first rank; Tijou, for instance, supplying the wrought iron railings and gates.

Later in life both the Duke and Duchess employed as their architect James Gibbs, a Catholic, Tory, baroque artist who worked for Catholic, Tory, baroque clients in the face of the neo-Palladianism of the Whig Establishment. The Duchess rebuilt her house at 16 Arlington Street (which still survives) to Gibb's design in 1734–5 and Gibbs also made additions to her villa at Chiswick. The Duke obtained designs from Gibbs for building a palatial new house at Arundel. These were not executed but the ruined residential ranges round the south quadrangle of the castle were patched up and given a new brick north front, possibly to Gibbs' design *circa* 1714, and some comfortable rooms contrived inside. The Duke only used the castle as a shooting lodge, visiting it for a couple of

John Vanderbanck. Edward, 9th Duke of Norfolk (1686–1777), and his wife Mary Blount at her needlework, 1732. She was considered the finest needlewoman of her day, as the long series of chair covers at Arundel still testifies.

weeks in the year, but this modest programme of restoration was the beginning of the process which was to lead to Arundel becoming the principal ducal seat before the end of the eighteenth century.

The 8th Duke died on 23 December 1732 at Norfolk House in St. James's Square, after a long and horrible illness. He was only forty-nine. Sir Thomas Robinson wrote to the Earl of Carlisle, who had always taken an interest in the well-being of the Duke from the time that he had acted as Deputy Earl Marshal on his accession: 'It is currently reported he was poisoned . . . his case entirely puzzled the doctors . . . he suffered as much pain as 'twas possible for any mortal to undergo for several weeks before his death.' He was succeeded by his younger brother Edward, as 9th Duke of Norfolk and last of the senior line of the Howards.

The accession of the 9th Duke of Norfolk and his talented forceful wife Mary was the beginning of a long, tranquil, uneventful stretch in the family history, a calm summer's afternoon after all the dramas of the previous three centuries; the traumatic reversals of fortune, the victories and martyrdoms, the riches and poverty, the treasons and glories, the high politics and devious religious diplomacy all led up to a shy, quiet, intelligent man and his energetic, admirable wife growing old together in harmonious wedlock, planting and building, decorating and collecting, praying and reading books against a princely backdrop of three major houses and four private chapels served by a succession of scholarly priests who, when not attending to the spiritual welfare of the ducal family, its household, tenants and dependants, were engaged in antiquarian and genealogical researches. Whereas in previous generations spectacular public and personal tragedies had dogged the head of the family bringing many to a premature end, the 9th Duke lived into his ninety-second year and it was only at the end of his life that shadows began to gather, with the great fire at Worksop and the death in turn of both his nephews and heirs in their early twenties.

Though the 9th Duke spent his long life in almost total seclusion from political life, he and his wife both played an active role in the fashionable social world. The Duchess in particular, who was the stronger character of the two and whom the Duke was happy to let take the lead, was gregarious and hospitable. Nor was their acquaintance restricted to their co-religionists: 'Her house was the centre of whatever was great and elegant, in either communion; and by familiarising them with one another, their prejudices were softened, and their mutual good will encreased.'[22] Soon after their succession they were received at Court by George II, tacit recognition of the fact that the Duke's Jacobite past was forgiven and forgotten. Lady Irwin wrote in January 1733: 'The Duke and Duchess of Norfolk were at Court on Friday where they were received with great distinction. The Duchess who is a sensible woman, and must act the man where talking is necessary, behaved much to her credit; she assured the Queen, though she and the Duke were of different religion, they had as much duty and regard for the King as any of his subjects, and should be glad of every occasion that gave 'em opportunity to show it.'

Mary, wife of the 9th Duke of Norfolk, was in many ways a remarkable woman; the daughter and co-heiress of Edward Blount of Blagdon, the early patron and correspondent of Pope, she was intelligent, energetic, charming, the possessor of natural good taste, an amateur of the arts, an ardent Catholic and something of a francophile who visited the Continent frequently and was received at the French Court by Louis XV. She could also be rather formidable: Horace Walpole referred to her as 'My Lord, Duchess'. Charles Butler wrote 'the duchess was gifted with great talents: was easy, dignified, and, when she pleased, singularly insinuating'.[23] She and the Duke spent much of their time discreetly improving the lot of their co-religionists; the Duke by financial help: building Catholic chapels, on his estates at Norwich and Sheffield, supporting students studying for the priesthood at the English colleges on the Continent or by gifts to Catholic establishments such as the altarpiece he gave to St. Mary's, Preston (later destroyed in an election riot); the Duchess by taking up causes and promoting them energetically. She became a great friend of William Murray, later the Lord Chief Justice, Lord Mansfield, and used him as an attorney on behalf of the Catholics; which may have been one of the reasons why the mob later burnt his London house in the Gordon Riots.

Their own life was in itself a major force making for religious harmony; open, charitable and tolerant themselves, they inspired similar standards in others. When Frederick, Prince of Wales and his wife, having quarrelled with George II, were ejected from St. James's Palace in September 1737, the Norfolks offered them shelter at Norfolk House, St. James's Square. It was there that the Princess's baby, the future King George III, was born in May 1738. This was in the old Norfolk House. Ten years after the birth of the future King on the premises, the Norfolks embarked on a large-scale reconstruction. The adjoining Belasyse House was bought, and both the old houses, apart from one detached range at the back, were demolished and the sites united to make room for a large new town house on a Continental scale of splendour.

The architect was Matthew Brettingham senior, who had constructed Holkham Hall in Norfolk. The shell was finished by 1751 though the fitting up of the interior with all 'the pomp of cost' and 'pride of art' took a further five years.

Brettingham's Palladian façade of white brick, with only a top balustrade and pediments to the first-floor windows for ornament, was reticent and dignified without being especially inspired. The interior however was another matter. It was one of the finest eighteenth-century rococo ensembles in London and its destruction in 1938 was a tragic architectural loss, quite apart from the house's historical associations. The excellent plan with the principal rooms arranged round a central grand staircase was due to Brettingham and was derived from the

Norfolk House, St. James's Square, London. Designed by Matthew Brettingham in 1748 and demolished in 1938.

Norfolk House. Monkey doorcase in the Great Room, designed by Giovanni Battista Borra and now in the Victoria and Albert Museum.

plan of the family and strangers' wings at Holkham. The decoration of the rooms, however, which was the special glory of the house, was largely designed by 'Mr. Bora', presumably Giovanni Battista Borra who arrived in London from Turin in 1751 and became 'court architect' to the Temples of Stowe who, like the Norfolks, were friends of Frederick, Prince of Wales. The colour schemes and furnishings were all devised by the Duchess herself and she was the driving force behind the whole project.

The simple entrance hall on the ground floor had a Doric frieze, with the heraldic animals of the Howards, Fitzalans and Talbots in the metopes, which was reproduced from a frieze at Arundel House and so may originally have been designed by Inigo Jones.[24] This outer hall gave access to the staircase hall which was embellished with amazing Italian rococo trophies of arms and armour designed by Borra and paralleled in the decoration at Racconigi near Turin. The principal rooms on the first floor comprised a continuous enfilade all round the house. The finest room was the Music Room with white and gold rococo panelling carved by John Cuenot and designed by Borra. The ceiling had magnificent plaster panels representing Music, Painting, Literature, Sculpture, Architecture, Astronomy and Surveying by Thomas Clarke who executed the plasterwork throughout the house.[25] Beyond were the drawing-rooms, each with a different colour scheme, the first hung with green damask and having a diagonally coffered ceiling designed by Brettingham and inspired by the chapel at Holkham, while the glorious carved and gilt pier glasses 'with mathematical trophies' were Cuenot's work. Beyond the drawing-rooms at right angles was the Great Room with wonderful doorcases designed by Borra with monkeys on top and the walls hung with four panels of Gobelin tapestry from the *Nouvelles Indes* series, bought by the Duchess in Paris and costing £9 a yard.[26] Then returning along the garden front were the state bedroom, dressing-room and closet with lighter gilt rococo ceilings similar to the family rooms on the ground floor. The bedroom chimneypiece was inlaid with jasper while the closet had niches in the walls for the display of china.

The most striking feature of these rooms were the enormous looking-glasses ordered from France, 'the largest plates . . . that were ever brought over'. Those in the Great Room alone cost £1,000 and were greeted with amazement by contemporaries. The carefully co-ordinated colours of the furnishings in all the rooms were worked out by the Duchess and the splendid carved and gilt furniture was also chosen by her. William Farington wrote to his sister in 1756 describing the different colour schemes in each room and commenting that 'the immense Grandure of the furniture is scarce to be conceived'. The state bedroom was hung with blue velvet and the bed was covered with peach coloured French silk embroidered with birds and flowers by the Duchess, who was considered one of the best needlewomen of her day. The dressing-room was 'intirely Chinese' with

Norfolk House. The music room, with carved panelling by Cuenot and plasterwork by Thomas Clarke. It is now in the Victoria and Albert Museum.

painted satin hangings 'in the most Beautiful India Pattern'. The seat furniture in the Great Room was upholstered in red velvet with gilt fringes.

The Norfolks gave a house-warming in February 1756. Mrs Delaney announced to her sister: 'The Duke of Norfolk's house in St. James's Square is finished and opened to the *grande monde* of London: 'I am asked for next Tuesday.' Horace Walpole was invited too, and left an inimitable description of the occasion:

All the earth was there. You would have thought there had been a comet, everybody was gazing in the air and treading on one another's toes. In short, you never saw such a scene of magnificence and taste. The tapestry, the embroidered bed, the illumination, the glasses, the lightness and novelty of the ornaments, and the ceilings are delightful.

He went on to quote a quip of Lord Rockingham's: 'Oh, there was all the company afraid of the Duchess, and the Duke afraid of all the company.'[27]

The good taste of the Duchess and the Duke's inclination for 'the cultivation of the fine arts', of which Norfolk House was so notable an expression, found an outlet in all the ducal properties: Arundel, London, Norwich, Sheffield and above all Worksop, the seat of seats. As already seen the Duke had established a Catholic chapel in Norwich on the site of the old palace. The Revd. Alban Butler

Worksop Manor, Nottinghamshire. The park front in 1745, the year the house was hurriedly vacated by the 9th Duke of Norfolk on the advance of the Young Pretender's Jacobite army.

was the priest there from 1745 till 1756 when he was appointed tutor to the Duke's nephew and heir-presumptive Thomas Howard, 'the Marcellus of the English Catholics'. Butler was a notable scholar whose *magnum opus*, *The Lives of the Saints*, was admired by Gibbon as 'a work of Merit, the sense and learning belong to the Author, his prejudices are those of his Profession'. A completely new chapel and priest's house were erected at Norwich in 1764 for the Revd. Edward Beaumont to the design of James Paine, an architect who was much employed by the Duke. The interior of the new chapel had an elegant segmentally coved ceiling with nice plasterwork and a gallery on columns at the west end.

Paine also redesigned the chapel at Arundel Castle as part of a scheme of renovation and redecoration of the rooms in the south wing in the 1760s. The Arundel chapel had a coved ceiling and an impressive white and gold altarpiece with Ionic columns and a pediment framing a Nativity by Benedetto Gennari from James II's chapel at Whitehall.

The Duke, partly because of his quiet life and lack of opportunity to waste money on political ventures such as the election campaigns which proved a drain on the purses of many eighteenth-century landowners, found himself in the happy position of getting richer all the time. The most important factor was the exploitation of the minerals and urban development of Sheffield on the northern estate, as industrialization gained momentum. The Duke commissioned splendid designs from Paine, and also from Thomas Atkinson, for laying out part of his estate with handsome squares and terraces; a start was made on building just before his death but the scheme was unfortunately abandoned and Sheffield never got its well-planned Georgian quarter.

The greatest portion of the increasing revenue was, however, poured into the embellishment of Worksop, the Duke's favourite estate. Before turning his attention to the house he had embarked on incredibly ambitious schemes for the park with the help of Lord Petre, an outstanding botanist and gardener. Petre's detailed planting scheme survives and is signed and dated 24 March 1738. The Duke also erected a number of decorative park buildings: a hemicycle, a Palladian Bridge and a Ziggurat as well as making a lake with two islands. This work continued for several years, over £1,000 a year being spent in 1743 to 1745. The Duke's gardening received an interruption in 1745 when the house was rapidly vacated on the approach of the Young Pretender's Jacobite army. Aware that he might fall under suspicion, the Duke went straight to London where he sought an interview with George II to pledge his loyalty.

In style and planting the garden at Worksop was of considerable interest, representing a transitional stage between the rigid geometry of the French school and the naturalism of the English, with a succession of glades and arenas of different shapes joined by serpentine walks. Lord Petre also made plans for adding wings to the house but these were not executed and the Duke and Duchess

Carved Rococo triptych made by John Cuenot as part of the furnishing of Norfolk House for the 9th Duke and Duchess of Norfolk.

contented themselves with a complete internal remodelling to James Paine's design. It was claimed that £12,000 a year was spent on these improvements over several years and that an army of workmen was kept constantly employed at Worksop. 'The Hall and all the apartments were newly finish'd by the present Duke of Norfolk. The Hall was Ornamented with Dorick Pil [asters] and Entablature, and the ceiling was extremely rich, as were those of the Apartments on the two Principal floors, all were design'd and finish'd under the direction of Mr. Paine.'[28]

The work was completed by summer 1761 and the Duke, now in his seventy-sixth year, gave a party in August at which the Duke of York was entertained with considerable splendour. The Norfolks then returned to London for the autumn. Hardly had they reached Norfolk House when news was brought to them of a terrible catastrophe. Worksop had been burnt to the ground and nearly all its contents destroyed. The fire had broken out in a small closet off the library and had soon got out of control. All the Duke's books, his special pride, were lost, also many of the paintings, most of the furniture and some statues from the Arundel Marbles recently excavated in London and sent to Worksop. The financial loss alone was computed at £100,000. The elderly Duke and Duchess received the news with stoical fortitude. The Duke said, 'God's will be done' and the Duchess said, 'How Many besides us are sufferers by the like calamity.'

The fire was the first of a series of blows to befall the elderly couple. Only a short time after, their nephew Thomas, son of Philip Howard of Buckenham by his first wife, and heir presumptive to the dukedom, died in Paris while on his Grand Tour with Fr. Alban Butler. However his half brother, called Edward after the Duke, and the son of Philip Howard by his second wife Henrietta Blount, sister of the Duchess, became the heir. As the nephew of both the Duke and the Duchess, he was their special favourite and almost more dear to them than a child of their own. So with him in mind the Duke and Duchess pushed on with their plans to rebuild Worksop on a scale which made it the largest country house commission since Blenheim. As at Norfolk House, the driving force was the Duchess. She had already designed a large Gothic farm called Castle Farm, which formed an eye-catcher in the view from the house. It was quadrangular, and as well as the usual offices contained the Duchess's dairy and a sitting-room for drinking tea where the Duchess kept most of her books on horticulture all bound up to match, and embossed on the spine in gold letters 'Castle Farm Worksop'. Horace Walpole referred to the farm in a letter to Sir Horace Mann in 1758: 'I am glad I am not in favour enough to be consulted by my Lord Duchess on the Gothic farm; she would have given me so many fine and unintelligible reasons why it should not be as it should be that I should have lost a little of my patience.'

The new house, designed by James Paine under the Duchess's supervision, was intended to be a visible proclamation of the Duke's position of premier duke.

Its plan is only paralleled in English architecture in the unexecuted schemes from Inigo Jones to William Kent and Sir William Chambers for royal palaces at Whitehall and Richmond. Worksop was to comprise a huge square block, each of its four fronts three hundred feet in length, with two internal courtyards divided by the central 'Egyptian Hall' 140 feet long. The north front was to contain the private apartments of the family, the south the main entrance and two state apartments, the east a Great Drawing-Room 130 feet long and the west a library 206 feet long.

The foundation-stone was laid on 25 March 1763 and the north range was covered in by July 1764, such was the speed of construction. Five hundred workmen were employed 'chiefly under the superintendence of the Duchess, who hardly quitted them'. Her plan was to concentrate on the north block making that habitable so that the family had a roof over its head, before embarking on the more ornamental and ceremonial parts of the building. This gave the Duchess much scope for her favourite activity of decorating and all the interior fitting up was done under her personal supervision. The rooms were neatly, rather than elaborately, decorated, each room with its co-ordinated colour scheme, the fabrics, wallpapers and upholstery matching as at Norfolk House. The First

William Hodges. Worksop Manor in 1777. This great house, designed by James Paine under the supervision of the Duchess of Norfolk to replace the Elizabethan mansion burnt in 1762, was never completed.

Drawing-Room was hung with crimson Lyons silk; the Great Drawing-Room had the Gobelins tapestry from Norfolk House brought to Worksop at this time, and the chairs were covered with needlework to match; the chairs in the dining-room were upholstered in red Morocco; the Duke and Duchess's bedrooms were hung with blue paper, while the bedrooms on the floor above had papers of different patterns, some of them Chinese. The staircase was painted in *trompe l'oeil* to represent sculptured panels of the Arts and Sciences by Theodore de Bruyn, a Flemish artist brought to England by the Duchess of Norfolk and who also painted decorative overdoors for the redecorated rooms at Arundel, now lost. De Bruyn stayed in England and among other schemes was responsible for the grisaille panels in the chapel of the Royal Naval Hospital at Greenwich, which still survive.

Several of the chimney-pieces and other architectural ornaments were designed by the Duchess herself including the sculpture in the pediments. Only that in the north pediment, showing the resurrection of Worksop after the fire, was executed; the south pediment with the 'Vision of Solomon' and the other ornaments, emblematic of the Howard family, remained ideas only. The office quadrangle, which survived the fire, was fronted with a new screen wall containing a triumphal arch in the middle; this was intended to support an equestrian statue of the 2nd Duke as victor of Flodden, but this was never installed.

All the work at Worksop ceased in 1767 when Edward Howard died, as a result of a fever caught while playing tennis after a bout of measles. The Duke and Duchess were deeply upset by the loss of their favourite nephew. The news 'affected the duchess almost to distraction . . . and she never recovered from the blow'. The next heir was a distant kinsman whom the Duke and Duchess hardly knew and though they invited his son Charles (afterwards the 11th Duke) to meet them, the contrast to their late nephew was so depressing that the poor Duchess burst into tears halfway through dinner and had to leave the room.

Having lost heart, the Duchess gave orders for building to cease and so only a third of the new Worksop was ever erected. Thomas Sandby, who visited it in 1774 to paint a picture of the menagerie, a decorative building in the park designed by the Duchess, was much impressed and commented on the overall scale of the project:

What then must the whole have been when compleated? too large surely for any Subject, and I am inclined to think the late Duchess of Norfolk began to think so herself; for, in her own handwriting, on the bottom of the plan, she says, that if the whole of that plan was finished, she wou'd still add one room more to it, wherein she might be confined as a mad woman.

This annotated drawing still hangs in the present house at Worksop which is formed out of the 8th Duke's court of offices, the incomplete Paine house having been demolished after its sale by the 12th Duke of Norfolk to the Duke of Newcastle in 1838. So it is only in Paine's engraved plans that the full scale of the 9th Duke's Worksop can now be appreciated. The only fragment of the new house still there, ironically, is the pediment which shows the resurrection of the house after the 1761 fire, now propped up on the ground near the site.[29]

The Duchess, though younger than her husband, died first in 1773; the Duke himself lived for ten years after the death of his nephew, dying in his ninety-second year at Norfolk House on 20 September 1777, and was buried at Arundel with his ancestors. He had continued active to the end, dressing fashionably, doing his own estate business as he had throughout his life as well as forming a new library of books to replace those lost in the Worksop fire, concentrating particularly on his own special interests: architecture, history, topography, the classics and horticulture. They remain the most substantial portion of the ten thousand books in the Duke of Norfolk's library at Arundel, and are a good example of informed eighteenth-century taste. Each book has the 9th Duke's bookplate together with a little printed card saying that it must remain an heirloom in the family forever.

The Duke, excluded from official Court and government positions, had for most of his life occupied his time by conducting his own estate business. The year before he died Lady Mary Coke reported that he had gone to Arundel to deal with the problem of sea encroachment on the Sussex estate as a result of the collapse of part of the sea-wall. Lady Mary Coke's journal gives the best impression of the Duke at the end of his long life. In September 1776 she called on him at Norfolk House where she found him in the company of the Spanish Ambassador. She was pleasantly surprised by the Duke's generosity, on being 'loaded with venison and fruit' when she left; 'how obliging at his time of life to have such attentions'. On another visit in the same month she found the Duke wearing a dark suit, thought he must be in mourning

and ask'd who it was for, 'I am not in mourning' said the Duke; 'yours is then the fashionable colour?' 'I believe I am, at least I told my taylor to make such a suit of Clothes in whatever colour was the most fashionable.' Is it not charming at ninety three years of age to desire to be in the fashion?[30]

There is something very touching about the last years of the 9th Duke's life, soldiering on to the end when, in Tierney's words, he had lived 'to behold the wreck of much that could have endeared existence to him', his wife and nephews already dead and the knowledge that the 'honours of his family were about to pass away from his own line to settle on that of a distant relative'.[31] On his death the Earldom of Norwich and the Barony of Howard of Castle Rising (both granted to the 6th Duke) became extinct, while the Baronies of Mowbray and Howard created by writ, and which could therefore pass through the female line, fell into abeyance between his nieces and descended to Lords Stourton and Petre, the Barony of Mowbray eventually being successfully claimed by Lord Stourton. The dukedom and the other titles in tail male passed to the next remaining branch of the Howards, the descendant of Charles Howard of the Deepdene and Greystoke, 4th son of Henry Frederick, Earl of Arundel.

The Greystoke Dukes

THE new Duke of Norfolk, Charles 10th Duke, was fifty-seven years old and a somewhat morose eccentric man, addicted to history, genealogy, gardening and claret. Nicknamed Anacreon by some of his contemporaries because of his preference for simple country life and facility with his pen, he was, in his own words, 'A whig Papist – a monster in nature.' Though a practising Catholic he believed strongly that religion had nothing to do with politics and resented his own exclusion from public life because of his personal religious beliefs. It was one thing to be a plain country gentleman, happily occupied with his own affairs, and altogether another to be an enormously rich duke unable to exercise the privileges of his rank or to play his allotted part in public life.

His elevation to a dizzy pinnacle at the head of the peerage and the accession to vast estates, instead of bringing him happiness seems ironically to have enhanced a natural tendency towards melancholia, and the contrast with what ought to have been exacerbated his distaste for the realities of contemporary life. 'I withdraw my eyes from hateful scenes of war and slaughter and retire to the tranquillity of my villa at Dibden (Deepdene) which I am now endeavouring to restore to its primitive state of rural elegance', he had written shortly after the spectacularly successful conclusion of the Seven Years War with its great conquests for the British Empire in East and West.

His character was perhaps best suited to modest seclusion and he never properly adapted to his new role, preferring to live quietly in his own house at the Deepdene rather than palatial Worksop, spending the summer in Surrey and the winter at Norfolk House. It would be wrong however to see him as a bucolic simpleton mooching ill at ease through the gilded state apartments of his predecessor, like the hermit pope Celestine V. On the contrary he was an intelligent, well-informed man, educated at the English College at Douai at a time when such denominational establishments were more efficacious than the moribund public schools and universities in England. He had an interest in the 'polite arts' and music, the latter shared with his wife, whose will makes mention

R. E. Pine. Charles,
10th Duke of Norfolk
(1720–86). Painted in
1784.

of her pianofortes and harpsichord. He was a Fellow of the Society of Antiquaries and the Royal Society, as well as being the author of several books which, though slightly pedantic, are not lacking in humour. The earliest, *The Memorial of Charles Howard Esq. of Greystock, and Miss Frances Howard of the Family of Norfolk of England*, was published in 1763 as a statement of his claim (under the 13th article of the Treaty of Utrecht which enabled Englishmen to inherit property in France), to the participation in the estate of an intestate Frenchman, Michel Toublet, a cousin of his mother's. Two other books, *Considerations on the Penal Laws against Roman Catholics in England and the new-acquired Colonies in America* (1764) and *Thoughts, Essays and Maxims, chiefly Religious and Political* (1768), summed up his views on the contemporary religious and political situation in England. But the most interesting of his writings is the *Historical Anecdotes of the Howard Family* (1769) dedicated to his son: 'These historical anecdotes of some of your ancestors are inscribed as patterns worthy of your imitation.' It was originally intended as an introduction to a new edition of the poems of the Earl of Surrey, but finding that Horace Walpole was already engaged on a similar project he expanded his memoir of the 'Poet Earl' to cover other members of the family and published it as an independent volume. It contains fascinating information, for example, about the Collector Earl and the dispersal of his collection, as well as the history of the 10th Duke's immediate ancestors, the Howards of Greystoke.

His grandfather, the Hon. Charles Howard, was the fourth son of Henry Frederick Earl of Arundel, and had had settled on him in 1652 the manor of Dorking in Surrey including the Deepdene. The Hon. Charles Howard was also able to secure to his own line of the family, as a result of a lawsuit against his brother Henry, the 6th Duke, in 1681, the Greystoke estate in Cumberland (which had come to the Howards in the sixteenth century through the marriage of St. Philip Howard, Earl of Arundel, to Anne Dacre, daughter and co-heiress of Lord Dacre of Gilsland). Though the Greystoke estate formed the basis of his territorial position and provided most of his income, it was the Deepdene which he made his home. There he built a single-storeyed cottage, described by Aubrey as a 'noble hermitage', with an oratory and laboratory, and laid out a famous garden admired by both Aubrey and Evelyn. In these arcadian surroundings he initiated the pattern of scholarly rural retirement that the 10th Duke also adopted in his own life. He pursued studies in chemistry and natural philosophy, experimented with the cultivation of saffron and a new method of tanning leather, on both of which subjects he contributed papers to the Royal Society, and formed a collection of dried wild flowers or herbarium, which he arranged in the alphabetical order of their Latin names in a leather-bound volume still at Arundel.

His garden was his principal achievement; it was of fifteen acres set in a natural amphitheatre, the sides terraced and planted with thyme, cherry trees and myrtle with some topiary but no statues; in the hillside were caves for the cool storage of beer for summer picnics. Aubrey thought the whole ensemble worthy of a pastoral poem and wrote a long description of the 'rare flowers and choice plants', the ingenious layout with avenues and 'boscages', and the 'two pretty lads his gardeners, who wonderfully delight in this occupation and this lovely solitude, and do enjoy themselves so innocently in that pleasant corner, as if they were out of this troublesome world, and seem to live in a state of innocency,' and summed up by describing the Deepdene as 'an epitome of Paradise . . . neat, elegant and suitable to the modesty and retirement of the proprietor, a Christian philosopher'.[1]

On his death in 1713 at the age of eighty-three the Hon. Charles Howard was succeeded by his eldest son Henry Charles, who had already been in occupation of Greystoke for a number of years and had built a new Baroque front on to the castle in 1710. He was a Jacobite, though not very active, and, as already seen, was one of the hardliners responsible for thwarting George I's attempt to secure some sort of concordat for his Catholic subjects. The 10th Duke, in an interesting attempt to protect his father's memory, attributes his own Whig-Papist views to his father in the *Anecdotes* and claims that Henry Charles was a supporter of Dr Strickland, but as the 12th Duke's chaplain Tierney has shown this is contradicted by the surviving documents. Henry Charles married Mary Aylward, the daughter of a London merchant and banker of Irish descent and it was their son Charles who became the 10th Duke.[2]

He inherited Greystoke and the Deepdene on the death of his father in 1720 and on both estates indulged his taste for gardening. At Greystoke he landscaped the grounds, damming the beck behind the castle to form a lake spanned by a pretty Chinese bridge (long since disappeared). At the Deepdene he bought some adjoining land and enlarged the property to a hundred acres, altering the garden and building a new house to the design of William Gowan, an obscure London surveyor, in the years 1768–75. The new house was a severe Palladian affair of thirteen bays with a central canted bow window, behind which was the drawing-room on the first floor taking advantage of the view, while on the ground floor were four principal rooms: a library, breakfast-room, dining-room and billiard-room. It was not a particularly enlightened piece of architectural patronage and it was the garden that really expressed the taste of the Duke and his wife Catherine, the daughter of John Brockholes of Claughton, Lancashire, an old Catholic family. She looks formidable in her portrait, even by the standards of eighteenth-century duchesses, but must have had a softer side as she was reported 'very fond' of gardens and was responsible for building the hermitage at the Deepdene 'with all the humble requisites for a holy anchorite'.[3]

Such was the 10th Duke's life and background before he became 'one of the highest rank of men – the least significant of Dukes'. As for his reign as Duke, Causton wrote dismissively: 'The repose of his short tenure of nine years was unbroken by any great act of nobility, of public scandal, or private censure.'[4] He was, however, responsible for two acts which determined the character and future of the family, though at the time they seemed modest enough. In 1778, along with other leading English Catholics, he signed the petition to George III which resulted in the first measure of religious relief and made the construction of Catholic places of worship legal. This was the harbinger of the complete emancipation which came in the early nineteenth century and opened the way for the unique and important role of the nineteenth-century Dukes of Norfolk in the English Catholic revival. The 10th Duke's other epoch-making decision was his private Act of Parliament in 1783 to secure the revenues from the renewal of the leases of the Strand estate in London for the restoration of Arundel Castle, thus securing its future as the principal ducal seat which it still remains. The 10th

Duke himself did not live long enough to take advantage of this and died, of drink, at Norfolk House on 31 August 1786; he was buried at Dorking.

There could be no greater contrast between the quiet hermit-like 10th Duke and his son Charles who succeeded him. The 11th Duke of Norfolk was a larger-than-life extrovert, coarse, aggressive, well-intentioned and generous; an Anglican, a Foxite Whig, friend of the Prince Regent, in taste a product of the Gothic North; Horace Walpole's 'Solomon' and Creevey's 'Jockey', known to posterity as 'the Protestant Duke' or the 'Drunken Duke'; a man whose inelegant figure, big and stout with immense whiskers, is so vividly described in the pages of contemporary diarists and letter-writers. 'Nature which cast him in her coarsest mould, had not bestowed on him any of the external insignia of high descent. His person large, muscular, and clumsy, was destitute of grace or dignity ... He might indeed have been mistaken for a grazier or butcher.'[5] Even the peculiarities of his pronunciation have come down to us – 'Airundel' for Arundel, 'Gairter' for Garter, 'Daiety' for Deity. Unwashed, sodden with claret, bubbling with contradictory ideas, a feudal-republican, he passed through life surrounded by parasites and illegitimate children, cheerful in his apostasy: 'I cannot be a good Catholic; I cannot go to heaven; and if a man is to go to the devil, he may as well go thither from the House of Lords as from any other place on Earth.'[6]

In many ways he is a figure more sympathetic to late twentieth-century taste than to Victorian writers, for whom he was the acme of all they most despised in the aristocracy, certainly not a Christian Gentleman. The nineteenth-century historian Causton dismissed him as 'vulgar in his ideas, licentious in his habits, coarse in his manners, vicious in his tastes, ungenerous in his patronage', and expressed the deepest disapproval of two rather pleasant attributes of his character: his 'deplorable' habit of drinking a toast to the prettiness of the ladies' maids after dinner and his preference for shabby old clothes, lack of hair powder and a threadbare coat of dirty plum-colour. 'A studied neglect of dress, even to a striking and grotesque singularity – a rude inelegance proper for a low and penurious sphere of life – seemed a trap for petty distinction – to excite inquiry and then surprise by the answer.'[7] But most detestable of all was the Duke's seeming hypocrisy in posing as a champion of liberal reform on the one hand, while trafficking in rotten boroughs on the other. He charged £4,000 each for the parliamentary seats in his patronage and considered it a great act of generosity to his penniless friend Sheridan to offer him one for a mere £3,000.

The Duke, like most rich, privileged 'liberals' was a mass of contradictions, and many of his points of view were not philosophically consistent or even rationally based, but this need not necessarily detract from a fair assessment of his character and achievement. Henry Howard of Corby, who knew him and had benefited from his generosity, painted a glowing portrait of the Duke, stressing his superior judgement, warmth of heart, good temper, fairness and indulgence to

ɔmas Gainsborough. Charles, 11th Duke of Norfolk (1746–1815).

others and particularly praising his disinterested behaviour to his third cousin and successor Bernard Edward, the 12th Duke. He did not hesitate 'in cramping his own enjoyments by leaving to his successors, though not nearly connected with him' the whole of the ducal patrimony intact and improved: Arundel, Worksop, Sheffield, Norfolk House and the Strand estate in London, Kenninghall and all the other estates, manors and properties which had accumulated over the centuries.[8]

The 11th Duke had spent his youth in Cumberland and it remained his favourite property throughout his life. It was the rugged northern landscape and the Dacre–Howard castles and traditions which nurtured his interest in the Picturesque and the Gothic Revival. Like his father, he was educated at Douai, but in 1780 at the age of thirty-four he conformed to the Established Church in order to contest an election at Carlisle, where he had already formed a party of Whig supporters against the all-powerful Tory interest of the Lowthers, Earls of Lonsdale, and he played an active part in politics for the rest of his life. He was elected MP for Carlisle in 1780 and immediately aligned himself in opposition to Lord North; he was made a Lord of the Treasury in the Rockingham administration of 1783, as well as Lord Lieutenant of the West Riding of Yorkshire. The following year, however, when Rockingham resigned and George III turned to Shelburne to form a new administration, he followed Fox into opposition and remained a Foxite for the rest of his life, becoming chairman of the Whig Club, but never holding office again. He adopted the stance of an advanced radical and, for example, strongly supported Dunning's motion 'That the influence of the Crown has increased, is increasing and ought to be diminished.'

He was not a good orator but was a forceful and aggressive speaker. After he succeeded to the dukedom in 1786 he attended regularly at the House of Lords and took a particularly keen interest in bills concerned with local and personal matters, paying great attention to divorce cases; 'he was always particularly solicitous to obtain a suitable provision for the unhappy female who had deviated from the strict line of chastity'. He had good reason to take a sympathetic interest in other people's marriages as the outcome of both his own was tragic. His first marriage, a love-match as a young man, was to Marian Coppinger, daughter of John Coppinger of Ballyvoolane, Co. Cork, in August 1767 but she died giving birth to a stillborn baby nine months later. His second marriage, in April 1771, to Frances Scudamore, daughter and heiress of Charles Fitzroy Scudamore of Holme Lacy, Herefordshire was perhaps even more unhappy in its outcome. The Scuda-mores had a strain of hereditary madness which shortly after the wedding made its appearance in the Duchess and she had to be confined as a lunatic at Holme Lacy for the whole of her life. She outlived the Duke by five years so it was impossible for him to remarry or to have a legitimate son to succeed him. He consoled himself with a series of mistresses, one of whom eventually became his 'official' mistress, Mary Gibbon, grand-daughter of the Dean of Carlisle and cousin of Edward Gibbon. They had five children, two of whom were appointed to the College of Arms as heralds. Edward Howard Howard-Gibbon (1799-1849) was in turn Mowbray, York and Norroy Herald and Earl Marshal's secretary. He was allowed by the 13th Duke of Norfolk to add the name and arms of Howard by Royal Licence with 'due distinction of illegitimacy'. His elder brother Matthew Charles Howard Gibbon (1796-1873) was Richmond Herald and lived near Arundel. A daughter, Mary Eliza, is buried near her father at Dorking and some of the Howard Gibbons later emigrated to Canada where their descendants still live.[9]

The 11th Duke's other great parliamentary interest was the committee for privileges, which appealed more to the feudal than the liberal streak in his make-up and which he considered part of his official business as Earl Marshal to attend. He had been appointed deputy Earl Marshal by his father in 1782 and on succession to the dukedom, as an Anglican, had been able to play his full role as Earl Marshal. Of all his family honours, the one he most prized was the Earl Marshal's Staff; he never appeared without it on any great occasion and his various portraits show him 'dangling the official baton in an attitude not remarkable either for grace or dignity'. In his attitude to claims before the committee of privileges he allowed his mind to be 'too much engrossed by the phantom of the exclusive greatness of the Howards' and did his best to stamp on the *nouveau* pretensions of more mushroom dynasties.[10]

He was a consistent opponent of the slave-trade and strongly favoured parliamentary reform, those two great rallying causes of the Foxite Whigs. But as already seen he did not allow the latter to stop him trafficking in boroughs. He used his own position as well as that of his wife's family to acquire a dominant interest in a number of parliamentary boroughs. He went about this in two ways, one of them by currying personal popularity and the other, simpler but more expensive, buying out the whole place. Gloucester is a good example of the former, and Horsham of the latter. At Gloucester the Duke made great efforts to win control by personal popularity, condescending to be elected mayor in 1810, renting a house in the city, giving lavish 'turtle dinners' to the Corporation and hobnobbing with the local shopkeepers, displaying the easy democratic manners of a Whig duke, calling on the baker, the butcher and the candlestick-maker for a glass of port or home-brewed beer and bread and cheese. At Horsham, on the other hand, he spent a fortune in acquiring the dominant political interest in the borough, which returned two members to parliament 'elected' by fifty-two 'burgesses', the owners of fifty-two houses within the ancient borough boundary. From the moment of his accession he set about buying these burgage houses, first those owned by the Irwins and finally in 1811 acquiring the Marquess of Hertford's share for £90,000, thus gaining complete control. The ducal position was further strengthened by the enclosure of the common. This hard-won control was affected, but not destroyed, by the Great Reform Act of 1832 which enlarged the constituency, but the voters of Horsham remained amenable to the ducal interest down to the Secret Ballot Act of 1872 and beyond.[11]

The 11th Duke was aware of the ambivalence of his position in posing as a champion of reform against such reprehensible Tory boroughmongers as the Earl of Lonsdale, while shamelessly buying and selling parliamentary seats and influence as if they were a species of private property. But he excused himself with the argument that while the present system was in force he had no option but to take part in it and that he would freely surrender his rights should the better system, which he hoped for, prevail.

In matters of religion the Duke was naturally liberal and for instance advocated complete freedom of worship for the Catholics in Ireland. His own Protestantism was no more than an adopted stance and rapidly slipped when he was drunk, as noted by Wraxall: 'When under the dominion of wine he has asserted that three as good Catholics sat in Lord North's last Parliament as ever existed, namely Lord Nugent, Sir Thomas Gascoigne and himself.'[12] George III was not deceived either; when the Duke, Thomas Carter and Sir Henry Englefield ganged together to ensure that James Wyatt 'the Destroyer' was blackballed from the Society of Antiquaries, he referred to it jocularly as a 'popish plot'. The Duke maintained his father's stipends to Catholic priests and kept open the Catholic chapels at Greystoke and Arundel Castles, merely moving them from the main house to one of the outbuildings. Nevertheless the conformity of the Earl of Surrey (as he then was), the heir to the chief Catholic family, was a great blow to the cause of the English Catholics. It has generally been considered to mark the nadir of the Church in England and was the immediate cause for Thomas Berington's book *The Present State of the Catholics in England* which analysed the decline of the Church in England in the eighteenth century. Perhaps more important for the future was that the defection of so important a member at that particular moment weakened the position of the Catholic laity leaving the lead to be taken by the clergy, a fact soon grasped and exploited by Bishop John Milner who deplored the cisalpine tendencies of the English Catholic gentry and strove to inject a strong dose of ultramontanism into the waning Church.

The Duke was generous and hospitable. At Arundel he had individual suites of rooms for his friends with their names painted on the door outside, such as 'Mr. Fox's Room'. His entertaining at his various houses was apt to be rowdy and drunken, due no doubt to the absence of the civilizing influence of a duchess. He, together with the Prince Regent, is reputed to have established the later hour for dinner, sitting down at six-thirty rather than three o'clock in the afternoon as had been the custom in the eighteenth century. The wine was good and the food plain, in the best English tradition. Creevey enjoyed the Duke's dinners, which were boisterous and jolly, and the conversation 'in the first style: the subjects infinitely various, from bawdy to the depths of politics' though he did add that at Norfolk House there wanted 'a few comforts – such as a necessary, towels, water etc. etc. to make the thing compleat'.[13] The Duke was noted for the vast quantities of claret and beer he could put away in an evening. 'Whoever has seen his massive silver porter cup full will wonder how a man of these degenerate days could lift it to his mouth.' Descriptions of his drinking achievements are legion and it will suffice to quote two, both at Brighton Pavilion. Creevey witnessed the first at Brighton in 1805:

It used to be the Duke of Norfolk's custom to come over every year from Arundel to pay his respects to the Prince and to stay two days at Brighton, both of which he always dined at the Pavilion. In the year 1804 upon this annual visit, the Prince had drunk so much as to be made very seriously ill by it so that in 1805 (the year that I was there) when the Duke came, Mrs. Fitzherbert, who was always the Prince's best friend was very much afraid of him being again made ill, and She persuaded the Prince to adopt different stratagems to avoid drinking with the Duke. I dined there on both days and letters were brought in each day after dinner to the Prince, which he affected to consider of great importance, and so went out to answer them, while the Duke of Clarence went on drinking with the Duke of Norfolk. But on the second day this joke was carried too far, and in the evening the Duke of Norfolk showed that he was affronted. The Prince took me aside and said – 'Stay after everyone is gone to-night. The Jockey's got sulky, and I must give him a boiled bone to get him in a good humour again.' So of course I stayed, and about one o'clock the Prince of Wales and Duke of Clarence, the Duke of Norfolk and myself sat down to a supper of boiled bones, the result of which was that, having fallen asleep myself I was awoke by the sound of the Duke of Norfolk's snoring.[14]

Thackeray describes a later drinking contest at the Pavilion where the Prince of Wales comes across as less good-hearted considering the difference in age between himself and the Duke:

Every person at table was enjoined to drink wine with the Duke – a challenge which the old toper did not refuse. He soon began to see that there was a conspiracy against him; he drank glass for glass; he overthrew many of the brave. At last the First Gentleman of Europe proposed bumpers of brandy. One of the royal brothers filled a great glass for the Duke. He stood up and tossed off the drink. 'Now,' says he, 'I will have my carriage and go home' . . . when his postchaise was announced, he staggered to it as well as he could, and stumbling in, bade the postilions drive to Arundel. They drove him for half an hour round and round the Pavilion lawn; the poor old man fancied he was going home. When he awoke that morning he was in bed at the Prince's hideous house at Brighton.[15]

The Duke was notorious for his aversion to soap and water and it was only when he was insensible with drink after dinner that his servants were able to get him into a bathtub and give him a good scrub. This was all light-hearted enough, but the trouble with his excessive drinking was that he tended to say things under the influence of alcohol which he later regretted, and sometimes there were serious repercussions. The most notorious occasion was at a dinner of the Whig Club in the Crown and Anchor Tavern to celebrate Fox's birthday on 24 January 1798, at a time when England was at war with Revolutionary France and Pitt's Government was ready to see subversive Jacobins behind every bush, if not beneath every coronet. Staggering to his feet after dinner to propose the customary toast to the King, the Duke announced: 'Our Sovereign's health – the majesty of the people.' George III was not amused, nor was the Government, and the upshot was that the Duke was dismissed from all his official positions including the Lord Lieutenancy of the West Riding.[16] The notification of his dismissal was brought to him at Norfolk House while the Prince of Wales was dining with him. Seeing the official letter from the Duke of Portland and Norfolk's change of expression, the Prince asked, 'What's up?' 'Read it', replied the Duke; and they both burst out laughing. The Duke subsequently did his best to explain away his behaviour in audience with George III at a levée, and the King expressed himself satisfied with exclamations of loyalty but it was not till January 1807 that he was officially reinstated; at that time he was appointed Lord Lieutenant of Sussex which he remained till the end of his life.[17]

An aspect of the Duke's character which does him credit was his generosity to young artists, scholars and writers. He appointed James Dallaway to be Earl Marshal's secretary at the College of Arms on the strength of a book he had written on heraldry which the Duke had read and admired. He financed both Dallaway's *History of the Western Division of Sussex* and Duncomb's *History of the County of Hereford*. He used his influence to get places for scholars he knew, writing generous references for anybody whose work he admired. A request for one such survives from an unexpected quarter after the Gordon Riots:

Lord George Gordon presents his compliments to the Duke of Norfolk and hopes His Grace is well. Lord George requests that His Grace will do him the Favour to acquaint him with the character of Mr. David Pugh, who has been introduced to Lord George as a literary and discerning man; but Lord George having heared that he was once in the service of His Grace as an Antiquarian and Librarian would be glad to know if he conducted himself with propriety, as Lord George's situation obliges him, having only one apartment, to make all his visitors, more or less, Table Companions.

Newgate.   Wednesday Morning.   Dec. 15th 1790.[18]

He interceded unsuccessfully for Shelley with the poet's irascible father, a neighbour in Sussex, and was extremely generous to Sheridan to whom he lent the Deepdene for some time before eventually selling it in 1790. When Sheridan left, he forgot the manuscript of his great speech at the trial of Warren Hastings in Westminster Hall, which had taken him five and a half hours to deliver and had

William Daniell. The quadrangle at Arundel Castle as reconstructed by the 11th Duke of Norfolk to his own design. On the left can be seen C. F. Rossi's 'exceedingly frightful' Coade stone relief of the institution of trial by jury by King Alfred. This picture is one of a set commissioned by the 12th Duke and exhibited at the Royal Academy, 1823.

Catherine Lyons. Watercolour view of the library at Arundel Castle in 1858 with the children of the 14th Duke of Norfolk.

made his reputation as a parliamentary orator. It was only when the 11th Duke died that Sheridan remembered he had left his manuscript behind and wrote to the Duke's executor Henry Howard of Corby who returned it to him, the late Duke having carefully preserved it. Sheridan was therefore able to reread his speech after an interval of twenty-five years with 'melancholy pride'.[19]

In the management of his estates the Duke showed a strain of shrewdness in dealing with tradesmen and business affairs that was probably inherited from his maternal merchant ancestors. He abandoned the 9th Duke's grand but unrealistic plan for Sheffield, realizing that what was perfect for Bath would not necessarily pay off in a smoky manufacturing town with a largely artisan population. He adopted the policy of *laissez-faire* but not inhumane management in Sheffield which determined the nineteenth-century character of the city as a place of unimaginative, but well-built, three- or four-room terraced brick cottages and small steel workshops; an entity that worked as an economic and social unit for a century and a half, though it was in no way a worthy architectural response to the noble landscape setting, perhaps the finest of any English city. He sold outright a portion of the town centre, including a site for the new General Infirmary at a specially low price, and used the proceeds to extend and improve the estates at Greystoke and Arundel, restoring the castles, creating the parks, planting trees and erecting interesting subsidiary buildings. In both cases he determined the present form of the estates and it is this which is his most long-lasting and worthwhile achievement.

At Greystoke he bought the adjoining smaller estates of Blencow, Greenthwaite and Johnby and added them to the Great Park making it up to five thousand acres, the largest in England, a deliberate challenge to Lord Lonsdale whose park at Lowther was a derisory four thousand acres. He encircled the new park with a stone wall and planted two hundred thousand trees making great use of the larch, then still something of a novelty in Cumberland.

He enlarged and remodelled the castle in the Gothick taste, largely to his own design, though he employed a local mason called Nixon to carry out his ideas. Most of his work at the castle has now disappeared, the main part having been remodelled by Salvin in the mid-nineteenth century and the subsidiary wing being demolished after the Second World War in order to make the castle more manageable. The 11th Duke's wonderfully dotty model farms, built in 1778 when the land east of the castle was enclosed, still survive and are named after events and personalities connected with the American War of Independence in order to cause maximum annoyance to Tory neighbours: Fort Putnam, Bunker Hill, Jefferson. They are all castellated in a highly entertaining way and are a monument to the Duke's sense of humour and political views as well as his enthusiasm for Gothic architecture. The most distinctive of them, Spire House, has a spire on top and was built as a practical joke on the tenant who belonged to a religious sect which worshipped in the open air and who had begun to bore the whole neighbourhood with his views on the lack of need for churches.

On a detached portion of the Cumberland estate overlooking Ullswater the Duke built a charming castellated folly called Lyulph's Tower after the legendary Saxon hero who is reported to have given his name to the lake. It is three-sided with little octagonal towers and was intended for shooting picnics and rural drinking parties. Enormous eighteenth-century claret bottles are still found there from time to time.

The Duke's greatest achievement, however, was his restoration of Arundel Castle and it is his work there that places him in the ranks of leading late eighteenth-century Gothic builders and collectors alongside Horace Walpole and William Beckford. His work at Arundel was specially notable because he acted largely as his own architect and showed a precocious interest in the revival of Norman architecture. As an amateur architect of some competence he deserves to be remembered. He turned his attention to the project as soon as he inherited and in the early stages before his own mind was made up he consulted various professional architects and experts on Gothic art about his proposals. In 1787 a correspondent of Richard Gough, the Oxford antiquary, reported while visiting Cumberland that 'At Greystoke Castle I found Mr. Hiorne the gothic architect whom the Duke of Norfolk had invited to consult with, relative to his intended repairs at Arundel Castle and we made a party to see Alnwick Castle etc. in Northumberland for Mr. Hiorne's information.' A prospect tower erected in Arundel park to Hiorne's design in 1787 is still called after him and gives a clear impression of what Hiorne's castle would have looked like. However, he died before his plans could be carried into effect, which was perhaps just as well, for, according to Dallaway, they would have involved the demolition of much of the original layout. Another Gothic expert consulted by the Duke was the ageing Horace Walpole, who in 1794 recommended to him James Wyatt, the most fashionable architect of the day, then restoring Windsor Castle for George III. The Duke, however, had no very high opinion of 'the Destroyer' and in the event he carried out his great scheme largely to his own ideas. 'After having long resolved in his own mind the idea of such a building, and resolved its various plans, he entrusted them for execution, solely to his ingenious master mason, and consulted none of the modern architects who have undertaken to revive the style and commanding effect of ancient English castles.'[20] This master mason was John Teasdale and, like the other craftsmen employed at Arundel, he came from Greystoke and had been sent to London at the Duke's expense to train under leading sculptors and architects, an unusual act of patronage. John Teasdale was assisted by his son, also John, who later moved to London to work on the restoration of Henry VII's chapel at Westminster so that his skills fostered by the Duke were of general benefit. Another Teasdale, James, acted as a surveyor and

The entrance hall and staircase at Arundel Castle built by the 11th Duke of Norfolk in 1796 and since replaced. From a nineteenth-century photograph.

Hiorne's Tower in Arundel Park, built by the 11th Duke to the design of Francis Hiorne of Warwick in 1787 as a trial run for his restoration of the castle.

drew the plans under the Duke's direction. The woodcarvers were Jonathan Ritson senior and junior whose excellent naturalistic capitals and bosses in the library can still be admired. After finishing at Arundel Ritson junior moved to another Sussex house, Petworth, where the 3rd Earl of Egremont employed him to restore the Grinling Gibbons carvings.

Before starting work on the castle the Duke made the park and landscaped the surroundings, creating the magnificent setting which still largely exists. The old park, sometimes known as the Rewell Wood, lay to the west of the town of Arundel completely separated from the castle. It was converted into the home farm and in its place the Duke bought 1,145 acres of rabbit-warren and rough grazing, previously in different ownership, adjoining the castle to the north; he enclosed it and created the present park from scratch. This ambitious project involved a three-mile diversion of the London road as well as considerable planting of forest trees, new drives, lodges and a boundary wall. The former mill-pond at Swanbourne was enlarged to form an ornamental lake. Dallaway described the results of the Duke's endeavours as 'presenting scenes worthy of Claude Lorraine or G. Smith'. The new park was freely open to the public from the start, as it has been ever since apart from a short period in the nineteenth century when it was shut by the 13th Duke. The castle was also opened to the public one day a week by the 11th Duke for a small charge, and the proceeds given to the poor.

The restoration of the building was drawn out over a long period and was the chief occupation of the Duke's leisure during the last twenty-five years of his life. Work began in 1791 with the addition of the south-east tower and proceeded methodically with the reconstruction of the south wing, containing the principal rooms, from 1795. The reconstruction of the east (library) wing began in 1801 and the ruins remaining from the Civil War on the west side of the quadrangle were cleared in 1806 and the foundation stone laid for the new 'Barons' Hall' and chapel. The substantial remains of the medieval castle: the barbican, gatehouse, shell keep on its conical mound, and the curtain walls round the upper bailey were left in a state of picturesque decay mantled with ivy and inhabited by a special breed of owls 'as large as eagles . . . with enormous eyes' introduced from America (another sign of the Duke's republican sympathies?) and now extinct, though several of them were stuffed. They all had political nicknames, for example, 'the Barons of the Exchequer' and 'Lord Thurlow'. The latter was the source of a typical country-house joke when the butler solemnly announced in the presence of suitably astonished guests, 'Your Grace, Lord Thurlow has laid an egg.'

The architectural style of the new parts of the castle was determined by the Duke's Whig principles; it was a hybrid of Perpendicular Gothic and Norman (then called 'Saxon') which were associated in the Duke's eyes with ancient liberty, and the whole building was in one sense intended to be a temple of liberty, a fact made clear (in Latin) on the foundation-stone: 'Charles Howard Duke of Norfolk, Earl of Arundel in the year of Christ 1806 in the sixtieth year of his age dedicated this stone to Liberty asserted by the Barons in the reign of John'. This theme was continued in the sculpture, painted decorations and stained glass, all of which celebrated the triumph of liberty over royal tyranny. Much of the sculpture was executed in Coade stone, a modern material which the Duke, as president of the Royal Society of Arts, adopted with enthusiastic relish. The *chef d'œuvre* was a large Coade relief of 'King Alfred instituting trial by jury on Salisbury Plain'. It was sculpted by J. C. F. Rossi in 1797 and dominated one side of the courtyard: Mrs Charles Stothard described it as an 'exceedingly frightful object', and it so embarrassed later generations with its blatant historical solecism that it was banished to a corner of the park and eventually used as foundations for a cricket pavilion.

The Duke's jolly stained glass windows were also a source of embarrassment to Victorian eyes. That in the Barons' Hall, 'the Great Norfolk Window', was designed by J. Lonsdale and made by Joseph Backler. It depicted King John 'with an expression of strong revulsion' being forced to sign Magna Carta by the Barons, all portraits of the Duke, his relations and friends. But it was the dining-room window which caused the deepest blushes. Designed by William Hamilton and made by Francis Eginton, it showed the entertainment of a buxom Queen of Sheba by King Solomon, in which Solomon was a portrait of the Duke, hence Horace Walpole's nickname for him.[21]

These windows, like much of the 11th Duke's work, were removed later in the nineteenth century, but his finest interior at Arundel, the noble library a hundred and twelve feet long, was rightly admired and survives as designed by him. It is fitted out entirely in carved mahogany like an inflated wooden model for a Gothic church. Here he brought together the 9th Duke's books and added many purchases of his own which included several of the most interesting and valuable books now in the library. He was known in his day as a bibliophile 'distinguished among the cognoscenti and amateurs'. He specialized in sixteenth- and early seventeenth-century English printed books of which he bought many including a first folio of Shakespeare, but also acquired several beautiful fifteenth-century illuminated manuscripts such as a version of Lydgate's 'Life of St. Edmund' (annotated by the sixteenth-century antiquary John Stow), making important purchases at Richardson's sale in 1803 and the Duke of Roxburghe's sale in 1812, where on both occasions he bid in person. This love of fine books is another facet of the 11th Duke's character which deserves to be recalled as an antidote to the prejudiced view of him as just a coarse drunkard.

The 11th Duke also began the process of buying back, having copied, or specially commissioning paintings and objects related to the Howard family and their history, a process which has continued down to the present and has reassembled at Arundel a family collection which while not in the same league as the Collector Earl's, is nevertheless one of the most fascinating surviving accumulations of late eighteenth- and nineteenth-century antiquarian taste.

The high point, not to say apotheosis, of the 11th Duke's career was the entertainment he arranged at Arundel in June 1815 to celebrate the six hundredth anniversary of the signing of Magna Carta, an event which coincided with the Duchess of Richmond's ball before the Battle of Waterloo, though it was some days before the news of Wellington's victory reached Sussex. This party was an interesting antiquarian event 'intended to renew and exhibit . . . "the pomp of olden days"' and preceded the Eglinton Tournament by about sixteen years. The new Barons' Hall was 'got up with all the upholstery necessary for the occasion' and the walls hung with 'arras' and bits of armour. The Magna Carta window was illuminated from outside to enhance the medieval spectacle and emphasize the *raison d'être* for the jollifications. The Duke gave a dinner for seventy-four people including twenty-three representatives of the different branches of the Howards – Norfolk, Suffolk, Carlisle and Effingham – followed by a ball and supper for a hundred and sixty guests. Twenty-five cooks were specially hired for the occasion and eighteen turtles, three oxen and five calves were consumed in the course of the evening.

Twenty genuine suits of armour were acquired from the Marquess Townshend, whose father had been a president of the Society of Antiquaries and an expert on medieval armour. Professional armourers were engaged from Birmingham to repair these and arrange them in all the majesty of ancient warfare. 'It was at first intended that the duke and barons should equip themselves in these awful habiliments of war; but on examining them they were found in so dilapidated a state that the idea was abandoned.' Instead the two best ones were hung on dummies to guard the elaborately accoutred 'Baron of Beef' on a side-table, while on another side-table was arranged a two-tier display of the ducal gold plate including the coronation cups.

The guests arrived at about half past five and dinner was served at six-thirty, the order of precedence being announced by the Earl Marshal's secretary. The arrival of the party in the Barons' Hall, after processing along the gallery from the library, was announced by a fanfare of trumpets from two bands of the Sussex Militia in the Minstrels' Gallery, and they continued to play martial music throughout the evening, punctuated by further fanfares to mark the entry of the more spectacular dishes including a whole roast stag carried in by two park keepers and the chief forester dressed in special neo-feudal suits of Lincoln green. The Duke himself, deprived of armour, wore his uniform as Lord Lieutenant of Sussex; which was perhaps just as well, for after dinner he opened the ball in person in the drawing-room with the Marchioness of Stafford ('Old Mother

The 11th Duke of Norfolk as an old man with horrible whiskers.

Stafford' as Creevey disrespectfully called her), and at his age and with his girth a creaky rusting suit of armour might have been the last straw. Tea and coffee were served in the library and supper followed in the Barons' Hall at one o'clock. According to contemporary accounts the Duke, an incorrigible radical even in his old age, did not toast the King but instead drank to the 'pious memory of the *twelve* Barons who compelled King John to sign Magna Carta'.[22]

The Magna Carta dinner was the old Duke's swansong and he did not long outlive its feudal-radical festivities. He died of 'water on the chest' at Norfolk House on 16 December 1815 after a short illness in which he faced death with certain qualms. 'It is whispered . . . that he refused seeing a priest of the Church of Rome, in his last moments, although it had been repeatedly proposed to him'; and one obituarist informed the world, in the manner of a tradesman's advertisement (Causton thought), that 'during the awful struggle that finally closed on 16th December, the duke is said to have sent to a bookseller's in Pall Mall, for

"Drelincourt's Consolations against the Fear of Death" – *a work that has gone through forty editions'.*[23] He was buried at Dorking with all the pomp of a deceased Earl Marshal, his broken baton of office being thrown into the grave after him.

Dying without legitimate issue he was succeeded by his third cousin, Bernard Edward Howard of Glossop, a descendant of the Hon. Bernard Howard, eighth son of Henry Frederick Earl of Arundel. As already seen, under the terms of the 11th Duke's will the whole of the ancient patrimony of the dukedom passed to the new Duke, but Greystoke once again became the seat of a cadet line of the Howards. It was bequeathed to Bernard Edward's younger brother Henry Thomas Howard Molyneux Howard and has since passed down through his descendants to the present owner Mr Stafford Howard. A younger son of the Greystoke family, Esme Howard, had a distinguished diplomatic career in the early twentieth century. He was British Ambassador in Washington from 1924 to 1930 and was created Lord Howard of Penrith.

Catholic Revival

THE Glossop Howards who inherited the dukedom in 1815, and who still hold it, have been the most consistently and strongly Catholic of the descendants of Henry Frederick, Earl of Arundel. For a hundred and fifty years they were faithful to an exiled dynasty and a proscribed faith. In the eighteenth century nearly every member of the family entered religion and lived abroad as nuns or priests; in each generation only one son married and carried on the line. Bernard Howard of Glossop I,[1] the eighth son of Henry Frederick, was educated at Douai and spent some time at the Court of Charles II. He went to France during the Titus Oates' Plot but returned under James II and was appointed a colonel in command of a troop of the Horse Guards and a Deputy Lieutenant for Wiltshire. Not much is known about him, save that he was a racer, and possibly a breeder, of horses and a skilled swordsman. He acted as a second in the notorious duel between the Duke of Buckingham and Lord Shrewsbury over the latter's wife (who turned up at the duel disguised as a pageboy and holding her lover Buckingham's horse), in which Lord Shrewsbury was killed and Bernard Howard had to take his place, killing in turn Buckingham's second, a skilled fencing-master called Jenkins. After the Glorious Revolution Bernard Howard's Jacobite sympathies landed him in trouble and he was committed to the Tower on three different occasions on suspicion of being involved in Jacobite plots, but perhaps against the odds he died quietly in his bed in October 1717.

All three of his daughters, Elizabeth Dominica, Mary Rose and Catherine Mary became Dominican nuns at Brussels. The second one, Sister [Mary] Rose Howard gained some notoriety as a Jacobite agent who regularly corresponded with the Old Pretender. The eldest son, Bernard II, was also an active Jacobite and lived with the Court in exile at St. Germains (where his portrait was painted by Belle) for several years, only returning to England when the Old Pretender moved to Rome. Bernard II had two daughters, one of whom died young while the other became a nun and eventually Abbess of the Blue Nuns in Paris, dying a prisoner there at the time of the French Revolution. Of Bernard II's four sons all except

A. B. Belle. Bernard Howard of Glossop II at the Court of the Old Pretender at Saint Germain.

Julian Story. Cardinal Edward Howard (1829–92), Arch-Priest of St. Peter's in Rome. Painted in 1884.

Henry, father of the 12th Duke of Norfolk, became priests. Bernard III, the eldest, was chaplain to the Vicar Apostolic in London; Thomas, after a spell as a page at the Court of the Elector Palatine, took Orders and became a canon at Douai; Charles, the youngest, was a Doctor of Divinity and rector of the English seminary of St. Gregory at Paris. His various theological treatises are still in manuscript and have never been printed.[2]

Henry Howard of Glossop was educated at Douai and became a wine merchant first in Dublin and later in Portugal, but his business failed and he would have gone bankrupt had not the 9th Duke kindly rescued him, paid his debts and appointed him agent to the northern estate, giving him a house in Sheffield (now the site of St. Marie's Church), and made him free of Worksop. At the age of fifty-one, Henry fell in love with, and proposed marriage to Juliana Molyneux, the daughter of Sir William Molyneux, a Protestant Whig neighbour. Her parents, not unnaturally in view of the differences in age and religion between them, opposed the union. But such an imbroglio of hopeless love was just the sort of problem on which Mary, wife of the 9th Duke of Norfolk, throve, and which she loved to solve. Before her imperious charm all difficulties melted away and the couple were duly married. They had three sons, Bernard Edward, Henry Thomas and Edward Charles, and so were able to effect a sensible compromise whereby the eldest and youngest sons were brought up in their father's religion, while the second son adopted his mother's religion, succeeded his uncle Sir Francis Molyneux to the Molyneux estates and added that name to his own. When on the death of the 11th Duke he also inherited Greystoke he added a further Howard, to become Howard-Molyneux-Howard. He lived mainly at Thornbury Castle in Gloucestershire, the unfinished seat of the attainted Staffords, Dukes of Buckingham, which he restored to the design of Thomas Willement, the stained glass artist. He died in 1824 and is buried at Arundel.

The youngest son, Edward Charles, was the grandfather of Edward Henry, Cardinal Howard, the *other* family cardinal whose career will be briefly followed here. He was born in 1829 and was educated at Oscott (where he was a contemporary of Mgr. Talbot, Pius IX's influential English adviser who eventually went mad) and then became a man-about-town and officer in the Life Guards, in the latter capacity leading the funeral procession of the Duke of Wellington in 1852. Shortly afterwards he resigned his commission and was ordained priest in the English College at Rome on the day that Pius IX defined the dogma of the Immaculate Conception. He had since early youth wanted to be a missionary and after his ordination he was soon sent to India with the difficult task of healing the schism that had broken out in the old Portuguese settlement at Goa. On his return to Rome, Mgr. Howard, as he now was, played a useful role

Bronze lamp from Cardinal Howard's private chapel (copied from one in the Jesù), now in the Brompton Oratory.

in assisting to conduct hesitating young Englishmen across the bridge which leads from Anglicanism to Roman Catholicism. He was an excellent proselytizer among a certain class of persons who are enchanted by the worldly good-breeding that lies at the heart of the spirit of Catholicism, at any rate as it is practised in Rome.[3]

In 1872 he was made Archbishop of Neocaesaria *in partibus* and five years later was elevated to the rank of Cardinal Priest, becoming in addition Protector of the English College and Archpriest of St. Peter's, the equivalent to the Dean of an Anglican Cathedral, responsible for the fabric and the liturgy. He particularly enjoyed this latter role as he loved the pomp and poetry of the traditional papal basilican liturgies (now, of course, all modified) and took a great interest in his own vestments, for instance using his mother's jewels for his mitre rather than the glass or paste imitations which more pinchbeck cardinals had to make do with. He was in every sense the sort of Catholic prelate that the Victorians most admired. Courtly and aristocratic, speaking Italian 'with wonderful correctness and fluency', and yet also very English with his roast-beef complexion, great height (his coffin is seven feet six inches long), his soldier's gait, his outspoken frankness, his habit of walking everywhere to the astonishment of the Romans, his taking an apple to his favourite horse every day after lunch, his secret frugality, only eating one meal a day. Towards the end of his life he fell ill and retired to Brighton where he died in September 1892. He was buried at Arundel, Vespers for the Dead and the dirge and requiem being sung in the Fitzalan Chapel. The coffin was draped with a violet pall on which rested his red hat, and was surrounded by six silver candlesticks; the Servite nuns held further tapers while the *Miserere* and *De Profundis* were sung in unaccompanied plain chant. The small congregation included the Duke of Norfolk and Lord Edmund Talbot (representing the family), Mgr. the Duc de Stacpool and Mgr. Lord Petre (representing the Pope) and two privates and a subaltern of the 2nd Life Guards (representing his regiment).

Bernard Edward, 12th Duke of Norfolk, the eldest son of Henry Howard of Glossop, was born in Sheffield on 21 November 1765 and was educated at Douai. He was a short, small-boned man, of quiet integrity in religion and politics, a cisalpine Catholic and a Whig. As heir-apparent to the dukedom, he bought Fornham Hall, a house designed by James Wyatt near Bury St. Edmunds in Suffolk, and that remained his favourite country house even after he became Duke. The great object of his life was Catholic Emancipation and this explains his attachment to the Whigs, the political party which favoured emancipation. All his efforts during the early part of his life were devoted to that end and are reflected in Creevey's letters. Creevey was a friend, a protégé and a bit of a toady; he frequently dined with the Duke at Fornham or at Brooks's (the Duke's club) and coined for the Duke the nicknames Barney, Twitch and Scroop. For a time Creevey sat for the Howard borough of Thetford, but was later removed by the Duke because he was not pulling his weight. Already before the death of the 11th Duke in 1815 leading political figures were guessing how the Duke would conduct himself. Brougham wrote to Creevey on 7 November 1815:

Now upon your friend B [ernard] Howard's succession to this important publick trust (for so I consider it), it is plain beyond all doubt that old Mother Stafford will be working by every means to touch him, at all events to neutralize him. She will make the young one turn Protestant – a most improper thing in his station; for surely his feeling should be – 'I *will* be in Parlt., but shall be by force of the Catholic Emancipation;' and viewing this as a personal matter to himself, he should shape his political conduct with reference to it. But I fear that is past praying for, and all we can hope is that the excellent father should remain as steady in his politics as he is sure to be in his adherence to his sect.[4]

In the event the new Duke more than fulfilled Brougham's expectations. Immediately on George IV's accession in 1820 he presented at a levee a petition from himself and his fellow Catholics urging the repeal of the surviving penal laws on the grounds that they encouraged popular prejudices, perpetuated religious dissension and prevented 'that general concord in the Empire so essential to its happiness, prosperity and independence'. He assured the King that the English Catholics recognized in the Crown alone the civil sword and had no allegiance to any foreign political power.

This was the opening of the final act and before the decade was out the whole anachronistic and unjust paraphernalia of persecution was swept away – not by the Whigs as it turned out, but by Wellington and Peel. Before that, the Duke had taken a step of his own to remove one of the impediments in his own life. On the

death of his Anglican brother, Lord Henry Thomas Howard-Molyneux-Howard, who had acted as Deputy Earl Marshal from the Duke's accession, he arranged for a private member's bill to be introduced into the Lords to allow him to exercise his office as Earl Marshal. Apart from a few old die-hards like the Duke of York, the majority of the Lords supported Norfolk's cause. Creevey describes the heated preliminaries before the bill was passed.

We are full of a battle that is to take place in the House of Lords between the Duke of York and our Scroop. Lord Holland had brought in a bill to enable Scroop, tho' a Catholic, to officiate in future as Earl Marshal. It was read a second time on Saturday, tho' the Duke of York and old Eldon were in a minority; but since then the D. of York has become perfectly furious, and has written to every peer he knows, calling upon him to come and protect the Crown against the insidious Scroop.[5]

The Duke of York lost and Norfolk won. As a result he was able to officiate as Earl Marshal at the coronations of William IV and Queen Victoria, though on both occasions the organization was a bit creaky and the latter ceremony was marred by the spectacular fall of an elderly peer from the top of the steps to the throne while kneeling down to make his homage. Another sign of the softening of the official attitude towards Catholics was the formal reversal in the same year of the attainder against Viscount Stafford.

On the passing of the Emancipation Act in 1829 the Duke was able to take his seat in the Lords, the first Catholic member of the family to sit there since the 6th Duke had withdrawn in 1678. Once again Creevey conveys something of the Duke's excitement as the bill passed on its tempestuous way through its various readings. 'Here is little Twitch, alias Scroop, alias Premier Duke, Hereditary Earl Marshal, who is sitting by my side and who reckons himself sure of franking a letter for you (a parliamentary privilege) before the session closes.'[6] The Duke was not unaware of the historic significance of this moment and had his portrait painted by Pickersgill wearing his parliamentary robes and with a copy of the Emancipation Act lying on a table beside him.

In Parliament the Duke remained a Whig and supported the Reform Bill. Even before 1832 he had refused to sell the parliamentary seats in his gift, but bestowed them on MPs he thought suitable, rather in the way that Anglican landowners disposed of the church livings in their possession. (The Duke of Norfolk's livings incidentally were, because he was a Catholic, administered by St. John's College, Cambridge, and still are.) While his party was in office in the 1830s the Duke received several honours, being appointed to the Privy Council, and in 1834 being made a Knight of the Garter.

The Duke's Catholicism was a major force in his life, but was of the old-fashioned English type that would hardly have been recognized as Catholic-

mas Gainsborough. Bernard, 12th Duke of Norfolk
6–1842), as a young man.

H. Pickersgill. The 12th Duke of Norfolk in Parliamentary robes, painted to mark the passing of the Catholic Emancipation Act in 1829. The robes are those still worn every year by the Duke of Norfolk for the State Opening of Parliament.

ism later in the nineteenth century. It was quiet, almost diffident, anti-triumphalist, anti-ultramontane, of the sort associated with the historian Dr Lingard and other clerics of the old school. Lingard, for instance, disapproved of the use of Holy Water and carrying the cross in procession and such-like 'un-English' practices. In 1824, the Duke appointed as his own priest at Arundel the Revd Mark Aloysius Tierney, a close friend of Lingard's and the doyen of old-style ducal chaplains, a considerable scholar who, like the Duke, was a fellow of the Society of Antiquaries and the Royal Society. In between his spiritual duties he devoted his time to archaeological and antiquarian researches, the chief fruit of which was his definitive *History and Antiquities of the Castle and Town of Arundel*, published in 1833 and still the standard history of Arundel. Tierney also continued Charles Dodd's *Church History of England* and contributed a memoir of Lingard to the sixth edition of his *History of England*.

The Duke's old-fashioned attitude is illustrated by the fact that he refused in 1838 to make a contribution towards the cost of the new Catholic cathedral in St. George's Fields, Southwark, on the grounds that he 'disapproved of large edifices'. This was not meanness; he genuinely thought that small chapels were more appropriate to English Catholic worship and on average he gave £7,000 a year towards the cost of acquiring sites and building chapels. Nor was his generosity restricted to his own denomination. He gave the sites on his Sheffield estate needed for Anglican churches and cemeteries. The visitant preacher at the opening of St. Mary's (C. of E.) church, Sheffield, was unaware that the site had been given by the Duke, and so not only failed to make any mention of it or to express gratitude, but took the opportunity in his sermon to attack the insolent spread of Catholicism in industrial towns. On it being gently pointed out to him afterwards that this might be construed as slightly discourteous to the donor, the poor man was overcome with embarrassment and wrote a grovelling letter of apology.[7]

Apart from his gifts to churches, the Duke was a substantial benefactor of poor Catholics, especially widows or paupers with large families who, because of their religion, were not able to benefit from many old-established almshouses and charities which had a specifically Anglican bias. A large proportion of his surviving correspondence is of this type, pleas from Irish maids with impossible Anglican mistresses or young married men in Wimbledon who had recently lost their job and had five children to feed. Many of them are just signed 'a Catholic layman' and would be of considerable interest to the student of nineteenth-century social history. The Duke decided whether a case was genuine or not and responded accordingly. He was able to be generous because, living on his own, his personal needs were by ducal standards modest and he had an income of £66,000 per annum gross (excluding Worksop), which even after necessary expenditure on estate repairs left him with £54,000 net.

It was not just a matter of money however but time, care and influence which he expended on behalf of his co-religionists. For instance, he took up the cause with the British Government of the interesting community of Catholics in India who were descended from Portuguese settlers and British (Irish) troops, but who were without priests, churches or schools, which the Duke thought should be provided, and campaigned to make the Government pay for them.

It is sad that such a kind and well-meaning man should not have found a wife to support and help him. Through no fault of his own, nor of his wife, his marriage had been a miserable failure. He had married in April 1789 the beautiful Lady Elizabeth Belasyse, daughter of the Earl of Fauconberg, but she was already in love with another man, the Hon. Richard Bingham, son of the 1st Earl of Lucan, and had been forced by her parents against her will to marry 'Barney'. In view of the outcome it seems a shame that Lady Elizabeth did not explain her predicament to her future husband who, from all that is known of his character, would surely have released her had he known the true circumstances. As it was, she went through with the charade of marriage though she did not love him. Her counsel stated at the divorce: 'this unfortunate woman was dragged a victim to the marriage bed, without the least love or smallest attachment for Mr. Howard'. She told her maid that 'she would rather go to Newgate than live with him'.

Bingham meanwhile had done the honourable thing and retired to Bath to try to forget Lady Elizabeth, but this merely impaired his health and did nothing to dampen his love. A son was born to Lady Elizabeth in 1791, but shortly afterwards she met Bingham again and they 'pursued their passion to a guilty conclusion'. The Howards separated on 24 July 1793 and she went to live with Bingham. The following year her husband took steps to obtain an Act of Divorce, for her benefit; as a practising Catholic he could not marry again in any case. He did not sue for damages and made it clear that he considered all the parties 'free from any severe censure'. The divorce was granted in May 1794. Bingham paid token damages of £1,000 and Lady Elizabeth married him within the month.[8]

In the management of his estate the 12th Duke continued the policies of *laissez-faire* growth in Sheffield and aggrandizement at Arundel initiated by his predecessor. He sold Worksop in 1839 to the Duke of Newcastle for £375,000 and used the proceeds to enlarge the Surrey and Sussex estate. The day-to-day running of affairs in Sheffield was left in the hands of the agent Michael Ellison whom the Duke appointed in 1819 and who was intelligent, conscientious, energetic and wholly devoted to what he saw as the best interests of the Duke and the town, chiefly the continuing provision of cheap, reasonably well-built artisan housing and the re-erection of the Shrewsbury Hospital on a better site in 1823. The Duke kept a keen eye on the overall conduct of affairs and, for instance, during the Chartist Riots in the town in the 1840s, Ellison wrote to him daily informing him of the outcome of events. At Glossop the Duke began the development of a completely new town, 'Howard Town', with a regular plan based on Norfolk Square and handsome public buildings including the Town Hall of 1838 and the Catholic church of 1836, both by Weightman and Hadfield. He was also one of the chief promoters of the new turnpike over the Snake Pass connecting Manchester and Glossop with Sheffield.

At Arundel the 12th Duke almost doubled the size of the estate, in 1827 buying Michel Grove to the south, anciently a seat of the Shelleys, demolishing the house and adding the land to his own holdings which he consolidated by enclosure, realigning roads and resiting buildings. He also extended the Great Park to the north west over land newly enclosed under an Act of Parliament of 1825. He began the programme of clearing away the buildings at the top of

Arundel High Street and realigning the London road south of the parish church in order to improve the castle grounds. This involved building a new neo-Norman town hall in 1836 for the town council, which had previously met in the old vestry of the Fitzalan Chapel, the mortuary chapel of the Howards and the Fitzalans which the 12th Duke repaired and refenestrated after years of neglect. These clearances included the Anglican vicarage, which might have been embarrassingly difficult for the Duke to get rid of, if God had not intervened directly and burnt it to the ground with a flash of lightning.

In all these works the Duke's architect was Robert Abraham, an erstwhile pupil of Nash who designed the Old Fire Office in Piccadilly Circus. He probably came to the Duke's attention through the Regent Street improvements which affected the rear of his property at Norfolk House. Through his recommendation, Abraham was able to build up quite a sizeable practice among Catholic clients in the years after Waterloo. For the Duke alone he added the portico to Norfolk House, repaired the College of Arms, made alterations at Fornham and repaired Worksop at a cost of £8,000 in 1818, as well as various works at Arundel. The latter consisted chiefly of outbuildings. Though he produced plans for partly remodelling the castle and making a new dining-room, these were not executed and the Duke in fact spent very little time at the castle, barely bothering to keep it in repair. Creevey who visited it from Goodwood, was shocked by the atmosphere of gloom and neglect and wrote that 'the devil himself could make nothing of the interior. Anything so horrid and dark and frightful in all things I never beheld.'[9] The grounds on the other hand were, apparently, beautifully kept up.

The Duke was a minor patron of contemporary artists from the early 1820s, when he commissioned a fine series of views of the castle from William Daniell, to 1841, when he bought C. R. Leslie's large oil painting of Fairlop Fair from the Royal Academy for £500. Perhaps his best purchases were the attractive watercolours which he brought together, a small but choice cross-section of contemporary talent with works by Copley Fielding, Prout, Varley, Joshua Cristall, William Collins and William Hunt. These hung at Fornham in his lifetime but are now at Arundel, Fornham having been sold by his son Henry Charles, 13th Duke, at auction almost immediately after his father's death in 1842.

Henry Charles, known in contemporary newspapers as old 'Pepper and Potatoes' had lived at Surrey House, Littlehampton, on the Sussex estate, a house improved for him by Robert Abraham, during his father's lifetime, but when he succeeded he moved straight into Arundel Castle. He was perhaps more pompously ducal than most Dukes of Norfolk. Like his father he was a Privy Councillor and Knight of the Garter, but was also an active courtier, at various times Treasurer of the Household, Master of the Horse, Captain of the Yeomen of the Guard and Steward of the Household. Thomas Greville described him as 'plain, unaffected and good natured'. That however was when he was young and

A. J. Oliver. Henry Charles, 13th Duke of Norfolk (1791–1856), painted as a young man in Paris.

HENRY CHARLES HOWARD, EARL OF SURREY, SON OF BERNARD ED-WARD DUKE OF NORFOLK. NAT. 1791.

he may have hardened as he grew older. Creevey, for instance, thought him 'odious'. His arrogance was perhaps partly caused by his being heir-apparent for so long (he was fifty-one when he inherited), by his good looks (inherited from his mother), and above all by his marriage in 1814 to Charlotte Sophia Leveson-Gower, daughter of George Granville, Marquess of Stafford and later 1st Duke of Sutherland, which immediately sucked him into the centre of the grandest of Whig connections as well as making him the son-in-law of the richest man in England.

At the Duke's suggestion his sons double-barrelled their name by Royal Licence to become Fitzalan-Howard in 1842, stressing their descent from the medieval Fitzalan Earls of Arundel as well as the Howard Dukes of Norfolk. This was indicative of his neo-feudalism, as was the fact that he shut the park at Arundel, which has otherwise always been freely open to the public, and made a very foolish 'let them eat cake' speech at an agricultural dinner after a cattle show at Steyning in 1845. (One contemporary wondered what it was about agricultural dinners which always inspired Dukes to make outrageously stupid speeches.) He had probably had too much to drink, but what he actually recommended with pompous gravity was that the starving poor who could not afford bread should eat curry because even if it was not enough to nourish them 'it is certainly warm and comfortable to the stomache'. He was twitted mercilessly in the press as 'a political economist the like of which the world has not lately witnessed' and heavily ironical articles about 'Norfolk *poudre*, or Ducal Condiment for the Poor' ran for months and months in the newspapers. *Punch* even published an excruciating poem which contrasted the Duke, to his shame, with John Howard, the prison reformer (no relation):

> Two Howards at two different periods born
> The happy isle of Albion did adorn
> The one was first in Chantry's fair list
> And earned the title of 'Philanthropist'!
> The other, also, was the first – among
> The lordly and hereditary throng;
> And when great Famine lowered his sapient head
> Devised a special substitute for bread
> (of which discovery none could be prouder)
> 'Instead of flour' quoth he, 'use curry powder'.

The Duke himself was a good farmer and ran his estates well, building many excellent new farm buildings, barns, piggeries and cowhouses, and personally planned the layout of the model dairy built at Swanbourne in 1845 with its attendant cattle-sheds and pretty octagonal milk room lined with blue and white tiles and with a little marble fountain in the centre. He also carried out various improvements to the castle in the 1850s constructing several new lodges round the park, erecting the rather ugly baronial curtain wall and gatehouse at the top of the High Street and modernizing the castle. His architect was William Burn (recommended through the Leveson-Gower connection), while the redesigning of the grounds, new kitchen garden and especially the layout of an elaborate formal parterre in the north bailey, or tiltyard, was the work of W. E. Nesfield.[10]

On the northern estate he continued his father's ambitious plan for New Glossop adding a market hall to the Town Hall in 1844 and providing the proudly classical railway station with the Howard lion over the entrance in 1847. Glossop Hall was enlarged in 1850 as a residence for the Duke's second son Edward, and an Anglican school and new parsonage added (for reasons which will be explained) at the same time. Hadfield, the architect of most of this, was a Catholic and a relation of the Duke's agent for the Derbyshire part of the northern estate. The well-planned layout and decent architecture of Glossop makes it one of the best small nineteenth-century industrial towns; the fact that it is all built of sand-

Formal parterre laid out by the 13th Duke in the tiltyard of Arundel Castle *circa* 1851. Destroyed. From a nineteenth-century photograph.

Design by William Burn for the main lodge and gateway to Arundel Castle, erected by the 13th Duke in 1851.

The Howard lion on the railway station at Glossop, built by the 13th Duke of Norfolk in 1847.

stone, not brick, also helps to raise it above the level of Sheffield where the Duke continued the successfully mediocre development of his predecessors under the direction of Michael Ellison. Ninety-nine-year leases were granted to small speculative builders to encourage the erection of cheap artisan housing close to the ever-expanding steel mills and cutlers' workshops in the Don valley.[11]

The great social event of the 13th Duke's life was the three-day visit of Queen Victoria and Prince Albert to Arundel Castle in December 1846. The castle was spankingly redecorated for the occasion by Morants, *the* fashionable decorators, the library being provided with well-upholstered red velvet sofas, the drawing-room hung with a smart new green and gold patterned paper, and a special set of white and gold Jacobean-style bedroom furniture including a spectacular state bed was made, with the royal arms at the head and the Norfolk arms at the foot and a red brocade canopy and hangings. The Queen had thoughtfully given two years' notice of her visit, presumably so that the castle might be made comfortable, but as the day approached the Duchess began to have qualms about Arundel's habitual wintry chill. What use the white and gold state bed, if royal toes froze to ice in the middle of the night! Fortunately the Duchess's sister was able to recommend a new-fangled invention, Joyce's stoves, which she had seen at Raby Castle. A great number of these were ordered immediately and distributed along the gallery, hitherto 'so impossible to warm', with instant results and an unaccustomed air of cosy warmth soon pervaded the interior.

All this careful preparation paid off and the visit was an unqualified success. The royal party entered Arundel from the Chichester road and were met by the mayor Edward Howard-Gibbon, York Herald. 'The Royal pair graciously acknowledged the salutations offered to them and appeared much gratified at the appearance of the children of the National School, who were drawn up in holiday attire opposite the residence of the mayor.' The entrance into the castle grounds had been transformed into an evergreen arch of 'gigantic dimensions and very effective design' with an inscription recalling the visit of the Empress Matilda in 1139, perhaps not very tactfully, as that Queen had had to leave with undignified haste when Stephen appeared before the castle with a large army. At dinner that night there was 'a gorgeous display of plate' including a gold dessert service, followed by fireworks 'whose orderly motion was, however, perpetually disturbed by the quantities of squibs and crackers, of rockets and other fireworks, that were let off in the public thoroughfares with indiscriminate liberality and mischievous fun'. The next day the Duke, the Prince and the other men in the party went shooting while Queen Victoria toured the grounds, being taken to the keep to admire Lord Thurlow and her companions and to see the new dairy at Swanbourne. Dinner that night was as magnificent as the previous night, but of course with a completely different display of plate, and was followed by an evening party in the library with entertainment by 'Ethiopian Serenaders'. The royal party, after planting two oak trees using a spade newly manufactured for the occasion by one of the Duke's Sheffield tenants, returned to Osborne on Friday leaving behind a general feeling of satisfaction.[12]

These happy feelings were dissipated by an event which occurred two weeks later. The Norfolks' third son and his mother's favourite, Lord Bernard Thomas Fitzalan-Howard, whose twenty-first birthday was due on 30 December, was away on his Grand Tour. After visiting Vienna, Salzburg, Munich, Rome, Naples and Malta he had gone to Egypt for the winter intending to return to Rome for Holy Week before coming back to England in the Spring. This was not to be. On 21 December he collapsed and died suddenly on the steps of his hotel after returning from a visit to the English consul Charles Murray. He had seemed in perfect health and the cause of death was discovered to be an internal haemorrhage and a clot of blood on the brain. He was buried in Egypt, the Catholic Bishop performing the service. The Duchess was deeply distraught by the news but scribbled with touching fortitude on the outside of the envelope of her son's last letter to her: 'My last letter from my beloved son Bernard of whose death at Alexandria I heared on 12 January. God's will be done.'[13]

The most conspicuous episode in the 13th Duke's career was his unexpected support for Lord John Russell's Ecclesiastical Titles Bill in 1851. The Duke had been in Parliament, first the Commons, then the Lords, since 1829. Immediately on the passing of the Catholic Emancipation Act the sitting member had surrendered the ducal borough of Horsham to him and he had at once taken his seat in the Commons, the first member avowedly of his Faith to sit there since the seventeenth century. He maintained his seat after 1832 but in 1841 was summoned to the Lords as Lord Maltravers, a year before succeeding to the dukedom. Throughout his political career he had been a conventional Whig, his only strong view being over the Corn Laws on which issue he was a Protectionist and voted against their repeal.

He reacted to the restoration of the Catholic Hierarchy in England by Pius IX and Wiseman in 1851 with unexpectedly strong feelings. He opposed it wholeheartedly and supported Lord John Russell's denunciation of the papal move as 'insolent and insidious . . . inconsistent with the Queen's supremacy, with the rights of the bishops and clergy, and with the spiritual independence of the nation'. The Duke voted for the Bill to forbid the assumption in England of 'ecclesiastical titles conferred by a foreign power' which was immediately rushed through Parliament and passed into law though it has never been put into effect.[14] The Duchess agreed with her husband and wrote to Queen Victoria criticizing the tone of the papal bull 'From the Flaminian Gate' which gave the impression that England was not a Christian country and spoke about her return to orbit in the ecclesiastical firmament after centuries in the outer darkness of heresy and barbarism. The Duchess also criticized the proselytizing of certain of the Catholic clergy and the whole new aggressive, triumphalist tone of the Catholic Church in England. The Queen replied moderately and sensibly: she saw 'no *real* danger' in the proceedings of the Roman Catholic clergy; it was the Puseyites who worried her.[15]

The Duke determined to make a stand. In the words of an obituarist, he 'felt so keenly (as did others of the Roman Catholic nobility) the attack upon the liberties of his country, that he not only voted in support of the Government measures, but quitted the Roman Communion, and conformed to the Established Church'.[16] The 8th Lord Beaumont (another of the present Duke of Norfolk's great-grandfathers) similarly joined the Church of England in protest against the 'Papal Aggression' at the same time.

The Duke of Norfolk's seemingly excessive reaction to the restoration of the Hierarchy, as well as expressing general patriotic distaste for 'foreign powers', was consistent with his, and his chaplain Tierney's, view of English Catholicism. He disapproved of proselytizing and converts. He did not like the new enthusiastic, ultramontane clergy, epitomized by Wiseman. His Catholicism was his own private affair, it was part of his historical inheritance like being a medieval Duke, both of which in his innermost heart he felt were a bit better than being an eighteenth- or nineteenth-century Anglican Duke (not that he would ever have admitted it), but it was no concern of anybody else's. Some gentlemen were Catholics and some were not and that was that. Like many of the English Catholic gentry he was a cisalpine in outlook who, while acknowledging the Pope's vague position as Head of the Church, Vicar of Christ, and the final arbiter on earth in all spiritual matters, considered practical interference in English Catholic affairs to be quite another matter, really none of the Pope's business at all.

The Duke's religious views were imbued with an aristocratic conservatism. He liked the Church the way it had developed in the recusant period. Its quietly beautiful neo-classical country-house chapels and missions; its dignified, and by Victorian standards, rather low-key services; the eighteenth-century French prayer books and missals with their gold tooled red morocco bindings and green silk endpapers; Kandler's ormolu rococo tabernacle (Tierney had just had it regilt); the gentlemanly scholarly priests, preferably secular or Benedictine, but possibly Jesuit, the four episcopal Vicars-General with their Marian blue, not purple, cassocks symbolic of the old tradition that England was the 'Dowry of Mary' and their wonderful romantic titles *in partibus infidelium*: Anazorba, Cambysopolis, Helenopolis, Hierocaesaria, Trebizond. Who would want to sweep all that away and replace it with Bishops of Salford and Birmingham, cheap Gothic churches in mean towns and uneducated Irish priests? How delightful by comparison the Established Church with its genuine medieval architecture, its sonorous language, its Oxonian clergy.

Another, and wholly creditable, reason for the Duke's objection to the restoration of the Hierarchy and the way it was announced, was the fear that it would stir up hostility and prejudice especially against poor Catholics who were in no position to defend themselves. He, after all, thanks to the letters which poured in week by week, knew what it was like to be a Catholic soldier in an English regiment or a Catholic servant in a non-Catholic household, whereas Wiseman, who had spent most of his life 'full in the panting heart of Rome', did not.

Despite his strong feelings over the Hierarchy issue, and his practical defection from the Church, the Duke never formally renounced his Faith. He contented himself with presenting a peal of eight bells to the Anglican parish church in Arundel and in building new Anglican schools there and on his other estates. He died a Catholic in February 1856, receiving the last sacraments at the hands of Canon Tierney as is testified by his coffin plate: 'Qui sacramentaliter absolutus, et unctionis sacrae praesidio munitus, ex hac vita migravit.'*

---

* 'Who departed this life sacramentally absolved (of his sins) and fortified with Extreme Unction.'

The Duke's stand over the Hierarchy was not shared by his two sons, Henry Granville, later 14th Duke, and Edward George, later 1st Lord Howard of Glossop. They, being of a younger generation, realized that the Church must change, that the growth of an urban Catholic proletariat as the result of northern industrialization and Irish immigration in the 1840s had drastically transformed its character in a way not immediately apparent from within the battlements of Arundel, not to mention the flood of highly educated Puseyite converts in the wake of Newman and Faber. To Catholics of the 14th Duke's generation Oxford was almost as interesting as Rome. As Earl of Arundel he had contested the Ecclesiastical Titles bill at every stage and had resigned his parliamentary seat of Arundel in order not to be beholden to his father, being adopted for the Irish seat of Limerick instead. Lord Edward Howard, though sharing his brother's views, was more moderate and attempted to reconcile the differences between his father and elder brother. He had an active political career sitting as MP for Horsham and Arundel for twenty years from 1848 to 1868. He was a liberal and a supporter of Gladstone. He was created a peer by the latter's recommendation in 1869, taking the title of Lord Howard of Glossop. He devoted his life to the cause of Catholic elementary education and with considerable success. He was chairman of the Catholic Poor School Committee in the 1870s and raised over £350,000 by private subscriptions, contributing £5,000 himself (though not a rich man) and securing £10,000 each from his nephew the 15th Duke of Norfolk and his son-in-law the 3rd Marquess of Bute. He married firstly Augusta, only daughter of the Hon. George Talbot, brother of the 16th Earl of Shrewsbury, and secondly Winifred, daughter of Ambrose Lisle March Phillipps de Lisle, the eccentric convert and patron of Pugin. Lord Howard of Glossop was described by Canon Tasker as 'honest, upright, truthful, earnest, energetic and self-sacrificing'.[17] He was the great-grandfather of the present Duke of Norfolk.

It is very difficult to write about his elder brother, Henry Granville Fitzalan-Howard, 14th Duke of Norfolk. It is not easy to describe a saint nor to write a panegyric. This Duke was described by Burke's Peerage as 'amiable, excellent and highly respected' and by his close friend Count Montalembert as 'the most noble, the most humble, the most pious layman of our time', while Fr. Faber wrote 'No Saint could have had a holier death.' He used his position entirely for the service of God and the poor; he twice turned down the Garter when offered it by Palmerston because he disapproved of his policies. He, and his wife, were the most perfect expression of mid-nineteenth-century English Catholic society. Rich, aristocratic, cosmopolitan and devout, austere, self-denying, and tirelessly devoted to good works. They formed part of a group which included Lady Georgiana Fullerton, the Baron Charles von Hügel and the Duchesses of Buccleuch and Argyll. They have been described as an aristocratic version of the Salvation Army, single-mindedly building churches and knitting vests for orphans, but perhaps a closer comparison is with those earnest post-tridentine Italian aristocratic saints of three centuries earlier, the Massimi, the Gonzaga, the Borromeo and the followers of St. Philip Neri.

There are three identifiable stages in the 14th Duke's life. First there is his conventional upper class upbringing; he was educated by private tutors and at Trinity College, Cambridge, before obtaining a commission in the Life Guards which he resigned on attaining the rank of Captain. Secondly there are his travels on the Continent in the late 1830s and early 1840s which were the most important formative influence on his life. Finally there is his brief reign as Duke, the saintly protector of the poor, the champion of all Catholic causes, the zealous promoter of the English Oratory, the close friend of Faber and Newman.

The key to the Duke's character lies in his Continental travels as a young man. He seems first to have been sent on a Grand Tour of the Continent at the age of twenty-three in 1838 in order to forget a Miss Pitt whom his parents did not wish him to marry. His grandfather was then still alive and he was known by the courtesy title of Lord Fitzalan, and indeed he was called 'Fitz' all his life by his brothers and sisters. Disraeli tells the story of what happened to him in Greece: 'Lord Fitzalan who was sent to Greece because he would marry a Miss Pitt, has returned engaged to Miss Lyon(s), daughter of our minister there. It is said he escaped from the Pitt to fall into the Lyon's mouth.'[18] This came about because he became seriously ill in Athens and was nursed back to health in the house of Admiral Sir Edmund Lyons (later 1st Lord Lyons), the British Minister, and fell in love with the Lyons's younger daughter Augusta Mary Minna. They were married in June 1839. Miss Lyons was at that time an Anglican, serious and pious, but later became a Catholic, bringing to her new religion all the proselytizing zeal of the newly converted.

The visits to France in the 1840s made the most profound impact on Fitz's character and beliefs, and in Paris he underwent something like a Pauline revelation. He was introduced to the small but influential Catholic party active in Louis Philippe's Government, especially Count Montalembert, a half-English, half-French aristocrat of great charm and romantic historical, religious and political views. Fitz also fell under the spell of the impressive preachers such as Père Lacordaire and Père de Ravignon who were then attracting large crowds to the leading Paris churches with their stimulating and profound sermons. It was all so different from his father's and grandfather's low-key, unintellectual, diffident English Catholicism. Here were vast churches full of eager and enthusiastic young people of all classes listening to well-argued sermons and taking part in services of an order of splendour not known in England; perhaps even more impressive was the charitable work among the poor, nursing and teaching, by nuns and friars, just like the Middle Ages.

Montalembert's own creed was an intoxicating and romantic evocation of the ancient Catholic world of Europe, such as it was before the triple invasions in the sixteenth century of the monarchy, legislative democracy and Protestantism. He wanted to recreate a society that was Catholic and aristocratic and gave scope to all the 'noblest faculties of the soul'. He was moved to tears by the ruins of monasteries and the decayed glories of the Catholic past, and inspired to ecstasy by backward rural areas like Brittany still peopled with a devout peasantry, landscapes in which he found 'so much faith and Catholic beauty of all sorts'. Montalembert saw Catholicism and 'real Conservatism' (by which he did not mean English 'Tory corruption' or the 'low servile monarchism' of the Continent) as being the same thing. All this had a considerable influence on Fitz. He would build churches; he would support the poor; he would fight for the oppressed Irish peasantry; he would restore 'true religion' on his estates. The Angelus would sound again at Arundel.* At last he realized what it was like to be a real Catholic. He now saw that he had been almost a Protestant and told Montalembert: 'I am not long a Catholic. You must look upon me as a convert.'

If the contemporary French Catholic revival was a revelation for Fitz he in turn was an inspiration to Montalembert's circle, for he was the embodiment of their ideal of the Catholic aristocrat. Montalembert became faint with emotion when he contemplated the history of the Howards, their long attachment to a 'conquered and proscribed church', their 'poetic *cultus* of the past' and the 'chain of the traditions' which identified their honour 'with fidelity to the ancestral religion'. He saw the Howards as the 'Montmorencies of England' but with something 'more religious and more touching in their glory by reason of the cruel and unmerited catastrophes of which they have been the victims'.

All this was heady stuff, but Fitz himself kept the romantic aspects of the Catholic revival firmly under control. To the likes of Pugin he was always to seem a milk-and-water compromiser, a man who could endure Mozart and fiddleback chasubles and did not even think that rood screens were essential. As Earl of Arundel, Fitz had intervened without success in the fiercest architectural controversy of the time, that between the Romans and the Goths. In May 1850 he had written with simple common sense to Ambrose March Phillipps (de Lisle):

Why do you call one particular branch of Art, however beautiful, Christian Art? It appears to me to be at least strange in a Catholic to forget that under the much abused Churches of Roman and Greek form so many Saints have received their inspirations; and that at this moment the spread of Religion in France is conducted entirely without reference to the external form of the building. There is nothing Gothick in the Church of Notre Dame des Victoires . . . I think variety pleasing, always within the limits that the Church willingly sanctions, and I confess in travelling I like to find in one place a Gothick, in another Grecian, and in a third a Byzantine Church . . . I cannot help thinking there must be many who hold this opinion and are heartily tired of unnecessary disputes.[19]

---

* It did for the first time since the Reformation in 1847.

The chapel in the Little Oratory at Brompton. Designed by Scoles and paid for by the 14th Duke of Norfolk. His arms impaling those of his wife can be seen in the centre of the ceiling. Fr. Faber, the superior of the London Oratory, was a close personal friend of the Duke's.

The Duke put his views into practice, on the one hand paying for the chapel of the Little Oratory at Brompton, an Italianate Classical design by Scoles, and on the other erecting a private chapel at Arundel Castle and his own mausoleum in the Fitzalan Chapel in the Gothic style to the design of M. E. Hadfield. His letters to the architect over the chapel at Arundel, which formed part of an abortive scheme for the reconstruction of the whole castle from 1859 onwards (halted by his premature death) give a clear idea of the Duke's architectural taste. He wished the work to be massive and simple and wrote: 'Hadfield I am very much afraid of the building being too elaborate in its details and I shall depend upon you to keep it as plain and massive in all its parts as possible.' He abhorred the style of the Houses of Parliament and Pugin's minute and fussy detail and told Hadfield that 'he would have nothing of that kind in the new building at Arundel'.[20] Apart from his architectural work at Arundel the 14th Duke also built a house at Sheffield called, rather inappropriately in view of its situation in one of the largest industrial towns in England, 'the Farm'. This was 'Jacobean' and also designed by

The Farm. The house built by the 14th Duke of Norfolk at Sheffield to the design of M. E. Hadfield. Demolished.

Hadfield. It marked the beginning of a new stage in the ducal attitude to Sheffield and one which was to be further developed by Fitz's son, the 15th Duke. Close personal interest in local affairs and residence for part of every year was to supersede the absenteeism and *laissez-faire* of the first half of the nineteenth century. This too was symptomatic of the Duke's serious view of his responsibilities as a Catholic landowner.

The 14th Duke's basically common-sense approach to religious matters is made clear in two pamphlets which he wrote: *A Few Remarks on the Social and Political Condition of the British Catholics* (1847) and *Observations on Diplomatic Relations with Rome* (1848). The former was intended to show the current position of the Catholic Church in England and Scotland, its claims and duties. It was essentially a plea for his poorer co-religionists, for example, that provision should be made for priests to be available to the Catholic inmates of prisons, workhouses and hospitals. He pointed out that though a third of all the soldiers in the British army were Catholics, there were no Catholic chaplains in the armed forces. The Duke also transcribed and published from the original seventeenth-century manuscripts in the Arundel muniment room *The Lives of Philip Howard, Earl of Arundel, and of Anne Dacres his wife* in 1857, a sign of his interest in the family's Catholic history. Philip Howard was his favourite ancestor and he shared Montalembert's view that he was 'the noblest and most ideal character ever produced by the British patricians'. He modelled his own life and his death on the example of his saintly ancestor.

He spent much of his day at his desk in the library at Arundel, sitting with his wife, who acted as his secretary, dealing with his correspondence from the poor, the sick, the lonely, a task which he tackled with 'heroic patience, good humour and unrivalled munificence'. He gave away most of his income to churches, schools, orphanages, almshouses, hospitals, convents, seminaries, the list is endless. 'He regarded himself as literally nothing more than the administrator of his goods for the benefit of God and his neighbours.'

Montalembert and the French Catholic revival of the 1840s had stimulated the Duke's original 'conversion', but the greatest religious influence on him later in his life were the Oratorians and it was the dual allegiance, on the one hand to the Romantic revival of medieval religion, and on the other to the full-blooded Roman practices of the Oratory which was responsible for the Duke's own impartiality in matters of church architecture, liturgy and music. The English Congregation of the Oratory had been founded in 1848 by a group of Tractarian converts to Catholicism under the illustrious leadership of Faber and Newman and had soon founded two independent houses, the Birmingham Oratory at Edgbaston under Newman, and the London Oratory under Faber which, after a spell in a gin warehouse near Trafalgar Square, moved to Brompton. These two Oratories were among the most important influences on the nineteenth-century

Table made by Morant & Co. as part of their redecoration of Arundel Castle for the visit of Queen Victoria and Prince Albert. The top of micro-mosaic by the Chevalier Barberi of Rome shows the arms of the 13th Duke impaling those of his wife, Charlotte Leveson-Gower.

Arundel Castle. The dining-room as redesigned by C. A. Buckler for the 15th Duke of Norfolk. It occupies the site of the eighteenth-century private chapel by James Paine.

Matthew Noble. Marble effigy of the 14th Duke of Norfolk on his tomb in the Fitzalan Chapel at Arundel.

Minna, Duchess of Norfolk, reading the *Tablet* in the drawing-room at Arundel *circa* 1880.

Catholic life of England. The Duke was a personal friend of both Newman and Faber and the most zealous supporter of the English Oratory in its early formative years. He paid for the Little Oratory and the library at Brompton and his arms impaled with those of his wife appear on the ceiling of the former. Faber became the Duke's confessor and spiritual adviser to the whole family. He received the Duchess into the Church in 1856 and it was through his influence that of their daughters, Lady Minna became a Carmelite nun, Lady Etheldreda a Sister of Charity, while Lady Margaret devoted the whole of her life to working among the poor in the slums of the East End of London. The two sons, Henry later 15th Duke of Norfolk and Edmund later Viscount Fitzalan of Derwent, were both educated at the Oratory School, Edgbaston, under Newman's immediate direction. Both Newman and Faber were regular correspondents of the 14th Duke, his wife and children throughout their lives, and during the last weeks of the 14th Duke's life Faber hardly left the castle.

The Duke when only forty-three contracted a painful and incurable disease of the liver and died two years later, though it was only in the last six weeks that he knew definitely that he was dying. Fr. Faber informed him that the doctors despaired of his recovery. 'Ah! Well, my father, since I have to die, it behoves me that I should at least make a good death.' Pius IX sent a last pontifical blessing. The Duke confessed his sins, received Holy Communion for the last time from Fr. Faber and died with his head on the shoulder of his wife on the feast of St. Catherine of Siena, 25 November 1860. His dying words were the same as St. Philip Howard's in the Tower in 1595.[21]

Duke Henry

HENRY, 15th Duke of Norfolk, died sixty-five years ago and already he seems to be of another race, another civilization. He is so close to us in time, yet in spirit he seems more remote than many of his ancestors: a man who built the present Arundel Castle as a place in which to live (even the 9th Duke's Worksop seems more cosy); volunteered to fight in the Boer War at the age of fifty-six; who devoted the largest part of his income throughout his life to the support of the Catholic Church in England, building cathedrals, churches and schools, subsidizing hospitals, convents, seminaries, as well as most charitable causes and an unknown number of private individuals in distress; whose *Times* obituary compared his influence on public life to that of Sir Thomas More. His presence is all-pervasive at Arundel. Apart from the fact that most of the architecture and a substantial proportion of the collections represent his personal taste, nearly every drawer, every corner contains some personal memento: a photograph, a prayer-book, an old invitation, sheafs of unused black-edged writing-paper from the long years of mourning. He seems inscrutable in his portraits, remote though not aloof, and the severity of his medieval bearded face is belied by the twinkle in his shy eyes, indicative of the duality of his character: saintly yet practical, serious yet jocular, genial yet melancholy, aristocratic yet humble. Few men have to endure in the course of their life such extremes of fortune. He had everything that life could bestow on an English Victorian duke, and few classes of men can have had a more enviable lot, but for many years he had to suffer great personal sadness, which he did with Christian fortitude and an unshaken faith in the essential benevolence of God and the rightness of His ways. Sir Almeric Fitzroy, secretary of the Privy Council, who worked with the Duke on several state occasions and knew him well, praised his fine character and unfaltering integrity:

In every obligation of life faithful to the highest ideals, a great nobleman and the leading Catholic layman, he is as punctual in the discharge of the most trivial courtesies as of the most solemn duties; an excellent man of business, an admirable host, a charming companion, and a most humble-minded Christian, he fills his position with a lustre and

Philip de Lázló. Henry,
15th Duke of Norfolk,
1908.

completeness, and yet with a modesty and self-effacement, for a parallel to which you must go back to St. Louis himself.[1]

Henry Fitzalan-Howard was born at his parents' house in Carlton House Terrace on 27 December 1847. His grandmother, the Duchess Charlotte, wrote from Arundel: 'Joy, joy, dearest Fitz and Minna. He has not been born on Christmas Day, nor on New Year's Day, but he has appeared on our marriage day. The bells have been ringing all through our walk, and with a fine echo near the wall, and the sunset was glorious!'[2] At the Duke's suggestion it was decided to use the old barony of Maltravers as the baby's courtesy title.

Henry was one of a large family of six girls and two boys; they had a happy and closely-knit childhood playing their own versions of the usual children's games, such as Christian martyrs refusing to sacrifice to Roman Emperors rather than cowboys and Indians. Another special family touch was that their Christmas tree, a newly introduced fashion, had the Howard crest instead of a star or whatever on top. Until their father inherited they lived in London but then moved to Arundel, only spending a small part of the year at Norfolk House where they played with the other children of St. James's Square in the central garden. It was in the course of one of these games that Henry failed to duck a stone and was hit in the mouth, breaking some teeth. This was the cause of an indistinct manner of speaking which he only overcame with great application and was one reason for his excessive shyness as a young man.

He succeeded his father in 1860 at the age of thirteen and in the same year he began his school life at Cardinal Newman's Oratory School at Edgbaston. The influence of the Oratorians was paramount in his development, for not only was he directly under Newman's supervision at school but at home Fr. Faber of the London Oratory was the family's spiritual director. So close was the young Duke to the Oratorians that it was rumoured in the newspapers that he was to become a priest. There is no evidence however that Faber or Newman advised him to take any such step. On the contrary they wished him to play the role of leading Catholic layman, to be the perfect Catholic version of the Victorian ideal of the Christian gentleman. On the Duke's fifteenth birthday Fr. Faber wrote to him with three pieces of advice which he was to follow all his life: be honest, be humble, be generous.

As a Catholic the Duke was not able to attend an English university because of a prohibition against non-Catholic educational establishments by the English Catholic Hierarchy. He always regretted not going to Cambridge, and in later life he used all his influence to have this short-sighted ban removed, as well as himself making provision for Catholic undergraduates at Cambridge by providing the site for a Catholic church. Debarred from university, he completed his education by a prolonged Grand Tour, to which he always looked back later as one of the happiest periods of his life. He spent a considerable time in Constantinople where his uncle, the 2nd Lord Lyons, was the British ambassador and from where he made trips to Broussa and Mount Athos. He also stayed at Rome, the traditional objective for all English young men on the Grand Tour, though by Duke Henry's time it had become an outdated convention. He spent the Easter of 1867 there and was warmly greeted by Pope Pius IX at a public audience.

The Duke came of age on 27 December 1868, an event which was celebrated by a week's festivities on his various estates. Almost his first act on attaining his majority was to carry out his father's intention of building a new Catholic church at Arundel dedicated to St. Philip Neri as an ambitious replacement of Tierney's

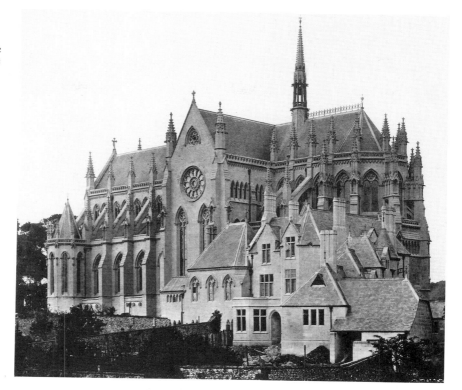

Arundel Cathedral.
Built by the 15th Duke
of Norfolk to celebrate
his coming-of-age and
designed by J. A.
Hansom.

Arundel Cathedral, the
interior looking east. It
was intended as a
'protest against the
spirit of the age'.

Silver casket presented to Arundel Cathedral by the 15th Duke of Norfolk. It incorporates seventeenth-century Flemish reliefs. The gilt statue of St. Peter on top was a present from Fr. Faber.

little chapel. This cathedral-scale fabric, now in fact a cathedral, was designed by J. A. Hansom in French Gothic style and was intended to be a dramatic, even triumphalist, demonstration of the Duke's faith. The mood it expressed is captured in the Duke's own words: 'I thank God with my whole heart that in His mercy I am a Catholic; I glory in belonging to the old faith.'[3] St. Philip's was opened in July 1873 in the presence of Cardinal Manning, the Bishop of Southwark and the Fathers of the London Oratory. In the Sermon Fr. Dalgairns of the Oratory stressed that this enormous stone church with vaults nearly as high as Westminster Abbey, with stained glass depicting the Mysteries of the Rosary, with its statues of symbolic saints, was 'a protest against the spirit of the age'.[4]

It was possible to underestimate the resolution of this shy young Duke. A contemporary cartoon shows him sitting diffidently on a bench in the House of

Lords, his beard not yet of the majestically unkempt medieval growth which it later attained, and the surprised comment beneath: 'That, my Lord of Norfolk? Yes.' But Duke Henry was single-minded in his determination to establish his Faith in England as a strong and respected force in national life, not just something to be grudgingly tolerated. He felt that the Church had not made the most of the opportunities offered to it by Emancipation and had persisted in its outdated introspective 'holes and corners' mentality. He feared that many English Catholics were so more as 'a family tradition than as a sacred and happy duty'. He was especialy disturbed by the mutual lack of understanding between Catholics and Anglicans, and hoped that this prejudice could be partly overcome by Catholics attending English universities, and by more social intercourse between people of different religious backgrounds.[5] He was determined to use his own rank, his fortune and his every effort to win respect for his co-religionists and to establish friendly relations between Catholics and Anglicans. In all this, of course, he was taking exactly the opposite stand to Cardinal Manning and many of the clergy, who wished to preserve and enhance the exclusive attitude of the English, and Irish, Catholics. The Duke however was never afraid of taking an independent line against clerical obscurantism. He was a founder member and first president of the English Catholic Union which was established in 1870, in response to the conquest of papal Rome, as an official body of leading Catholic laymen with the means of making their influence felt in Church and national affairs. In the last resort he was prepared himself to act as the protector, and treasurer, of the English Catholic Church, when for sectarian reasons the Government refused to take action. An example of this was his intervention in 1876 to save the Venerable English College in Rome, the oldest English institution abroad. Founded in 1362 as a hostel for English pilgrims, it had been converted into a theological college by Cardinal Allen in 1579 and rebuilt by Cardinal Norfolk in the late seventeenth century. Following the capture of Rome, the College, and its property, was confiscated by order of the Committee for the Liquidation of the Ecclesiastical State of Rome. Despite strong representations, the British Government refused to intervene on the grounds that the College was ecclesiastical rather than national property: 'H.M. Government finds no justification in extending its protection to the English College' runs the characteristically negative memorandum. It was sold at public auction and bought for 59,000 lire by the Duke of Norfolk 'for and on behalf' of the English College. It was bequeathed to the College in his Will and when he died in 1917 the British Government, which had failed to recognize it as English national property in 1876, now changed its mind and levied death duties on the bequest.[6]

Duke Henry established the position of the Duke of Norfolk as the active leader of the Catholic laity in England, a role he assumed from the moment he came of age. One of his earliest acts was to ask Newman to reply to Gladstone's recently published pamphlet attacking the dual loyalty of Catholics. How could they be true patriots if they owed allegiance to a foreign power? The result was Newman's celebrated *Letter to the Duke of Norfolk* published in 1875 which is the classic defence of the Catholic position. Newman wrote to Duke Henry: 'It will be a great satisfaction to me, in the last thing probably I shall write, to end my say with the great House of Norfolk on my tongue.'[17] Five years later the Duke was able, at a private audience, to recommend that the Pope recognize Newman's great work for the Church in England by bestowing on him a cardinal's hat. The Duke explained, 'It appeared to me that in the cause both of justice and of truth it was of the utmost importance that the Church should put her seal on Newman's work.' On the new Cardinal's return from Rome where he had received his hat in the majestic ceremony, the Duke gave a two-day reception for him at Norfolk House.

The Duke gradually came to act as the principal link between the British Government and the Vatican, a role for which he was ideally fitted. Though there was no official British representative at the Vatican till the First World War, there was increasing rapprochment between the English Crown and the Holy See in the late nineteenth century, made necessary by Britain's world role and especially the problems of the large Catholic communities in different parts of the Empire: Africa, Australia, Canada, Ireland and Malta. It was essential for the British Government to have a discreet means of putting its views across to the Pope on any occasion where British interests and Catholic issues were involved. The Duke of Norfolk was entrusted with much of this confidential business and opened communications with Cardinal Rampolla at the Vatican. The chance to establish cordial relations between the greatest political power and the greatest ecclesiastical power on earth occurred at the time of Queen Victoria's Golden Jubilee. The Pope on his own initiative asked whether he could send his congratulations to the Queen. The Duke approached Lord Salisbury with the suggestion. Salisbury was at first dubious because if the Pope's congratulations were accepted it would mean that Queen Victoria would have to reciprocate on Leo XIII's Golden Jubilee as a priest and that might revive anti-Popery feelings among 'the English non-Conformists of every degree'. When consulted however the Queen 'was much gratified at the suggestion' and merely stipulated that the Prelate sent should be a foreigner and not a British subject. 'I daresay', wrote Lord Salisbury to the Duke, 'you could convey this hint quite unofficially and confidentially to the proper authority.' The outcome was that Queen Victoria's Golden Jubilee celebrations were graced by the presence of Mgr. Ruffot-Scilla, the titular Bishop of Petra, whom the Duke entertained for the occasion at Norfolk House. Lord Salisbury explained on 19 June: 'My instructions are to present the Monsignor at 3.15 tomorrow. He comes after the dusky potentates of the East but before the special Ambassadors and Envoys.'[18] This all went off very well and in December 1887 the

Queen in return sent the Duke of Norfolk as her special envoy to Leo XIII. It was the first time that a British Sovereign had officially sent an envoy to the Vatican since Lord Castlemaine's disastrous embassy from James II. The Duke conveyed to the Pope a cordial letter written in the Queen's own hand and a golden ewer copied from a piece of plate at Windsor. On his return Lord Salisbury congratulated him on his conduct of affairs: 'Everything seems to have gone off admirably; only the Pope's remark that the Queen's present would do for use at Mass was tactless.'

These preliminaries having been gone through close relations were maintained, via the Duke, with the Vatican during Lord Salisbury's administration and during Balfour's. This contact was especially important to the British because of the Irish question. It was essential for peace in Ireland that the Vatican should not recognize or promote overtly republican clergy as this would antagonize further the powerful Protestant minority in Ireland. It was important also that the Vatican should know the English Government's point of view on Irish affairs and not just be fed one-sided information by the Irish Hierarchy. The Duke had all the necessary qualifications for this difficult role. He was a strong Catholic, but was also a perfectly honourable, sensible, moderate and intelligent man with a position carrying as great weight in Rome as in England. Another sensitive issue where he was able to exert his influence was Catholic missionary activity in Africa. French missionaries based in Algeria sought to represent to the Africans that if they embraced Catholicism they were French. This could have led to much awkwardness as the British were then consolidating their position in Africa. The Duke with Cardinal Vaughan, the Vatican and the Foreign Office was able to solve this problem by creating a new Catholic Vicariate based on Mombasa, and it was made perfectly clear to the Africans that the fact they were Catholic did not mean they could not also be British.

As well as visiting Rome on official business, the Duke frequently led pilgrimages of his countrymen to the Holy City. One such was in May 1877 when a group of English Catholics went to Rome for the episcopal jubilee of Pius IX. The Duke read an address to which the Pope replied extempore and with a dramatic flourish; Pius IX usually sat on these occasions because of old age but after a few words he rose to his feet and lifting his hands, according to Abbot Oswald Hunter-Blair of Fort Augustus, said 'in that strangely sweet and resonant voice, which no one who heard it ever forgot: "Inghilterra! Inghilterra! io prego sempre per Inghilterra." The effect on his audience was extraordinary. I saw the Duke's eyes fill with tears, and others present were not less moved.'[9] Among these others was Lady Flora Abney-Hastings, daughter of Lord Donington and the Countess of Loudon (in her own right).

In September 1877 the Duke, now twenty-nine, became engaged to Lady Flora while staying at Derwent Hall, his house in Derbyshire. The Duke's mother

Derwent Hall, Derbyshire. The 15th Duke's house on his northern estate restored for him by J. A. Hansom. It was submerged under Ladybower Reservoir in 1935.

wrote from Arundel: 'The school-children here appear to think you are going to marry Flora to please them because she was so nice at the School Feast.' The wedding took place at Brompton Oratory on 21 November and was in many ways a high point of the nineteenth-century Catholic Revival in England. The Bishop of Southwark performed the ceremony, assisted by the Superior and Fathers of the Oratory. At the Nuptial Mass the white and gold Arundel vestments which the Duke's mother had presented to Fr. Faber as a thank-offering for her reception into the Catholic Church were worn. The bride wore a pearl necklace which had belonged to Mary Queen of Scots and was accompanied by no less than twelve bridesmaids. The signing of the register was witnessed by Disraeli whose entrance into the church caused something of a stir. He told Lady Bradford: 'There was as great a crowd from Hyde Park Corner to Brompton as on Lord Mayor's Day. When I arrived it was supposed to be the Bride, and the whole Church, very long and very full, rose, and were sadly disappointed when it was only I in a fur coat and your rustic stock.'[10] The honeymoon was spent at Arundel which was illuminated with electric light for the first time, in celebration of the event. The Duke's wedding present from the Marquess of Bute was a pair of jewelled ivory hair – brushes designed by William Burges.

To commemorate his marriage, the Duke decided to build another church. 'Shortly after my most happy marriage I wished to build a church as a thank-offering to God' and chose Norwich as the chief city of the county 'of the title I hold'. Of the dozens of churches which the Duke built in his lifetime the 'great Gothic fane' at Norwich was his favourite architectural enterprise. He chose the Early English style because it was not already represented in Norwich and he wanted his church to be a notable addition to the Norman and Perpendicular styles represented in the City's existing church architecture. George Gilbert Scott Junior was appointed the architect on the recommendation of Cardinal Newman, who had received him into the Catholic Church. After G. G. Scott went mad the work was completed by his brother J. Oldrid Scott. Duke Henry took a close personal interest in the designing of his church and made various suggestions which Scott incorporated in his plans: 'one feature may be looked on as essentially the Duke's own design, namely, the grand triple lancets in the end wall of the north transept. It may confidently be said that nothing finer has been accomplished in modern architecture than these noble windows.'[11] The foundation-stone was laid on 17 July 1884 and work continued for twenty years, the church finally being opened in 1910 after an expenditure of £250,000. Long before the church was completed however the *raison d'être* for building it had disappeared.

The Duke's marriage which had begun so auspiciously was to be attended by great sorrow. Both the Duke and Duchess were very fond of children and much wanted a large family of their own. Quite soon however the young Duchess's health began to fail and it was doubted whether she would be able to bear children at all. By 'a miracle' a son was born in September 1879 and christened Philip to great rejoicing. Congratulatory letters poured in from all sides. They make sad reading with hindsight. For this only son was born blind and epileptic and his mind never developed beyond an infantile state though he did not die till he was twenty-three. The Duke said later to his sister: 'If I had been told that I should have a blind and epileptic child I should have thought I could not bear it; but God can enable us to bear trials, and I can bear it.'[12] There was no human cure for their son but the Duke and the Duchess, while she lived, never gave up hope of a miracle. They took the boy to Turin to see St. John Bosco who was famous for his work with children and orphans, and also took him every year to Lourdes. Once at Lourdes the Duchess with a friend met a procession chanting the Magnificat. They sang 'Esurientes implevit bonis sed divites dimisit inanes'.* The poor Duchess could not keep back her tears. 'Did you hear that,' she said, 'we shall get nothing.' Well might she contribute an altar to the Brompton Oratory with the inscription 'Of your charity pray for the soul of Flora, Duchess of Norfolk, who

---

* 'He hath filled the hungry with good things, but the rich He hath sent empty away.'

Brompton Oratory, London. The altar of St. Philip Neri designed by Herbert Gribble, a gift from the 15th Duke of Norfolk who also contributed £20,000 to the cost of building the church.

The Cathedral church of St. John, Norwich. Designed by G. G. Scott Junior and J. Oldrid Scott 1884–1910 for the 15th Duke of Norfolk as a thank-offering to God for his happy marriage. It cost £250,000.

The interior of St. John's looking east. It was the 15th Duke's favourite architectural work.

put up this altar to the Mother of Sorrows that they who mourn may be comforted.' She also founded the little convent of the Poor Clares at Cross Bush on the Arundel estate in the woods across the valley from the castle, its bell clearly audible in the still of summers' evenings calling the nuns to vespers or to compline. Its community was a spiritual substitute for the children the Duchess could not have. 'You see, Father,' she explained to Abbot Vaughan of Fort Augustus, 'God has not given me a family, but as the Mother-Foundress, all the nuns are my children, so I have plenty now.'

The Duchess's own infirmity increased gradually during the ten years of her marriage and she died on 11 April 1887 after being unconscious for two days. She was only thirty-four when she was buried in the Fitzalan Chapel. The route of the funeral procession was lined with two hundred and fifty children from the schools in Arundel. The Duke erected to her memory the stained glass east window of the Fitzalan Chapel which depicts a requiem Mass for her, the coffin lying in the foreground under a pall with coronet, the Duke and his little son kneeling on either side of the priest at the altar while all around are serried ranks of ancestors and saints, an evocation of the profound grief that lies at the heart of all things.

Philip, Earl of Arundel and Surrey, was eight when the Duke was left to care for him alone in his vast Gothic castle. Lady Etheldreda Fitzalan-Howard, a nun, later wrote of the Duke:

The most pathetic feature in his life was his devotion to his poor afflicted child . . . No father could have loved the most attractive and perfect child more than he did his afflicted one. He said 'I love him much more than if he had been all right, it is a delight if I wake in the morning and feel that I am in the same house.' After the child's death his fortitude almost gave way; he once said to me: – 'I feel as if I could not live without the little boy.'[13]

The Duke found some solace for his bereavements in architecture. William Beckford had once remarked: 'Some men drink because they are unhappy. I do not drink, I build.' Duke Henry could have said the same. The 1880s and 1890s saw the high point of his architectural activity; they were decades in which he immersed himself in his churches and castles. He had a great love and knowledge of Gothic architecture and his family had always given him English and French books on architecture for his birthday presents, works by Viollet le Duc, Seroux d'Agincourt, Rickman, Pugin, Street, Ruskin and Scott, all still preserved in the library at Arundel on the shelves where he placed them, the affectionate inscriptions on their flyleaves as fresh as if written yesterday.

Duke Henry started his great reconstruction of Arundel Castle in the late 1870s with the extension of the east wing to contain an independent group of private rooms: drawing-room, breakfast-room and billiard-room, for occupation

Arundel Castle. The main staircase by C. A. Buckler with carvi
Thomas Earp. The Gobelins tapestry is one of a set of the *Nouve*
Indes series bought by the 9th Duchess in Paris for £9 a yard.

by the family when no party was staying. He continued in the 1880s and 1890s with the reconstruction of the south and west wings, rebuilding the staircase, dining-room, Barons' Hall and the Chapel. The latter is perhaps the finest of the late Victorian interiors at Arundel. It is Duke Henry's personal Sainte Chapelle, influenced by Westminster, Lincoln and Salisbury, richly adorned with columns of Purbeck and Frosterly marble, excellent stiff leaf carving by Thomas Earp and richly coloured stained glass depicting scenes from the life of Our Lady by John Hardman Powell. Duke Henry's taste was for an austere, serious, timeless and self-effacing historicism rather than the flamboyant eccentricity of William Burges or the originality of the Arts and Crafts. He chose as his architect Charles Alban Buckler, grandson of the well-known topographical artist, a Catholic, a Knight of Malta, and Surrey Herald Extraordinary. His work has not lately been admired by the architectural cognoscenti mainly because it lacks the 'modernity' of the more progressive late-Victorian architects and patrons. But modernity was not something for which either the Duke or Buckler were striving. They were creating an appropriate seat for the hereditary Earl Marshal of England and an expression in stone of the family history with all its associations, religious as well as baronial; statues of Our Lady stand in canopied niches alongside displays of the almost infinite quarterings of the ducal heraldry. The genuinely medieval parts of the castle and the Fitzalan Chapel were restored with painstaking archaeological accuracy while the unfinished patchwork of late eighteenth- and mid-nineteenth-century Gothic which formed the residential part of the castle was sweepingly reconstructed to form an evocation of what a medieval castle should look like. Sir Almeric Fitzroy who visited the castle in May 1902 when Duke Henry's work was only recently completed, shows a more intelligent grasp of what had been achieved than most modern architectural critics.

We spent Sunday at Arundel, a place where the traditions of a stately and reverent life still survive. The castle has been restored by the present owner with a scrupulosity of sentiment it is impossible to praise too highly. The assimilation of the spirit of the past has taken the place of the sterile reproduction of its letter, with the result of elevating and subduing the mind to the reception of the most living lessons of history. No more fitting fabric could, indeed, enshrine the story of the great house, for centuries feudal Earls of Arundel, an honour transmitted, with the ancient heritage of the Fitzalans, to the son of the Duke of Norfolk who suffered under Queen Elizabeth.[14]

The work went on for years, and during much of the middle period of the Duke's life the castle quadrangle was a builders' yard, filled with huts, scaffolding, piles of materials and mud. One contemporary compared the castle to Portsmouth Dockyard, with its army of workmen trooping in and out of the gate morning and evening over the years. The builders became quietly attached to the Duke and used to send him little hand-painted cards on his birthdays and a touching letter on the death of his son.

ndel Castle. Duke Henry's Sainte-Chapelle.

As well as Arundel Castle, Duke Henry had a house on the northern estate. He gave up his father's house, the Farm in Sheffield, because of its proximity to the Midland Railway, and bought instead an old Jacobean house, Derwent Hall (the 'er' pronounced by him as in Derby) set in beautiful country mid-way between Glossop and Sheffield and so very convenient for management of the northern estate. He restored and enlarged this house to the design of J. A. Hansom and built a Gothic chapel at the back decorated by Westlake.[15] He used to go to Derwent Hall every year in September for the shooting and Sheffield business; early summer he spent in London at Norfolk House, where he had the eighteenth-century rococo decoration refurbished by Charles Nosotti, and the winter at Arundel, where after his wife's death one of his sisters kept house for him. Duke Henry also had a yacht, the 'Star of the Sea', built in Leith in 1882 and furnished with a portable altar. This was a great pleasure to him for he loved scenery and would go up the West Coast of Scotland, seeking solace in the beauties of the mountains, lochs and isles.

The Duke's major architectural interest was his churches, and in this he differed from his contemporary and cousin by marriage, the 3rd Marquess of Bute, who was a much more single-minded house builder. As well as the major churches at Arundel and Norwich, by Hansom and Scott respectively, Duke Henry built a series of churches at Sheffield designed by Charles Hadfield, of which St. Joseph's, Handsworth, with its adjoining presbytery and school is a characteristic example. He also commissioned churches in memory of Duchess Flora: Our Lady Star of the Sea at Lytham, Lancashire, by P. P. Pugin, and Our Lady of Lourdes at Ashby-de-la-Zouche, Leicestershire, in the Norman style by F. A. Walters. He built a series of smaller churches on the Sussex estate such as St. Wilfrid, Angmering, and the school and church at Shoreham. He was the major benefactor of both Westminster Cathedral and Brompton Oratory and presented a large number of chapels, altars, stained glass windows to other churches includ-ing the beautiful Abbot's Chapel by P. P. Pugin at Fort Augustus or the east window (destroyed in the Second World War) of St. Etheldreda, Ely Place, London. The Duke had a reputation in his family as an expert on Gothic architecture and was consulted by his relations when they were building churches. For instance, when his nephew James Hope-Scott rebuilt the Catholic church at Herons Ghyll to the design of F. A. Walters the Duke recommended Climping church near Arundel as a suitable model. In his patronage as a church builder, it is possible to see the Duke's taste developing from a more florid fourteenth-century French-inspired Gothic towards the 'pure beauty' of the Early English style. The Duke's interest in architecture was combined with a great historical sense and any old pieces which came to light during new building or alterations the workmen had instructions to preserve, with the result that bits of stained glass and sculptured fragments, old iron spurs and nails, and other items of archaeological interest

Top. Arundel Castle. The reconstruction of the quadrangle *circa* 1890. A contempor compared the castle to Portsmouth Dockyard with its armies of workmen trooping and out of the gate, morning and evening year after year.
Bottom. Arundel Castle. The drawing-room, reconstructed to the design of C. A. Buckler, who was also responsible for the heraldry, 1875. The chimneypiece is Thomas Earp.

accumulated in corners at Arundel, while the herbaceous borders in the garden of the Works' Yard in Sheffield used to sport a fine crop of Gothic pinnacles and Cromwellian cannon-balls amid the phlox and delphiniums. He bought back various ancient sites connected with the family history including the castles at Clun and Bungay. He also added substantially to the collections at Arundel, buying pictures, furniture, books and armour, especially if they had family associations or related to Howard history. He bought in addition old ecclesiastical plate and vestments for St. Philip's church at Arundel.

Though he never sat as an MP because he inherited the title so young, or became a member of the Cabinet, Duke Henry had an active public life, but one which cannot be accurately measured by listing the official appointments he held. It was his influence that counted, and as the years rolled by he came to occupy the informal position of viceroy for almost all Catholic affairs in the British Empire. As a young man he followed recent family tradition and supported the Liberals. In March 1878 he turned down the Garter when offered it by Disraeli as he did not at that stage wish to leave the Liberal party though he foresaw that the occasion might one day arise when it would be his duty to do so: 'I have always thought that I should some day join the Conservative Party and it is easy to see at this time that questions may come up at any time which would make me feel it to be my duty to do so at once. Were I to do this however I should be breaking with the tradition of my family.'[16] Gladstone's incompetent government between 1880 and 1886, the death of Gordon at Khartoum, the exacerbation of the Irish question, finally decided the Duke and he left the Liberals and joined Lord Salisbury and the Conservative party. In a speech in Sheffield in 1885 he said that he had nothing but 'anger, scorn and disgust for a Government which, when it was out of office, talked itself into the confidence of the Country by high-sounding sentiments, and which, since it had come into office, had been playing tricks with the Interests of our Country and the lives of her children'. The Garter was offered to him again by Lord Salisbury in February 1886 and this time he accepted the honour.

He regularly attended the House of Lords though he spoke infrequently as a result of natural diffidence, confining himself to subjects on which he had strong views such as education, matters affecting his co-religionists and especially Irish affairs. It was Gladstone's Home Rule policy which was the strongest factor in driving the Duke into the arms of the Conservatives, for though a Catholic he was a whole-hearted Unionist and felt deeply about any proposals to dismember the United Kingdom. On 5 September 1893 he made a long speech in the House of Lords in support of the rejection of the second Home Rule Bill. He did not deny

that there had been much of evil in the past in the government of Ireland, for which amends had to be made but the remedy was not, having taken from Irishmen all power to arrange their own affairs, and having sapped and undermined their strength, to give them this pretended boon at a time when it was sure to be used by one Party against another in that unhappy country.

As a Catholic the Duke was much in demand on the platform of Unionist meetings in England to show that the Irish Question was not simply Protestants against Catholics. He only went to Ireland once, in 1904 for the consecration of the Catholic Cathedral at Armagh. It is one of the tragedies of modern British history that he was not appointed Viceroy of Ireland under Salisbury and Balfour from 1895 to 1905, but at that time it was still not possible for a Catholic to be Irish Viceroy. With his special gifts and position, had he been viceroy at the time that George Wyndham was chief secretary, it would have formed a powerful combination in favour of reconciliation and might have avoided the disaster of partition. As it was this religious disqualification was only repealed by the Irish Home Rule Act of 1920 and in 1921 the Duke's younger brother, Edmund, Viscount Fitzalan of Derwent, became Viceroy of Ireland, but by then it was too late.

The Duke instead of becoming Viceroy of Ireland was made Postmaster-General in 1895. Lord Salisbury wrote on 30 June from Hatfield:

My dear Norfolk,
   Your letter gives me an idea that you might possibly accept an office of detail. I know you will not accept one of dignity. The Post Office is available. Are you disposed to become Postmaster-General? You will have plenty of work, and you will have no one over you; on the other hand the office is as non-democratic as you could possibly desire.[17]

The Duke was also made a member of the Privy Council. At first his appointment was the object of radical criticism as the Post Office, it was said, 'is one department of the public service, which must nearly concern the people at large, and where if at all, the talents and experience of the most skilled administrator are urgently needed, and yet the post is given to a gentleman without official training or proved capacity for affairs, simply because he is the Premier Duke of England'. The Duke, however, was able to prove his critics wrong. After he had been in office for some time the *Saturday Review* hailed him as 'the best Postmaster-General the Department has seen for a long time'. The Duke and his family took a characteristically jolly view of his elevation to public office and a little caricature (probably by one of his sisters) shows the Duke ascending to Heaven on a cloud in the guise of a saint, supported by angels holding the Howard crest and a mailbag respectively. He resigned the Post Office in 1900 in order to enlist as a captain in the Imperial Yeomanry going out to fight the Boers in South Africa, a gesture showing more patriotic fervour than sense for a man in his fifties. Perhaps fortunately he was hurt in a fall from his horse shortly after arriving in South Africa, was invalided home and so was spared being shot by a Boer bullet.

The Duke sat frequently on Royal Commissions and associated public committees; he was generally considered to be among the best chairmen of his generation, but he had had plenty of practice. He was chairman of the important Royal Commission on Army Reform set up by Balfour in 1903.[18] In 1908 he was a member of the English delegation which accompanied the Prince of Wales (later King George V) to Canada to celebrate the tercentenary of the founding of Quebec where he was 'most useful as a uniting link in the atmosphere of a Catholic Province', and in 1909 was president of the committee which organized the British–Japanese exhibition in London.

He naturally took a strong interest in his hereditary office of Earl Marshal of England and was successful in defending his prerogatives as well as being able to restore several aspects of ancient ceremonial which had fallen into neglect during Queen Victoria's long reign. At the funeral of Queen Victoria in 1901 he was able to insist that it was the Earl Marshal's responsibility, as a Great Officer of State, to make the arrangements for the ceremonial rather than the details of these being in the hands of the Lord Chamberlain, as the latter had asserted they should be. It required some courage on the part of the Duke 'so far to overcome his natural modesty' to fight off an encroachment of a department of The Royal Household which had been entrusted with a number of Royal Funerals, although not the Sovereign's, in the past. At Queen Victoria's funeral he had only ten days to prepare, and received no help from the Lord Chamberlain's officials. There was a certain amount of confusion as a result, but he was able to perfect the ceremony for the funeral of King Edward VII in 1910, that last gathering of the crowned heads of Europe. For the coronation of King Edward VII, the Duke used the service of 1838 as a basis, but had to compose certain aspects of the ceremonial from scratch, while the length of the service was restored to its ancient form. The illness of the King and postponement of the coronation was a great boon and the Duke reported that without that welcome respite and much-needed further rehearsal 'only a miracle could have averted a fiasco'. He worked extremely hard in the preparation of these ceremonies and told a friend after Edward VII's funeral in St. George's Chapel, Windsor, in 1910, that he had had no more than three hours' sleep a night for a fortnight. There was a further attempt at the coronation of King George V to disestablish the Earl Marshal's department with its seemingly antiquated cortège of heralds and to transform the office into the titular direction only of state ceremonies, the real responsibility to be given to a new standing committee of officials representing the great departments of the Household and State. The Duke took exception to this and fought for his rights, threatening to take the matter to the Court of Claims. He won and retained his own independent officers, secretary and staff as in the past. It is largely as a result of Duke Henry's determination between 1901 and 1911 that the office of Earl Marshal is the only one of the medieval Great Offices of State which still properly functions and has not been reduced to an empty honour.[19]

Another field in which the Duke played an active public role, perhaps at first sight rather surprisingly, was local government. He became a member of the London County Council in 1892, was the first Lord Mayor of Westminster from 1900 to 1901, and president of the London Municipal Reform Association. In order to understand this aspect of the Duke's public life it is necessary to see it in the context of his Sheffield estate. He owned altogether about fifty thousand acres, chiefly at Arundel and Sheffield, but also with smaller estates in Surrey, Norfolk and London. Though not large in area by late nineteenth-century standards (twenty-eight peers had estates of over a hundred thousand acres in 1883) it was exceptionally lucrative as it included a lot of urban property, Arundel, Littlehampton, Dorking, the Strand estate in London, and above all substantial portions of Sheffield. After the Marquess of Bute he was the richest Catholic peer and among the top twenty landowners in the kingdom in terms of income. When he inherited in the 1870s his estates produced over £100,000 gross per annum and his income increased throughout his life. Over half came from Sheffield, not just from rents but also from mineral rights and the markets, which he owned as lord of the manor till 1899 when he sold them to the Corporation.[20] As has been seen already the Norfolk connection with Sheffield in the earlier nineteenth century had been distant and *laissez-faire*, but under Duke Henry there was a great revival of the family interest and he rather than Lord Fitzwilliam (the other great Sheffield landowner) became 'the node of reverential politics' in the town. He presided over his northern industrial fief with a mixture of sound business sense, Christian philanthropy and medieval splendour which was only paralleled in the late nineteenth century by the 3rd Marquess of Bute at Cardiff.

Duke Henry restored the ancient monuments which belonged to him in the town, such as the gatehouse of Sheffield Manor Lodge in 1873 and the sixteenth-century memorials to the Earls of Shrewsbury in the parish church (now the Anglican cathedral) in 1880. He gave churches, schools, recreation grounds and parks, of which Norfolk Park, next to the Farm, was the finest and which he maintained at his own expense. He played an active role in establishing the university and was its first Chancellor as well as receiving its first honorary degree. He made some effort to redeem the architectural meanness of the city by various splendid new buildings, of which the Corn Exchange, built 1878–82, was the finest. This was a large quadrangular complex entered through a gatehouse and contained, as well as the Exchange, a hotel, commercial premises and the Duke of Norfolk's estate office. It was designed in a rich Tudor style by Charles Hadfield, whose secular masterpiece it was, while the heraldic decoration was designed by J. F. Bentley.[21] This splendid building was unfortunately gutted by fire in 1947 and demolished in 1964 by the Corporation in order to make way for a traffic roundabout. Not all the Duke's ventures were as solid as this; one more

Sheffield. Triumphal arch of canvas and timber erected by Duke Henry to the design of Charles Hadfield for the visit of the Prince of Wales in 1875.

Sheffield Town Hall. Designed by Mountford and opened by Queen Victoria in 1897 at the time that Duke Henry was first Lord Mayor. From a nineteenth-century photograph.

ephemeral was a Gothic triumphal arch built for the visit of the Prince of Wales (later King Edward VII) in 1875 with *tourelles* and coats of arms all of canvas and wood. It was garrisoned for the occasion of the royal visit by schoolboys 'in warlike attire',[22] and rich currant buns were distributed to all the children in the town.

Duke Henry's role in Sheffield is a good example of the way in which the traditional landowning classes adapted to life in the world's most advanced industrial society and not only survived but prospered in the nineteenth century. While to urban radicals the Duke might have seemed the incarnation of hostile privilege, he was idolized in general as all that was good, grand and genial. The apotheosis of his role in Sheffield came in the 1890s when he was elected Mayor, and then in 1897 the city's first Lord Mayor and the city's first Freeman. He gave Sheffield its mayoral chain of office and its mace, designed by Omar Ramsden under his personal supervision. The new town hall was built to Mountford's design during the Duke's mayoralty and is the only really good surviving building in Sheffield, a magnificent free classical affair with Arts and Crafts touches, a tall tower, excellent sculpture, alabaster lined walls and art nouveau brass light fittings. The Duke's statue in white marble by Onslow Ford still survives at the foot of the staircase wearing the mayoral chain tucked into his Garter sash. Should it stir into life it would find its immediate surroundings unchanged, but would be well advised not to step outside and look around there.

At the Duke's invitation Queen Victoria visited the city in 1897 and opened the New Town Hall, an event which more than anything marked the late nineteenth-century reconciliation between the old aristocracy and the new urban industrial England. The appointment of titled mayors in the 1890s, the Marquess of Bute at Cardiff in 1891 was among the earliest, was a sign of the rapprochement between the Town Corporations and the landowners following a bout of radical hostilities in the 1870s, though this had not been as bad as the Chartist troubles in the 1830s and 1840s. When the 14th Duke of Norfolk had died in 1860 he had received a six-line obituary in the local paper. When Duke Henry died in 1917 he got a whole page obituary, the Lord Mayor went to Arundel for the funeral and there was a requiem at St. Marie's in Sheffield attended by every dignitary and official in the city.[23]

After the death of his son the Duke considered the possibility of re-marriage, and for a time seems to have thought of marrying Lady Gwendolen Cecil, the daughter of the Marquess of Salisbury. In the event, seventeen years after the death of his first wife, he married in January 1904 a Catholic cousin, Gwendolen Constable-Maxwell, daughter of Lord Herries and heiress to that barony and estates in Yorkshire and Scotland. They were married at Everingham, the Constable-Maxwell seat in the East Riding. Among his wedding presents on this occasion was a large gold Gothic monstrance designed by Westlake and made

E. Roberts. Gwendolen, Duchess of Norfolk and her eldest daughter Lady Rachel Pepys.

The Fitzalan Chapel, Arundel, which dates from 1380. It is the burial place of the Earls of Arundel and Dukes of Norfolk. The stained glass in the east window is a memorial to Flora, first wife of the 15th Duke. His own monument with a bronze effigy by Sir Bertram Mackennal occupies the foreground.

by Hardman's of Birmingham, the gift of all the Catholics in England and paid for by penny subscriptions. The Duke was consulted beforehand about its form and he suggested that it should be Gothic rather than of the Baroque sunburst variety, so it is directly expressive of his personal taste: 'I should like it to be a Gothic Monstrance of early fourteenth century type of design. Mr. Westlake would probably obtain this from some reliquary of the period.'[24]

This second marriage ushered in the last and happiest phase of the Duke's life. His castle was completed, his churches were built, and now at last he received the reward of the family he had always wanted. Three daughters and one son, Bernard Marmaduke, Earl of Arundel and Surrey (afterwards 16th Duke of Norfolk), Lady Rachel, Lady Katherine and Lady Winefride. Duke Henry was happiest surrounded by a houseful of children, taking part in their games, playing 'sardines' or 'hare and hounds' or romping around on the floor with his own children and his nephews, nieces and god-children. He was notably unconstrained and easy-going as a private person and many stories are told of his shabby clothes and utter lack of pretension. Waiting for a guest at a railway station he was accosted by a lady who mistook him for a railway porter and gave him her case to carry. This task achieved she grandly pressed a small coin into his hand with the words 'There, my good man, there's the first penny you've ever earned.' 'Yes, indeed it is,' he replied with a smile.

He could, however, be sharp if he thought it necessary. When, at the coronation of Edward VII in Westminster Abbey, the jurisdiction of the Dean and Chapter was suspended in the traditional manner and replaced by that of the Earl Marshal's Court, and the Dean inundated the Duke with tiresome grumbles, he replied that *his* sympathies were entirely with the Benedictine monks whom the Dean and Chapter had superseded.

He was made Lord Lieutenant of Sussex in 1905 and this was his last important appointment. Thereafter he gradually tried to reduce his burden of public business. He wrote in 1909 that he had 'for some time felt obliged to refrain from accepting any fresh appointments or offices'. In mid-life, after the death of his first wife, he had told a friend that he did not find life pass quickly enough to its end. But in his sixties he found that it was increasingly difficult to find time for all he was called on to do: answering letters, estate business, public duties, as well as the demands of his young children. The outbreak of the First World War disturbed the peaceful pattern of his life and he found himself swept up once more in new activities such as organizing the reception of Belgian refugees in England. Though none of his immediate family was killed in the fighting, several of his cousins and god-children were. He did not live to see England's victory but died on 11 February 1917 at Norfolk House after a short illness. He was buried in the Fitzalan Chapel at Arundel which he had restored under Buckler's supervision and where his fine bronze monument by Sir Bertram Mackennal now forms a centrepiece. At the same time as the funeral at Arundel concurrent Requiem Masses were sung at Westminster Cathedral, Brompton Oratory and all the major Catholic churches in England:

Thus it hath pleased Almighty God to take out of this transitory life unto His Divine Mercy the late Most High, Mighty and most Noble Prince Henry Fitzalan Howard, Duke of Norfolk, Earl Marshal and hereditary Marshal of England, Earl of Arundel, Earl of Surrey, Earl of Norfolk, Baron FitzAlan, Baron Clun and Oswaldestre and Baron Maltravers, Knight of the Most Noble Order of the Garter, One of His Majesty's Most Honourable Privy Council, Knight Grand Cross of the Royal Victorian Order, His Majesty's Lieutenant and Custos Rotulorum of the County of Sussex, A Knight of the Order of the Golden Fleece, of the Noble Order of Christ, and of the Order of the Golden Spur.[25]

THE TWENTIETH CENTURY

I HAVE chosen to end this book with the death of the 15th Duke of Norfolk in 1917 because it makes a good place to break, leaving a decent gap between the historical past and the present, where objectivity may be distorted by respect for the feelings of the living. It is usual in a book of this type to choose some date in the twentieth century and to give the impression that that is the end of the story and that the rest, which the reader is to be spared, is just a tale of ruin and decline. This is certainly not the case with the Norfolks. The 16th Duke of Norfolk who died in 1975 after a reign of nearly sixty years inherited from his father an excellently run estate comprising nearly 50,000 acres and over forty manors, and from his mother the Herries barony, houses and estates. Norfolk House in London was given up and demolished in 1938, but otherwise the 16th Duke ran his estates on traditional lines, maintaining the standards of an Edwardian aristocrat up to the last quarter of the twentieth century. In 1960 he built a new Georgian style house in Arundel Park to which he moved from the castle, and this remains the home of his widow Lavinia Duchess of Norfolk who followed her husband as Lord Lieutenant of West Sussex, the first woman to hold this post. She has also been created a Lady of the Order of the Garter.

As Earl Marshal of England Bernard, 16th Duke of Norfolk, became a well-known and popular public figure through the televising of State occasions. He was responsible for the organization of the funerals of King George V, George VI and Sir Winston Churchill, the coronations of King George VI and Queen Elizabeth II and the investiture of Prince Charles as Prince of Wales at Caernarvon. As the leading Catholic layman he represented the English Crown on various occasions in Rome including the coronations of Pope John XXIII and Pope Paul VI, and was involved with many religious charities and institutions in England. He saw his father's church at Arundel raised to cathedral status, and the canonization of his ancestor St. Philip Howard by Pope Paul VI. Duke Bernard like his father was Lord Lieutenant of Sussex, a Knight of the Garter and member of the Privy Council. Though he held many public offices and appointments, his chief interests were cricket and the turf. He was president of the MCC and manager of the English Cricket team during the 1962-3 tour of Australia and New Zealand. He was Senior Steward of the Jockey Club, Her Majesty's Representative at Ascot for twenty-seven years, and a keen breeder and racer of horses, winning the 1974 Ascot Gold Cup with 'Ragstone'. He married in 1937 the Hon. Lavinia Strutt, daughter of Lord Belper, and had four daughters, Lady Anne, Lady Mary, Lady Sarah and Lady Jane Fitzalan-Howard. On his death in 1975 his eldest daughter succeeded as Lady Herries while all the other titles passed to his cousin and male heir Major-General Miles Francis Fitzalan-Howard, 12th Lord Beaumont and 4th Lord Howard of Glossop, the great-grandson of the second son of the 13th Duke who, as has been seen, was MP for Horsham, chairman of the Catholic education committee, and Deputy Earl Marshal during the minority of the 15th Duke.

In the lifetime of the 16th Duke various peripheral family properties had been disposed of, including woodlands in Surrey and ground rents in Littlehampton, as well as Norfolk House, in order to pay estate duty and his father's substantial bequests to various Catholic charities, notably capital endowments for the great Victorian churches at Arundel and Norwich. The nucleus of the family estates, however, including Arundel, Sheffield, the Strand and Norfolk survived into the 1950s. Various steps were then taken to secure their future at a time of very high personal and capital taxation which posed a threat to the continuance in England of all such hereditary properties.

In 1956 the Arundel Estates Act was passed by Parliament and this enabled the entail, created by the Collector Earl in the seventeenth century, to be broken and part of the family property to be transferred to discretionary trusts for the benefit of the 16th Duke's four daughters and the present Duke's eldest son, the Earl of Arundel, thus avoiding several potential tranches of death duties which might have wiped out the estates entirely. Long-term thought was also given to securing the future of the castle as a significant historic entity, open to the public, and negotiations were opened with the National Trust but had not been completed at the time of Duke Bernard's death in 1975.

The new Duke did not wish the castle to pass out of family hands to an institution like the National Trust and instead explored the possibility of establishing an independent trust for the preservation of the fabric of the castle and opening it to the public. This proved possible under recently revised legislation for educational charities. The new castle trust was established in 1976 with the Duke as chairman, and with its own endowment from the renewal of the leases of the Strand estate in London. The principal contents of the state rooms were made available to the castle trustees on a long loan agreement, and the buildings themselves thoroughly repaired at family expense under the direction of Seely & Paget. So successful has this arrangement proved that it has subsequently been copied by many other major houses in Britain including Chatsworth, Harewood, Wilton, Burghley, Grimsthorpe, Hopetoun and the Royal Collection. Since the great storm in 1987 the park has been almost completely replanted, many miles of park wall rebuilt, the lodges and other subsidiary buildings repaired.

The future of the estates was an even more intractable problem than the castle itself as their ownership had become fragmented to avoid death duties, and the 16th Duke's personal estate had been left to his widow, not to his successor in title.

A far-seeing strategy was adopted of securing, as far as possible, that the heart of the Arundel estate and the urban property in London and Sheffield would pass with the dukedom. This involved the sale of the Norfolk land around Kenninghall in order to buy out the other beneficiaries. Seven years later, thanks to the enterprise and hard work of the duke's eldest son, it proved possible to repurchase the historic Kenninghall estate (for rather less than its sale price). After a series of family transfers most of the family lands have been preserved with the dukedom including those in Yorkshire, the Strand, Norfolk and half the Sussex estate; there has even been some augmentation, Lord Arundel himself also having purchased the Arkengarthdale estate in Yorkshire.

Miles, the 17th and present Duke of Norfolk, like many of his earlier ancestors was a professional soldier, having served in the Army for thirty years. He was Head of the British Military Mission to Russian forces in Germany 1957-9. He commanded the 70th brigade of the King's African Rifles just before the independence of Kenya in 1963 and later commanded the First Division in the Rhine Army 1963-5. Through his mother he inherited the barony of Beaumont and Carlton Towers in Yorkshire, an old house of the Stapletons sensationally Victorianized in the 1870s to the design of E. W. Pugin and J. F. Bentley.

Since inheriting, the 17th Duke has played a role in public affairs similar to the nineteenth-century Dukes of Norfolk, taking an active lead in English Catholic affairs and frequently attending the House of Lords where he has spoken on similar subjects: education, Catholic issues and Ireland. As Earl Marshal he presides over the College of Arms and is responsible for the annual State Opening of Parliament, on which occasion he wears the robes made for his great-great-great-grandfather following the Catholic Emancipation Act in 1829. Like many of his ancestors the present Duke of Norfolk is a Knight of the Garter, and has also been presented with the G.C.V.O. by the Queen. The Duke of Norfolk is married to Anne Mary Constable-Maxwell, and has two sons and three daughters, Edward, Earl of Arundel and Surrey, Lord Gerald, Lady Tessa, Lady Carina and Lady Marcia. In 1987 the Duke's eldest son Edward married Georgina Gore. Two years later they moved back into Arundel Castle, after an extensive programme of internal modernisation and redecoration had been completed. They have four children, Henry Lord Maltravers, Thomas, Rachel and Isabelle, and for the first time in forty years the castle is once again a family home.

The Duke's younger son Lord Gerald Fitzalan-Howard and his wife Emma have taken on the other historic family house, Carlton Towers in Yorkshire, which has also been gradually restored and brought back to life as a family home.

Carlton Towers, Yorkshire, inherited by Miles 17th Duke of Norfolk from his mother, Baroness Beaumont in her own right.

They have three children, Arthur, Florence and Grace. Altogether the present Duke of Norfolk and his seven brothers and sisters (all their names begin with M: Miles, Michael, Martin, Mariegold, Miriam, Miranda and Mirabel) have over fifty grandchildren between them. In the different branches of the Howard family there are nearly two hundred heirs to the dukedom. So at the end of the twentieth century the future of England's oldest non-royal dukedom looks as secure as can reasonably be expected of any human institution.

GENEALOGICAL TABLE I

THE EARLY HOWARDS

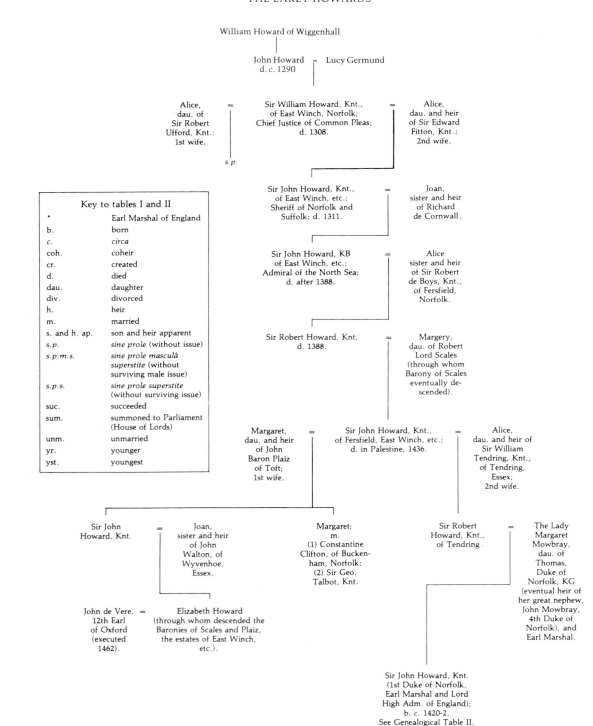

William Howard of Wiggenhall

John Howard = Lucy Germund
d. *c.* 1290

Alice, = Sir William Howard, Knt., = Alice,
dau. of   of East Winch, Norfolk;   dau. and heir
Sir Robert   Chief Justice of Common Pleas;   of Sir Edward
Ufford, Knt.;   d. 1308.   Fitton, Knt.;
1st wife.   2nd wife.

s.p.

Sir John Howard, Knt., = Joan,
of East Winch, etc.;   sister and heir
Sheriff of Norfolk and   of Richard
Suffolk; d. 1311.   de Cornwall.

Sir John Howard, KB = Alice
of East Winch, etc.;   sister and heir
Admiral of the North Sea;   of Sir Robert
d. after 1388.   de Boys, Knt.,
of Fersfield,
Norfolk.

Sir Robert Howard, Knt. = Margery,
d. 1388.   dau. of Robert
Lord Scales
(through whom
Barony of Scales
eventually de-
scended).

Margaret, = Sir John Howard, Knt., = Alice,
dau. and heir   of Fersfield, East Winch, etc.;   dau. and heir of
of John   d. in Palestine, 1436.   Sir William
Baron Plaiz   Tendring, Knt.,
of Toft;   of Tendring,
1st wife.   Essex;
2nd wife.

Sir John = Joan,   Margaret;   Sir Robert = The Lady
Howard, Knt.   sister and heir   m.   Howard, Knt.,   Margaret
of John   (1) Constantine   of Tendring.   Mowbray,
Walton, of   Clifton, of Bucken-   dau. of
Wyvenhoe,   ham, Norfolk;   Thomas,
Essex.   (2) Sir Geo.   Duke of
Talbot, Knt.   Norfolk, KG
(eventual heir of
her great nephew,
John Mowbray,

John de Vere, = Elizabeth Howard   4th Duke of
12th Earl   (through whom descended the   Norfolk), and
of Oxford   Baronies of Scales and Plaiz,   Earl Marshal.
(executed   the estates of East Winch,
1462).   etc.).

Sir John Howard, Knt.
(1st Duke of Norfolk,
Earl Marshal and Lord
High Adm. of England);
b. *c.* 1420-2.
See Genealogical Table II.

Key to tables I and II

*	Earl Marshal of England
b.	born
c.	*circa*
coh.	coheir
cr.	created
d.	died
dau.	daughter
div.	divorced
h.	heir
m.	married
s. and h. ap.	son and heir apparent
s.p.	*sine prole* (without issue)
s.p.m.s.	*sine prole masculâ superstite* (without surviving male issue)
s.p.s.	*sine prole superstite* (without surviving issue)
suc.	succeeded
sum.	summoned to Parliament (House of Lords)
unm.	unmarried
yr.	younger
yst.	youngest

NOTES

ABBREVIATIONS

AC	Arundel Castle	fol.	folio
BM	British Museum	Harl. MS	Harley Manuscript
ed.	editor	PRO	Public Record Office
f.	following	SP	State Papers

CHAPTER I

1. Henry Howard, *Memorials of the Howard Family* (1834), Appendices I–IV. Henry Lilly, 'The Genealogie of the Princelie Familie of the Howards', MS 1638, preserved in the library at Arundel Castle.
2. J. Gairdner (ed.), *Paston Letters* I (1901), 337, 340–1.
3. ibid., Supplement, 117.
4. ibid., II, 422.
5. Rot. Parl. VI, 168–70 17 Edward IV A⁰ 1478.
6. J. Payne Collier (ed.), *Household Books of John, Duke of Norfolk* (Roxburghe Club, 1844), 277.
7. Rot. Pat. 18 Edward IV Pt.2 m.9; Calendar p.137; Rot. Pat. Richard III Pt.1 m.7, Pt.3 m.10; Calendar pp. 364, 418.
8. Payne Collier, op.cit. (n.6).
9. Sir George Buck, *Life of Richard III* (1619), 568. This book was dedicated to the Collector Earl of Arundel.
10. Gairdner, op.cit. (n.2), III (1901), 320.
11. Quoted in Gerald Brenan and Edward Phillips Statham, *The House of Howard* (2 vols., 1907) I, 56.

CHAPTER 2

1. John Weever, *Ancient Funerall Monuments within the United Monarchie of Great Britaine, Ireland, and the Islands Adjacent* (1631), 834–40.
2. As the word attainder is going to appear frequently in the following pages it will be as well to define it here: it is an Act of Parliament registering a person's conviction for treason and declaring all his property forfeit to the King and blood 'corrupted', that is, incapable of inheriting titles of honour etc. Only in 1539 did it come to be used in lieu of a trial as a result of one of Thomas Cromwell's 'reforms'.
3. Payne Collier (ed.), op.cit. (ch.1, n.6).

4. W. Camden, *Remains of a Greater Worke* (1614), 283.

5. W. Campbell, *Materials for History of Henry VII* I (1872), 480.

6. Katherine of Aragon later gave the cup to the 3rd Duke of Norfolk and it remained in the Howard family till this century.

7. The sword, dagger and ring reputedly taken from the body of the Scottish King at Flodden were placed at the College of Arms on permanent loan by the 6th Duke of Norfolk. The 'Flodden sword' displayed at Arundel is merely representational and largely dates from the eighteenth century. The authenticity of all these relics has been doubted by scholars.

8. To quote the wording of his epitaph. There has been a certain amount of later quibbling as to whether the 1514 patent was a restoration or re-creation. In fact it gave the Duke precedence from 1397 and included the Mowbray Dukes as his predecessors, not just his father. The exact Howard precedence of the Dukes of Norfolk from 1483 was restored in the patent of restoration by Charles II in 1660/1661.

9. Brenan and Statham, op.cit. (ch.1, n.11), I, 105–6.

10. Thomas Martin, *History of Thetford* (1739), Appendix VIII.

CHAPTER 3

1. Diarmid MacCulloch, 'Kett's Rebellion in Context', *Past and Present* (August 1979), 53–7.

2. F. R. Grace, 'The Life and Career of Thomas Howard 3rd Duke of Norfolk 1473–1554', MA thesis, University of Nottingham 1961, 205.

3. PRO, L and P, Henry VIII, XIV I/16.

4. BM, Cotton MS Titus BI, 394 f.

5. PRO, SP I/115, fol. 80–1.

6. PRO, SP I/2, fol.98.

7. PRO, SP II/53.

8. PRO, SP II/61.

9. PRO, SP I/115, fol.244–5.

10. PRO, SP I/118, fol.216–7.

11. MacCulloch, op.cit. (n.1), 55.

12. PRO, LR2, fol.116; Revd C. R. Manning, 'Kenninghall', *Norfolk Archaeology* VII (1872), 294–6; XV (1904), 51–8.

13. Laurence Stone and Howard Colvin, 'The Howard Tombs at Framlingham, Suffolk', *Archaeological Journal* CXXII (1966), 159–71. The 3rd Duke's interest in his ancestral tombs is demonstrated by the fact that he obtained permission from the Venetian *Signoria* in 1532 to remove the bones of Thomas Mowbray, Duke of Norfolk, who had died in exile in 1399, from the Basilica of St. Mark for reinterment in England. The design of the 3rd Duke's tomb is identical to the upper tier of the choir stalls in Toledo Cathedral.

14. Grace, op.cit. (n.2), 226–39.

CHAPTER 4

1. Richard Howlett, 'The Household Accounts of Kenninghall Palace in the year 1525', *Norfolk Archaeology* XV (1904), 51; G. F. Nott ed., *The Works of Henry Howard Earl of Surrey . . .* (3 vols., 1815–16) I, Appendix III.
2. Hester Chapman, *Two Tudor Portraits* (1960), 40. Edward Cassady, *Henry Howard Earl of Surrey* (New York, 1938), 34–47.
3. Brenan and Statham, op.cit. (Ch.1, n.11), II, 383.
4. Nott, op.cit. (n.1), I, 178.
5. ibid., 224.
6. ibid., Appendix XLVII.
7. J. S. Symonds, *Blank Verse* (1895), 16.
8. *Archaeologia* XXIII, 62.
9. Lord Herbert of Cherbury, *Life and Raigne of King Henry VIII* (1649), 562.
10. Chapman, op.cit. (n.2), 121.
11. Rot. Pat. 20 Richard II (4).
12. BM, Harl. MS 1453. A 'drawing of arms Howard Earl of Surrey, for which he was attainted', shows a larger number of quarterings and suggests that Surrey was engaged in nothing more harmful than heraldic doodling.
13. Henry Howard, op.cit. (Ch.1, n.1).
14. Herbert, op.cit. (n.9), 565.
15. AC MS G5/25.

CHAPTER 5

1. William Camden, *Historie of Elizabeth* (1630), 153–4.
2. Neville Williams, *Thomas Howard Fourth Duke of Norfolk* (1964), 104–10.
3. ibid.
4. Quoted in Brenan and Statham, op.cit. (Ch.1, n.11), II, 453.
5. *Dictionary of National Biography* III, 213.
6. Survey of London: *The College of Arms* (1963), 3–4.
7. Williams, op.cit. (n.2), 141.
8. Hatfield House Cecil Papers 5/70, Thomas 4th Duke of Norfolk to Queen Elizabeth, 21 January 1572; Conyers Read, *Mr Secretary Cecil* (1955), 447–52.'
9. Charge against the Duke of Norfolk 1571, quoted in Williams, op.cit. (n.2), 226.
10. Francis Edwards S. J., *The Marvellous Chance* (1968), 45–9.
11. Williams, op.cit. (n.2), 224.
12. Edwards, op.cit. (n.10), 204.
13. Brenan and Statham, op.cit. (Ch.1, n.11), II, 455. Hatfield House Cecil Papers 5/70.
14. Camden, op.cit. (n.1), 140.
15. AC MS G1/22.
16. This *New Testament*, published by Richard Jugge in 1566, is preserved in the library at Arundel.

CHAPTER 6

1. 14th Duke of Norfolk, ed. *The Lives of Philip Howard and Anne Dacres, His wife* (1857). The original MS of *circa* 1630 is preserved in the muniment room at Arundel.
2. ibid., 5.
3. BM, Harl. MS 787.
4. M. A. Tierney, *History and Antiquities of Arundel* (1833), 376.
5. Norfolk, op.cit. (n.1), 53.
6. ibid., 57–65.
7. Tierney, op.cit. (n.4), 395.
8. Godfrey Goodman, *The Court of King James the First . . . To which are added letters illustrative of the personal History of the most distinguished characters in the court of that monarch and his predecessors* I (1839), 141–2.
9. Tierney, op.cit. (n.4), 397.
10. Norfolk, op.cit. (n.1), 112–13.
11. ibid., 117.
12. ibid., 115.
13. Tierney, op.cit. (n.4), 407.
14. BM, Lansdowne MS XCIV, fol.4, 9.
15. Richard Gough, *British Topography* III (1780), 127.

CHAPTER 7

1. Sir John Laughton, ed., *State Papers relating to the defeat of the Spanish Armada* (1894).
2. The barony of Howard of Effingham survived in the descendants of the Lord Admiral's younger brother William Howard. The 5th Lord Howard of Effingham was Governor of Virginia, and in 1713 Gen. Francis Howard, 7th Lord Howard of Effingham, was created Earl of Effingham. This earldom in turn became extinct on the death of the 4th Earl in 1816 and was revived in 1837 for the 11th Lord Howard of Effingham.
3. Edward Hasted, *History of Kent . . . Hundred of Blackheath* (1886), 91.
4. This was later Northumberland House and was demolished in 1874.
5. *State Trials* I, 266.
6. PRO, PCC 55 Lane; N. E. McClure, ed., *Letters of John Chamberlain* I (1939), 541.
7. ibid., I, 548.
8. Lawrence Stone, *Family and Fortune* (1973), 271–5.
9. McClure, op.cit. (n.6), II, 144.
10. BM, Cotton MS Titus CVI; McClure, op.cit. (n.6), I, 478.
11. Stone, op.cit. (n.8), 282.
12. ibid., 168 f.
13. *Country Life* (25 March 1911). Much of his work was destroyed in a disastrous fire in 1844 but Naworth was subsequently restored by Salvin.
14. Henry Howard, op.cit. (Ch.1, n.1), Appendix XI, 'Lord William and Lady Elizabeth Dacre'.

CHAPTER 8

1. Lord Clarendon, *History of the Great Rebellion* I (1702), 44.

2. BM, Harl. MS 6272, fol.168.

3. Clarendon, op.cit. (n.1), I, 44.

4. Mary Hervey, *Thomas Howard, Earl of Arundel* (Cambridge, 1921), 60.

5. ibid., 77.

6. Kevin Sharpe, ed., *Faction and Parliament, Essays on Early Stuart History* (1978) VII 'The Earl of Arundel', 211.

7. *House of Lords Debates*, 1621, 73, 4.

8. Sharpe, op.cit. (n.6), 210–43.

9. Hervey, op.cit. (n.4), 356–65.

10. Sir Edward Walker, *Historical Discourses* (1705), 212.

11. BM, Cotton MS Julius C III fol.205.

12. James I may have given the Earl a discreet permission for this visit; at least he paid no attention to the stories of Arundel's enemies who informed the King of the Earl's 'crime'.

13. Walker, op.cit. (n.10).

14. *Survey of London* XVII (1936), 46–54. It was at the Arundels' villa in Highgate that Francis Bacon died of pneumonia contracted from his experiment of stuffing a fowl with snow to preserve it.

15. David Howarth, 'Thomas Howard Earl of Arundel Collector and Patron', Ph.D Thesis, Cambridge, 1978, 90.

16. AC MSS, Autograph Letters, Inigo Jones to Earl of Arundel *re* St. Paul's Cathedral; Howarth, op.cit. (n.15), 168.

17. It has been lent by the Duke of Norfolk to the London Museum. Van Dyck's 'Continence of Scipio' is at Christ Church, Oxford.

18. Hervey, op.cit. (n.4), 398.

19. Clarendon, op.cit. (n.1), I, 44.

20. AC MS 79.

21. Clarendon, op.cit. (n.1), I, 44.

22. In the library at Arundel, having been given back to the 15th Duke of Norfolk by the 5th Marquess of Northampton whose ancestor had acquired it in the late-seventeenth century following the dispersal of much of the Earl of Arundel's collection.

23. William Harvey accompanied the Collector on the embassy to the Emperor in 1636 and caused consternation by going off on his own to look for botanical specimens despite the danger of wolves. (Aubrey, *Letters of Eminent Persons*.)

24. Clarendon, op.cit. (n.1), I, 44; AC MS MD59.

25. Hervey, op.cit. (n.4), 126.

26. Clarendon, op.cit. (n.1), I, 91.

27. The helmet is at Framlingham church, Suffolk, the sword was placed on permanent loan at the College of Arms by the 6th Duke of Norfolk, the tournament shield is still at Arundel Castle.

28. This exclusion has the effect that should the senior line of the Howard family ever become extinct the dukedom would pass to the Suffolks and the earldom of Arundel to

the Carlisles. This exclusion may have been because of the Earl of Suffolk's disgrace, or more likely, was the Collector Earl's retaliation for the alienation of some of his estates into Suffolk's hands.

29. Hervey, op.cit. (n.4), 438.

CHAPTER 9

1. Hervey, op.cit. (Ch.8, n.4), 161. Thomas Coke of Trusley, Derbyshire, was the brother of Sir John Coke, Secretary of State under James I, and had entered the Earl of Arundel's service after the death of the 7th Earl of Shrewsbury, in whose household he had been originally.
2. AC MSS, Autograph Letters, Aletheia Countess of Arundel to Lord Andover, 14 September 1648.
3. They had married in October 1652.
4. Tierney, op.cit. (Ch.6, n.4), 516.
5. William Bray, ed., *Memoirs of John Evelyn* (1812) I, 19 June 1662.
6. ibid., 10 August 1655.
7. ibid., 17 October 1659.
8. Tierney, op.cit. (Ch.6, n.4), 525.
9. *Philosophical Transactions* XII (1677), 907–17; T. Barbo, *Metallurgie* I, 308.
10. Evelyn, op.cit. (n.5), 11 January 1662.
11. Lord Braybrooke ed., *Pepys's Diary* 1828), 17 January 1668.
12. John Burbury, *A Relation of a Journey of the Rt. Hon. Henry Howard from London to Vienna and thence to Constantinople* (1671).
13. *Letter from a Gentleman of the Lord Ambassador Howard's Retinue* (1670).
14. BM, Sloane MS 1906, Edward Browne's Journal.
15. Evelyn, op.cit. (n.5), 17 October 1671.
16. Ernest A. Kent, 'The Houses of the Dukes of Norfolk in Norwich', *Norfolk Archaeology* XXIV (2) (1930), 84.
17. Evelyn, op.cit. (n.5), 23 August 1678.
18. AC MS MD 1278, 1241, A962, A967, A1267, Conveyances of estates to trustees (Lord Howard of Effingham, Sir Paul Rycaut and Dr Cuthbert Browne) and their accounts.
19. Godfrey Anstruther, 'Cardinal Howard and the English Court', *Archivum Fratrum Praedicatorum* XXVIII (1958), 319–20.
20. ibid., 322–41. The Earl of Peterborough stood proxy for James at the wedding at Modena.
21. Henry, 6th Duke of Norfolk to Philip, Cardinal Howard, quoted in C. F. Raymond Palmer, *The Life of Philip Thomas Howard, O.P., Cardinal Norfolk* (1867), 170.
22. ibid.
23. Westminster Cathedral Archives XXXVI No. 27 (20 January 1693).
24. Michael E. Williams, *The Venerable English College, Rome* (1979), 47–9.
25. Gilbert Burnet, *History of His Own Time* (2 vols., 1724–34) I, 661.
26. ibid.
27. *Catholic Record Society* XI, 105.

CHAPTER 10

1. They were Dr Cuthbert Browne, Symon Fox and Sir Paul Rycaut.
2. *Complete Peerage.*
3. Burnet, op.cit. (Ch.9, n.25), I, 684.
4. Monson MS: 7th Duke of Norfolk to Lord Effingham 10 Sept. 1687. I am grateful to Professor Warren Billings for drawing this to my attention.
5. Charles Howard, *Anecdotes of the Howard Family* (1769), 110.
6. Evelyn, op.cit. (Ch.9, n.5), III, 379, April 1700.
7. Verelst's portrait of the 7th Duke of Norfolk is at Arundel Castle, that of the Duchess is at Drayton.
8. S. F. K. Causton, *Howard Papers* (1862), 251.
9. Burnet, op.cit. (Ch.9, n.25), II, 127.
10. *Complete Peerage.*
11. Causton, op.cit. (n.8), 252.
12. ibid., 254.
13. ibid.
14. Evelyn, op.cit. (Ch.9, n.5), 28 February 1692.
15. ibid., April 1700.
16. Causton, op.cit. (n.8), 207.
17. AC MS G1/31.
18. AC MS A119–22.
19. Causton, op.cit. (n.8), 274.
20. Henry Howard, op.cit. (Ch.1, n.1), 8.
21. Tierney, op. cit. (Ch. 6, n.4), 555–9.
22. ibid., 564.
23. Charles Butler, *Memoirs of the English Catholics* III (1821), 282.
24. When Norfolk House was demolished, sections of this frieze were rescued and are in store at Arundel Castle.
25. When the house was demolished, the music room was given to the Victoria and Albert Museum.
26. They were taken later to Worksop and are now at Arundel.
27. *Survey of London* XXIX (1960), 192–202; *Country Life* (25 December 1937); Desmond Fitzgerald, *The Norfolk House Music Room* (Victoria and Albert Museum, 1973).
28. *Gentleman's Magazine* XXXI (November 1761), 531–2.
29. James Paine, *Noblemen and Gentlemen's Houses* II (1783), 1–5; Arthur Young, *Tour in the North of England* I (1768), 367; *Country Life* (22 March 1973).
30. Unpublished Journal of Lady Mary Coke, 16 July, 11 and 14 September 1776. In the possession of Lord Home, to whom I am grateful for permission to quote this passage.
31. Tierney, op.cit. (Ch. 6, n.4), 565.

CHAPTER 11

1. John Aubrey, *Natural History and Antiquities of Surrey* IV (1688), 164. There is a plan of the garden in the Bodleian Library, Oxford: MS Aubrey 4, fol.49–50.
2. The Aylward Papers are preserved in the muniment room at Arundel Castle and are

interesting documentation of the life and transactions of a seventeenth-century London merchant. The absurd Victorian upper-class prejudice against 'trade' is contradicted by the history of the Howards, for not only were the Dukes of Norfolk and other members of the family directly involved in a series of mercantile projects from the fifteenth to the eighteenth centuries, but on several occasions they married into merchant families.

3. Doris Mercer, 'The Deepdene, Dorking', Surrey Archaeological Collections LXXI (1977).

4. Causton, op.cit. (Ch.10, n.8), 414.

5. Sir Nathaniel Wraxall, *Historical and Posthumous Memoirs* I (1884), 29.

6. *Oxford Dictionary of Quotations*, New Edition (1979).

7. Causton, op.cit. (Ch.10, n.8).

8. Henry Howard, op.cit. (Ch.1, n.1), 48.

9. College of Arms MS, Howard Gibbon.

10. Causton, op.cit. (Ch.10, n.8), 418.

11. AC MSS, Horsham borough papers, HO1–2397; W. Albery, *A Parliamentary History of . . . Horsham 1295–1885* (1927).

12. Wraxall, op.cit. (n.5), 29.

13. St. John Gore, *Creevey* (1948), 94.

14. ibid., 31.

15. W. M. Thackeray, *The Four Georges* (1861), 117.

16. AC MSS, Howard Letters and Papers 1636–1822, II. Notification of dismissal from all his public appointments; Minute of the 11th Duke of Norfolk's interview with King George III following his republican toast; Extracts from the 11th Duke's diary 1798–9.

17. AC MS G2/43.

18. AC MSS, Howard Letters, 1760–1816, I.

19. R. C. Rhodes, *Harlequin Sheridan* (1933), 247.

20. AC MS, James Dallaway 'An account of the Festival held in the Barons' Hall of Arundel Castle on the fifteenth day of June 1815. Written June 16th 1815.'

21. J. M. Robinson, 'Gothic Revival at Arundel 1780–1870', *Connoisseur* (March 1978), 163–71.

22. AC MS, op.cit. (n.20).

23. Causton, op.cit. (Ch.10, n.8), 491.

CHAPTER 12

1. All the heads of the Glossop Howard family were called Bernard after Lord Bernard Stuart, Earl of Lichfield (brother of Elizabeth Stuart, wife of Henry Frederick Earl of Arundel), who was killed at Chester fighting for Charles I.

2. J. Gillow, *Biographical Dictionary of English Catholics* (1885) III, 418, 421.

3. Obituary, *The Standard* (17 September 1892).

4. *Creevey Papers*, II, 147, 7 November 1815.

5. ibid., 250, 22 June 1824.

6. ibid., 306, 7 February 1829.

7. AC MSS C533–45. Correspondence of 12th Duke of Norfolk.

8. AC MSS, Newspaper cuttings relating to the 12th Duke's divorce. He took the opportunity through his counsel to say that he did not question the legitimacy of his son.

9. Creevey, op.cit. (n.4), II, 162.

10. Robinson, op.cit. (Ch.11, n.21).

11. H. J. Dyos and Michael Wolff, eds., *The Victorian City* I (1973): D. J. Olsen 'House upon House', 338–45. The Chemist's shop at Glossop still displays a nineteenth-century warrant 'By Appointment to the Duke of Norfolk'.

12. AC MS C518. Duchess of Norfolk to Miss Coutts 14 December 1846. *Illustrated London News* (5 December 1846); *Morning Post* (4 December 1846).

13. AC MS C630.

14. It remains on the Statute Book with the risible result that the coats of arms of all the Catholic bishoprics are illegal and cannot be granted by the Kings of Arms.

15. A. C. Benson and Viscount Esher, eds., *The Correspondence of Queen Victoria* II (Longmans, New York 1907), 325–6, 331–2. The Duchess's letter appears only in the American edition. The contemporary English edition published by John Murray is slightly abridged.

16. *Annual Register* (1856).

17. Gillow, op.cit. (n.2), III, 422–6.

18. *Complete Peerage*.

19. 14th Duke of Norfolk to Ambrose March-Phillipps (de Lisle) 11 May 1850, quoted in M. R. Trappes-Lomax *Pugin* (1933), 227. There is a draft of the original letter in the 14th Duke's correspondence among the AC MSS.

20. AC MS MD20, MD2042–3.

21. Count Montalembert, *Memoir of the 14th Duke of Norfolk* (1860).

CHAPTER 13

1. Sir Almeric Fitzroy, *Memoirs* (2 vols. 1926) I, 85.

2. AC MSS, correspondence of Charlotte, wife of 13th Duke of Norfolk.

3. AC MSS, papers and letters of 15th Duke of Norfolk.

4. Francis Steer, *The Cathedral Church of St. Philip at Arundel* (1973).

5. It is difficult now to envisage the sort of religious prejudice with which the Duke and his contemporaries had to contend, but a letter received by the Duke's father-in-law Lord Donington when he became a Catholic gives some idea. The writer told Lord Donington that he disapproved of Catholics because they belonged to an inferior race, a race inferior to the Teutonic; they could not colonize, and the Teutons could and did. 'Clearly', said Lord Donington to the Duke, 'he thinks the Apostles ought to have colonised and it was an omission on their part not to have done so.'

6. Michael Williams, *The Venerable English College Rome* (1979), 133–7.

7. AC MSS, op.cit. (n.3); C. S. Dessain, ed., *Letters and Diaries of John Henry Newman* XXVII, 177.

8. AC MSS, op.cit. (n.3).

9. Sir David Hunter Blair, Bart., OSB, *A Medley of Memories* (1919).

10. G. E. Buckle, *The Life of Benjamin Disraeli, Earl of Beaconsfield* VI (1910), 196.

11. Anon. (J. W. Picton?) *A Great Gothic Fane* (1913), 166.
12. Lady Margaret Fitzalan-Howard to Mr Bernard Holland for inclusion in his life of the 15th Duke of Norfolk which was never published; the MS is preserved in AC MSS.
13. Lady Etheldreda Fitzalan-Howard to Mr Bernard Holland.
14. Fitzroy, op.cit. (n.1).
15. Derwent Hall was submerged under the Ladybower Reservoir in 1935.
16. AC MSS, op.cit. (n.3).
17. ibid.
18. J. K. Dunlop, *Development of the British Army 1899–1914* (1938).
19. Fitzroy, op.cit. (n.1), I, 43, 46, 79, 96, 97; II, 408, 416, 417, 419; AC MSS, Earl Marshal's Papers.
20. AC MSS, op.cit. (n.3).
21. *The Builder* (29 July 1882).
22. *The Graphic* (21 August 1875).
23. David Cannadine, *Lords and Landlords* (Leicester 1980), 44–55.
24. AC MSS, op.cit. (n.3). A monstrance is an elaborate piece of church plate used for displaying the Consecrated Host at Benediction. Duke Henry's Monstrance is at Arundel Cathedral and is still used every year for Benediction on the Feast of Corpus Christi.
25. To quote the style read by Garter King of Arms at the 15th Duke of Norfolk's funeral.

SELECT BIBLIOGRAPHY

From the late-fifteenth up to the mid-seventeenth century the Howards are so closely involved with national history that almost every general history book contains some reference to the family. Thereafter their story is synonymous with English Catholic history and all the standard works on that subject are relevant to a study of the family. The following is restricted to the chief works on individual members of the family.

Early Howards

Lilly, Henry, 'The Genealogie of the Princilie Familie of the Howards', MS, 1638.
Howard, Henry, *Memorials of the Howard Family* (1834).
Brenan, Gerald, and Statham, Edward Phillips, *The House of Howard* (2 vols., 1907).

2nd Duke of Norfolk

Tucker, M. J., *Life of Thomas Howard, Earl of Surrey and 2nd Duke of Norfolk* (1964).

3rd Duke of Norfolk and Queen Katherine Howard

Grace, F. R., 'Life and Career of Thomas Howard 3rd Duke of Norfolk', MA thesis Nottingham University, 1961.
Smith, L. B., *Tudor Tragedy* (1961).

'The Poet' Earl of Surrey

Chapman, H. W., *Two Tudor Portraits* (1960).
Cassady, Edwin, *Henry Howard, Earl of Surrey* (New York, 1975).
Steer, F. W., *Henry Howard, the Poet Earl of Surrey* (1977).

4th Duke of Norfolk

Sampson, T., *A discourse touching the pretended match betwene the Duke of Norfolke and the Queene of Scottes* (1571).
   A Brief History of the Life of Mary Queen of Scots, and the Occasions that brought her and Thomas Duke of Norfolk to their tragical ends . . . (1681).
Brown, J., *The Tryal of Thomas Duke of Norfolk . . .* (1709).
Williams, N., *Thomas Howard, 4th Duke of Norfolk* (1964).
Edwards, F., *The Marvellous Chance* (1968).

St. Philip Howard, 13th Earl of Arundel

Norfolk, 14th Duke of, ed., *The Lives of Philip Howard, Earl of Arundel, and of Anne Dacres, his wife* (1857, 2nd. edn. 1861).

Pollen, J. H. and MacMahon, W., eds., *The Venerable Philip Howard, Earl of Arundel* (Catholic Record Society 1919).

Waugh, M., *Blessed Philip Howard* (1961).

1st Earl of Suffolk

Lawrence Stone, *Family and Fortune* (1973).

'The Collector', 14th Earl of Arundel

Walker, Sir Edward, *Historical Discourses* (1705).

Tierney, M. A., *History and Antiquities of Arundel* (1833).

Hervey, M. F. S., *The Life, Correspondence and Collections of Thomas Howard, Earl of Arundel* (Cambridge 1921).

Howarth, D. J., 'Lord Arundel as Patron and Collector', PhD Thesis Cambridge University, 1978.

6th Duke of Norfolk

A Letter from a Gentleman of the Lord Ambassador Howard's Retinue . . . (1670).

Burbury, J., *A relation of a journey of . . . my Lord Henry Howard from London to Vienna, and Thence to Constantinople* (1671).

Cardinal Norfolk

Palmer, C. F. R., *The Life of Philip Thomas Howard, OP, Cardinal of Norfolk* (1867).

7th Duke of Norfolk

The Duke of Norfolk's Case: or the doctrine of perpetuities fully set forth and explain'd (1688).

The Tryal between Henry Duke of Norfolk, plaintiff, and John Jermaine defendant . . . (1692).

The Proceedings upon the Bill of Divorce between His Grace the Duke of Norfolk and the Lady Mary Mordant (1700).

The Greystoke Howards

Norfolk, 10th Duke of, *Anecdotes of the Howard Family* (1769).

11th Duke of Norfolk

Causton, H. K. S., *Howard Papers* (1862).

14th Duke of Norfolk

Montalembert, Count, 'The 14th Duke of Norfolk', *Merry England*, June, July 1890, 118–33, 247, 248.

15th Duke of Norfolk

Norfolk, Gwendolen, Duchess of, ed., *Henry Fitzalan-Howard, 15th Duke of Norfolk* (1917).

The main source for a history of the Dukes of Norfolk is the vast accumulation of private and estate papers stored in the six muniment rooms at Arundel Castle. For a detailed list of these the reader is referred to the four volumes of *Interim Handlists to the Arundel Castle Archives* prepared by my predecessor Dr F. W. Steer and published by the Sussex County Record Office (Chichester 1968–80).

INDEX

Note: Duke = Duke of Norfolk; peers are indexed under their family names